D. M---

Gypsy politics Traveller identity

edited by Thomas Acton

a companion volume to
Romani culture and Gypsy identity

published by
University of Hertfordshire Press

First published 1997 in
Great Britain by
University of Hertfordshire Press
University of Hertfordshire
College Lane
Hatfield
Hertfordshire AL10 9AD

ISBN 0 900458 75 5 (paperback)
ISBN 0 900458 80 1 (hardback)

Designed by
Beverley Stirling

Cover design by
John Robertshaw

based on a photograph by
David Gallant
of the meeting of the Praesidium of the International Romani Union
in Brno in April 1993

Page layout by
John Robertshaw

Printed by
Antony Rowe Limited

Contents

Introduction
Thomas Acton, Editor

Chapter 1
Page 7
Theorising sedentarism: the roots of anti-nomadism
Robbie McVeigh, Researcher, Centre for Research and Documentation, Belfast

Chapter 2
Page 26
Why do Gaujos hate Gypsies so much, anyway? A case study
Sinéad ní Shuinéar, Researcher and Translator, Dublin

Chapter 3
Page 54
Somebody like you: the images of Gypsies and Yoroks among some Bulgarian Muslims
llia lliev, Researcher, Universities of Sofia and Greenwich

Chapter 4
Page 61
The Criminal Justice and Public Order Act and its implications for Travellers
Luke Clements , Solicitor, Thorpes, Hereford
Sue Campbell, Traveller Research Unit, Cardiff Law School

Chapter 5
Page 70
Sites of resistance: places on the margin – the Traveller 'homeplace'
Sally Kendall, Lecturer in Geography, University of Leeds

Chapter 6
Page 90
Razor blades amidst the Velvet? Changes and continuities in the Gypsy experience of the Czech and Slovak lands
Chris Powell, Lecturer in Criminology, University of Wales

Chapter 7   Foreign Gypsies and British immigration law after 1945
Page 100   *Donald Kenrick, Researcher and Consultant, London*

Chapter 8   Burakumin in contemporary Japan
Page 111   *Ian Neary, Professor of Japanese Studies, University of Essex*

Chapter 9   "New Age" Travellers: identity, sedentarism and social security
Page 125   *Colin Clark, Lecturer in Social Policy, University of
Newcastle upon Tyne*

Chapter 10   The theory of Gypsy law
Page 142   *Thomas Acton, Reader in Romani Studies,
Susan Caffrey, Lecturer in Sociology and
Gary Mundy, Researcher, University of Greenwich*

Chapter 11   The social construction of Romani identity
Page 153   *Nicolae Gheorghe, Researcher, Institute of Sociology, Bucharest,
and Vice-President, International Romani Union*

Afterword   *Sir Angus Fraser, Researcher and Consultant, London*
Page 172

Introduction

How do politics and policy shape the identity of Gypsies and groups like the Gypsies?

In the era of the nation-state, ethnic loyalties often seem primordial and fixed, and ethnic conflicts ineradicable. But if this perception is true, it would mean giving up on Gypsy politics.

During 1993 and 1994 a small group of scholars, professionals and Gypsy activists met regularly at a series of seminars funded by the Economic and Social Research Council at the University of Greenwich. The idea was that Romani studies, instead of stagnating in a series of repetitive books (usually based on PhD theses) by isolated scholars, should develop into a cumulative and collaborative effort which would end the marginalisation of Romani studies in the world of knowledge. Our aim was both to challenge the easy assumptions of academic study in and of nation-states and to serve the teachers, community workers and activists seeking to remedy old injustices and bring to an end ancient quarrels.

Near the beginning of the seminar series, Robbie McVeigh confronted us, through the concept of sedentarism, with a new way of theorising the manner in which non-Gypsy politics constrains Gypsy identities, while Nicolae Gheorghe, in a tour de force of a speech delivered at lightning speed without notes and transcribed here with almost no revision, forced upon us the paradoxes of the Romani intellectual in politics. All the other chapters, written and rewritten over the past three years, try to bring some answers to the questions raised by the first and last chapters.

The answers range widely. The shock of recognition of the forms of Burukamin Liberation politics in Japan shows us that the answers come from political analysis, not from any description of a supposed essential character of the Romani peoples. Our understanding and our liberation have to come from the understanding of the relations between groups within our common humanity.

The quarrels may occur within the Romani community as well as outside it. The cover of this book shows a meeting of the Praesideum of the International Romani Union in Brno in April 1993, chaired by its President, Rajko Duric. At the previous meeting there had been calls for the expulsion of two of the contributors to the ESRC seminar series, Nicolae Gheorghe and Ian Hancock, for various alleged irregularities. Only a rearguard action by Peter Mercer, president of the Gypsy Coucil for Education, Culture, Welfare and Civil Rights in England limited the action against them to suspension. This suspension was lifted at the Brno meeting, after the suspicion of irregularities was shown to be a product of the cultural misunderstanding by East European Roma of the way lobbying politics has to work in the West. Common political action by Romani groups against oppression cannot wait upon some mythical resolution of what Romani culture really is, or the achievement of a universally accepted standard Romani language.

None of this is to deny the joy and pleasure and specificity of culture. A companion volume to this one, *Romani culture and Gypsy identity*, reflects the work of the group on cultural themes. But culture must not be turned into a prison; and politics must set culture free, not divide it into warring camps.

Thomas Acton, Editor

Chapter 1   Theorising sedentarism: the roots of anti-nomadism

Robbie McVeigh, Researcher, Centre for Research and Documentation, Belfast

On Tuesday 1 June 1993 the *Daily Star* front page headline screamed, "£1 MILLION WASTED ON SCUM". The story quoted Tory MP Michael Colvin who "stormed":

> "The situation is becoming intolerable. We have to start getting tough with people. The sooner we get new legislation the better".

The *Star* spoke of "unwashed scroungers", leading the police a "right dance" on their "slimy path" as they "thumb their noses at decent folk". The *Star's* leader column went on to demand that,

> "Instead of DSS officials meekly handing out cash, the scum army should be told they can only collect in John O'Groats. *After crawling over broken glass.*" (original emphasis).

Of course, such intemperate language is commonplace in the British tabloid press. Moreover, it is almost standard when the press addresses tensions between nomadic and sedentary people. However, it was significant that this was not a racist attack on European Roma or English Romanichals or Irish Travellers: rather it was an assault on New Age Travellers. The story referred to 'Operation Nomad', an attempt by police to prevent the Avon Free Festival taking place.

New Travellers have become the subject of an intensifying moral panic in Britain and Ireland. Constructed as a plague or blight, these nomads have come to be regarded as the bane of the 'decent folk' in the 1990s. At one level of critical analysis this should provoke nothing more than a healthy *schadenfreude:* there is a rather pleasing sense of the Traveller as the nemesis of the Thatcherite dream – even in the commuter belt there is no escaping the dispossessed ever eager to scratch one's Range Rover and shit in one's garden. However, there is also a more sobering aspect to anti-Traveller hysteria – it is becoming an increasingly useful tool of authoritarian populism. The moral panic around New Travellers played a key part in engineering support for the Criminal Justice Act 1994 which now threatens the survival of New Travellers and other nomads alike. Furthermore, as the state gears up systematically to repress nomads through this Act and other measures, the attendant erosion of liberties and paramilitarisation of policing will have consequences for every community in resistance.

This process of demonising New Travellers as part of a package of reaction is not easy to understand in terms of traditional categories. Perhaps more than any other oppression, the experience of New Travellers illustrates the complexity and contradictions of the race/class nexus. However, it is important to make sense of this confusion – *to begin to take anti-nomadism seriously*. And this needs to be done for the sake of the civil liberties of the whole community rather than out of a patronising sympathy for the marginalised and alienated New Travellers. The legitimation of repression associated with the Travellers is part of the construction of a coercive hegemony which is dangerous to sedentary and nomad alike.

Travellers are subject to a whole series of stereotypes which combine to render them hugely problematic: they are criminals by 'nature', they come from outside the community, they are dirty, they are dishonest, they are immoral and amoral and, most importantly, they are 'nomadic'. Most of these contemporary constructions of nomads draw on a long history of establishment fears about the travelling dispossessed and the threat they pose to the moral and political order. There are obvious parallels with historic discourse about vagrancy and itinerancy. More particularly there are parallels with the old notion of 'dangerous classes': New Travellers are seen to be more dangerous than individual 'tramps' or 'vagrants' precisely because they are a class (or at least a community) – they travel together in numbers. Historically the 'vagrant underworld' included a wide range of social categories and occupations:

> "the young ... beggars ... peddlers and tinkers, soldiers and mariners, many entertainers, students, unlicensed healers and even fortune-tellers... Gypsies and the Irish were also treated as vagrants." (Beier 1985:10)

The idea of a travelling underworld has been a source of concern to European states for centuries. And the efforts of the state apparatus to 'deal with' this supposed threat have always constituted a brutal and undemocratic project. Yet the enduring attempt to control the 'dangerous classes' has been one of the least theorised aspects of state repression. This leaves many people struggling to make sense of the current moral panic around New Travellers, despite the obvious parallels with the long-standing notion of the 'dangerous classes'.

Similarly, the contemporary parallels between the experience of New Travellers and what might be termed 'ethnic nomads' – like Scots and Irish Travellers and *Roma* (or 'Gypsies') – have been undertheorised. Much of the content of anti-New Traveller discourse is indistinguishable from traditional anti-nomadic discourse. 'Gypsies' and Irish Travellers have long been subject to accounts of their dishonesty and shiftlessness. They have also been seen as harbingers of filth and pollution and contamination. This is not to argue that the experiences of different nomads should be collapsed; while broader notions of biological inferiority or incompetence are sometimes used to 'explain' New Travellers, they have *not* been racialised. (There is an interesting exception to the non-racialisation of New Travellers in Ireland where the 'Englishness' of New Travellers has been an important element in their pathologisation – they have been identified as "dirty foreign scroungers" (Callanan 1995) – some New Travellers have themselves identified this as racism). But ethnic nomads and New Travellers *are* problematised in similar ways. So why do New Travellers inspire so much dread and loathing? And what is the connection between their experience and the parallel marginalisation and pathologisation of ethnic nomads and individual vagrants? To answer these questions we need to employ novel explanatory concepts. Interesting exploratory work on the nomadic/sedentary interface has been done by Deleuze and Guattari (1988) around the notion of 'nomadology' and Sinéad ní Shuinéar explores the functions of anti-nomadism in the next chapter. I have already suggested that anti-nomadism is not reducible to racism. Nor is it simply about class, at least in any conventional sense. I want to argue that anti-nomadism is best characterised as *sedentarism* – a concept which has been developed to an extent with reference to the specific experience of 'ethnic nomads' (Liégeois 1995; DTEDG 1992).

What is 'sedentarism'?
Sedentarism will be defined here 'as that system of ideas and practices which serves to normalise and reproduce sedentary modes of existence and pathologise and repress nomadic modes of existence.' This notion of sedentarism obviously includes the active and intentional incitement of fear and hatred of nomads witnessed in campaigns against Travellers. However, it also includes a host of other less tangible ideas, actions and structures which construct being sedentary as the only possible mode of existence within contemporary society.

In the context of our definition, 'nomadic' is used in the widest sense – it includes all those who lead a mobile way of life, independent of its economic specificity. This is not to suggest that a way of life is ever autonomous of its economic specificity, simply that nomadism is problematised within sedentary society *whatever* the dominant mode of production of the nomads involved. Thus nomads may be primarily involved in food-extracting, food-producing, the provision of services or dependent on welfare benefits. This definition therefore includes as nomads: hunters and gatherers, pastoral nomads, commercial nomads and also – provisionally – individual travellers (tramps or vagrants). The term characterises contemporary power relations at the interface between sedentary and nomadic ways of life.

Sedentarism needs to be situated in terms of the long history of sedentary/nomadic tension involved in the transition of the *predominant* mode of existence from nomadism to sedentarism. The theorisation of the transition from non-sedentary to sedentary modes of existence has been distorted by social evolutionism. This is particularly crude in some Marxist writing but it occurs in most post-Enlightenment thought. Social evolutionism assumes that somewhere in history societies shifted from travelling to sedentary modes of existence. In addition, it assumes that this shift was both total and irreversible. Furthermore, social evolutionism almost inevitably regards this shift as a 'good thing' – as a movement upwards towards civilisation, security and modernity.

After accepting the obvious truth that at some point in the histories of most peoples the dominant mode of existence became sedentary, we can begin to critique such evolutionism in three particular ways:

1 The transition from non-sedentary to sedentary modes of existence was never absolute or irreversible. There are many survivals of nomadic modes of existence and sedentaries can become nomads just as nomads can become sedentaries.

2 The transition was never inevitable or unproblematic. There is much evidence of nomadism providing a profound threat to sedentary modes of existence.

3 The transition was not necessarily a positive, civilising development. There are atavistic residues of loss and alienation within sedentary societies which illustrate the powerful attractions of nomadism.

Attention to these three critiques begins to situate sedentarism – whether directed towards ethnic nomads or New Travellers – in terms of a long-standing and deeply-rooted history of anti-nomadism. The contemporary moral panic around New Travellers draws directly on this history. It is rooted in the fact that the very existence of New Travellers challenges hegemonic ideas about the victory of sedentarism over nomadism. New Travellers are emblematic of the survival and resilience of nomadism. Moreover, they have a specific importance because they represent something more than the survival of ethnic nomads on the margins of the modern state. They illustrate the possibility of the re-birth of nomadism within a sedentary society convinced of its triumph over nomadism. For contemporary societies steeped in sedentary conceit, the re-emergence of nomadism is profoundly disturbing prospect.

Partiality and reversibility of nomadic-sedentary transition
The idea that the transition from nomadism to sedentarism was absolute and irreversible does not stand up in the face of different extant nomadic modes of existence. The nomadic-sedentary shift was never as total as social evolutionism implies – there are survivals of nomadic modes of existence in every sedentarist social formation – whether these are commercial nomads (like Travellers in Ireland), pastoral nomads (like the Masai in Africa or the Bedouin in North Africa and the Middle East) or individual travellers. Each of these groups is evidence of at least residues of non-sedentarist modes of existence within contemporary sedentarist social formations. So the idea of a total transition implicit within a stages theory of history is simply wrong – it did not happen. At any given time there are

groups of nomads in most sedentary societies.

This is true for most contemporary social formations but it is even more clearly the case with earlier formations. Nomads have always played a crucial part in different societies. While the historical evidence about nomads often appears deliberately frustrating – it seems that we have found 'ethnic nomads' and yet we are unable to be completely certain – we need to turn this on its head. We need to realise that the 'lack of evidence' is crucial to the whole nomadic/sedentary debate. It is sometimes less than certain that we are referring to nomads precisely because, very often, that certainty did not exist. The boundaries between the nomadic and the settled person were much less precise. The conceptual distinction between nomad and sedentary is simply harder to make about historical subjects.

I am not suggesting that at some stage ethnic nomads were not 'really ethnic'; that they had not 'evolved', as it were, into an ethnically distinct group. For example, when 'Gypsies' arrived in Britain around 1500 they were immediately ethnically distinct – the racialised interface between them and the indigenous population was already in place. But it may be the case that their 'nomadism' was less distinctive. The nomadic/sedentary interface was not nearly so obvious or easy to identify at that time.

More generally, the common confusion about nomadic/sedentary difference must be read as symmetrical. If at times it is difficult to be certain whether different historical groups were nomadic or not, it is equally difficult to be certain whether they were sedentary or not. To put it another way, it seems likely that at certain points in the history of different social formations, the sedentary/nomad distinction was much more ambiguous than it is in contemporary societies. It is possible that everyone was semi-nomadic. It is possible that, where distinctions can be made, the difference might more properly be made between nomad and 'proto-sedentary'. Certainly these pre-modern societies appear more fluid than contemporary societies – despite the absence of a comparable transport infrastructure. There is continuous movement in pre-modern times: people are travelling on pilgrimages, on crusades, in search of work or alms. Indeed, as I will argue later, one of the defining characteristics of modernisation was that it settled people – it turned them into sedentaries.

So, historically, nomadic/sedentary distinctions may have been much less clear cut than social evolutionism suggests. But, even when this distinction does become unambiguous – when nomad and sedentary become recognised as profoundly different modes of existence – it bears emphasis that nomadic-sedentary transition is not a one-way process. Just as people can exchange a nomadic for a sedentary existence, so they can exchange a sedentary for a nomadic existence. This is precisely what the New Travellers have done. And, in doing this, they have challenged deep-seated sedentarist ideas about the irreversibility of the nomadic-sedentary transition and the inevitable 'extinction' of nomadism.

Contingency and difficulty of nomadic-sedentary transition

If inherited wisdom about the irreversibility of nomadic-sedentary transition is fundamentally flawed, ideas about the ease and inevitability of this transition are equally problematic. Again there is an implicit assumption that the sedentary was *so* superior in terms of social power and organisation that the transition happened with little resistance. This in turn implies that the nomad never threatened the sedentary, that the defeat and departure of the nomad was unproblematic given the huge disparity between the capacities of sedentaries and travellers. But this received wisdom flies in the face of reality – in truth travelling modes of existence were able to defeat, dominate and indeed terrorise developing sedentary formations for centuries. At one time nomads were as convinced of their superiority as sedentary people are now.

There are manifestations of this still around. Despite their marginalisation and subordination and the internalisation of anti-Traveller racist stereotypes, many Gypsies and Travellers still believe in their own superiority. The use of the words 'Country people' and 'Gaujos' (which means bumpkin or clod-hopper) to describe all settled people, rural or urban, illustrates the nomad's sense of his or her privilege and superiority *vis-à-vis* all settled people. I want to stress that this should not be taken too far. Clearly what is of contemporary interest in terms of the operation of sedentarism is not the vague symmetry between the use of pejorative words by both sedentaries and nomads to describe each other but rather the asymmetry in terms of social power available to them. We must contrast the capacity of the overwhelmingly dominant settled population to racialise, marginalise and discriminate against the nomad with the incapacity of the nomad to operationalise any anti-sedentary prejudice he or she may hold.

However, it is also important to remember that this contemporary power differential is neither inevitable or unchanging. Folk memories of the historical power of nomadism are evidenced in the contemporary construction of travelling people. Thus myths persist about the magical qualities of nomads: they are fantastically empowered, put curses on people, 'steal children' and so on. This aspect of their construction represents not the more familiar anti-Traveller discourse about inferiority and wretchedness but rather the threat they once presented to sedentary society. Historically there are more obvious examples – the continuing emotive power of half-remembered nomadic symbols like Attila the Hun or the Golden Horde attest to this. Indeed, the fall of Rome assumed a pivotal position in the history of Western consciousness – an event illustrating the vulnerability of sedentary society to the *power* of nomadism. Khazanov points to the long-standing dependence on nomads of many different sedentary societies (1984:222-7). Furthermore, he argues (1984:222) that:

> "until the modern period with its revolution in things military, sedentary states were unable to find any permanent solution to the military problem of how to defend themselves against the raids of nomads. It is this fact that explains the following paradox: in different regions and in different historical periods sedentary states built expensive defensive systems on borders with the nomadic world but again and again nomads have shown that these systems were ineffective...."

Ibn Khaldun's (1980) seminal philosophy of history *The Muqaddimah* is based upon this central dialectic of nomadic/sedentary interaction. And, rather than pathologising the destructive capacity of nomadism, he points (1980, (1) 250) to its rejuvenative qualities within the indulgence and complacency of sedentary existence. To him:

> "Sedentary people" means the inhabitants of cities and countries, some of whom adopt the crafts as their way of making a living, while others adopt commerce. They earn more and live more comfortably than Bedouins because they live on a level beyond the level of bare necessity and their way of living corresponds to their wealth."

However, Ibn Khaldun (1980, (2) 296) regards their comfort as a corrupting influence:

> "The goal of civilisation is sedentary culture and luxury. When civilisation reaches that goal, it turns towards corruption and starts being senile, as happens in the natural life of living beings."

Examples of social theory like this expose the myth of ease and inevitability attached to nomadic-sedentary transition. Attention to this myth begins to situate contemporary anti-nomadism in terms of the history of a much more real and extensive 'threat' posed by nomads to sedentary societies.

Alienation and unease of the nomadic-sedentary transition

So the nomadic-sedentary transition was neither irreversible nor inevitable. And neither was it unambiguously positive – even for the people being sedentarised. Despite the virulence of sedentary attacks on the uncivilised nature of the nomad, there is evidence to suggest that sedentarisation was far from emancipatory for formerly nomadic groups. To begin with there are the old truths about the ease and relaxed nature of existence in hunter/gatherer and pastoral societies. There is a genuine freedom involved in 'primitive communism' which is lost in sedentary 'civilisation'. And the equation of 'civilisation' and 'sedentarisation' is itself problematic since some nomadic societies produced states and cultures which were just as sophisticated as their sedentary counterparts. So there is nothing inevitably good or civilising about the nomadic-sedentary transition.

Furthermore, while sedentarism may have been unambiguously advantageous for an emerging dominant class, this is no reason to suggest that it was good for the whole society. (There is a similarity here with the way in which individual property rights benefit a minority class while expropriating the vast majority of the people.) So a very large question mark has to be placed alongside the notion of advantage and progress and civilisation involved in nomadic-sedentary transition. Furthermore, there is much evidence to suggest that the transition was actually associated with a profound sense of loss and unease. Indeed, there is a whole historical subtext to the transition which is characterised by a sense of loss and envy among the sedentarised. This is deeply rooted in the historical consciousness of Jewish, Christian and Muslim culture. Many key biblical myths concern nomadic/sedentary difference – the whole notion of the Fall of Man is a fine example of the unease associated with sedentarisation.

Agriculture required sedentarisation and introduced work into social life. It may have ensured a more secure food supply but it also entailed the end of nomadic freedom – the expulsion from the Garden of Eden. (We get, simultaneously, the creation of one of the first patriarchal myths – women are blamed for the expulsion from the garden or, decoded, the invention of agriculture.)

These arguments should not be taken too far but it is clear that elements of this sense of loss remain with us. The contemporary construction of nomads continuously emphasises the freedom of the 'Gypsies' or New Travellers. Even when it is palpably clear that sedentary prejudice, discrimination and repression is making the lives of nomads anything but free and easy, commentators refer constantly to the liberatory aspects of nomadism. Traditional stereotypes about nomadic identity occur *ad nauseam* – even in serious or quality reportage. For instance, in 1992 the *Observer* reported the expulsion of thousands of Romanian Gypsies from Germany under a headline of: "King of the Gypsies refuses to give a royal pardon to worst of his subjects". Based on the spurious testimony of a Romanian Gypsy 'Royal family', the article proceeded to uncritically reproduce almost every existing anti-Traveller stereotype.

" 'Gypsies' are 'feckless', deceitful, incapable of organising to defend themselves, 'unscrupulous' and 'aiming at big families to take advantage of family allowance". Their pathological dishonesty has obvious benefits: one *Observer* informant is, "dripping gypsy gold in a sweeping polka dot shirt", another has, "gold-spangled hands". We are told that these *Roma* show no:

> "fine liberal outrage at German discrimination against their
> gypsies. They do not label Romanians racist, nor do they dredge
> up the crime committed against their people by the Nazis. Like
> any Romanian, they know that gypsies tend to be feckless and are
> liable to steal." (15 November 1992)

The report further repudiates "liberal outrage" and the "dredging up" of best-forgotten Nazi crimes in fine style. We are told, "gypsies as a rule refuse to take advantage of the free education Romania provides. No asset to any factory, they are among the first to be made unemployed now". Nonetheless, "many [Gypsies] are better qualified than most to profit from the unscrupulousness that is the Romanian economy today". Finally, we are reassured that, "the vast majority of those being returned may be the victims of discrimination but not of persecution". If reports like this were not appearing in the context of intensifying European racism, their reproduction of absurdly inaccurate caricatures of Roma and other nomads would be laughable. In the face of the resurgence of anti-Traveller discrimination and pogroms across Europe, such reporting plays an invidious part in the continued oppression of Europe's oldest racialised minority population.

This kind of (mis)reporting also evidences the continuing construction of nomadism as 'the great romantic alternative to modern life'. This reproduces wider sedentary notions about nomadic 'freedom' – social, cultural and sexual. There are obvious echoes here of nineteenth century romanticism when the Gypsy was a central motif in anti-modernist discourse. It bears emphasis, however, that nomadism is not an alternative to modern life but rather an alternative modern way of life. And nomadism is often far from being romantic – not because of its intrinsic qualities but because the sedentarism which forces nomads onto illegal, unsafe, unhealthy and unserviced sites precludes this. It is wrong to use notions which reproduce the dichotomy between 'good' Travellers (ethnic, exotic, romantic, free) and bad travellers (non-ethnic, dispossessed and debased sedentaries, subcultures of poverty). In fact, the suggested dichotomy between the construction of the romanticised 'Raggle Taggle Gypsy' and the pathologised 'itinerant' is a false one. Both simultaneously inform contemporary ideas about and the treatment of, *all* nomadic peoples. While arguments about Traveller inadequacy may dominate, other elements recognising the power and freedom of nomadism continue to be a subtext. These draw on the deep-seated and long-standing alienation attached to sedentarisation. They suggest that even for sedentaries the sedentary condition continues to be characterised by unease and dissatisfaction.

Nomadism and ethnicity

I have already suggested that, while the focus on sedentarism has emerged from the theorisation of anti-nomadic racism, there is a connection between the construction and treatment of 'ethnic' Travellers and travelling people who are not 'ethnic nomads' (Okely 1983). This suggests that there are crucial similarities between the sedentarism which informs anti-Gypsy practice and the sedentarism which informs anti-vagrant practice. This is not to deny the centrality of nomadism to the ethnicity of many Travellers who are indeed ethnically distinct from the sedentary population with which they have most contact (McDonagh 1994; Ní Shuinéar 1994). I am certainly not arguing that ethnic nomads and New Travellers are the same. I am, however, suggesting that the sedentarism which attempts to control and eliminate both these groups is essentially the same and that it needs to be theorised with each of these groups in view. This raises questions about the connection between sedentarism which focuses on ethnic nomads and can be theorised as racism and the sedentarism which attaches to nomads and Travellers who are 'not ethnic' (at least at present). What is the connection between nomadism and ethnicity? And, how far are ethnic nomads and 'vagrants' separated in the sedentarist mind?

The beginnings of an answer to this are found in accounts of the 'vagrancy problem' in England at its height in the sixteenth and seventeenth centuries and the way that vagrants and ethnic nomads were constructed. Beier (1985:64) in his *Masterless Men* suggests that at the time, "although they roused fear and loathing, gypsies and the Irish were few in number compared with English vagrants." But he also argues that Gypsies and the Irish travelled in large companies and to some extent family-type units were formed among English vagabonds by taking new partners and stealing or adopting children. But it was exceptional to find vagrants in very large troops and even when couples and their children increased in number in the early Stuart period they rarely accounted for more than a third of the total. Above all, vagrancy was a crime of the young male (1985:68).

Beier suggests, therefore, that there are four key points concerning the profile of the whole vagrant community. Firstly, there is a clear distinction to be made between what he calls 'alternative societies' which are capable of reproducing themselves physically and culturally over time and individual vagrants who are not. Secondly, most members of the whole vagrant community are individual vagrants rather than members of 'alternative societies'. Thirdly, this minority vagrant population of the 'alternative societies' are either ethnic nomads – the Irish and the 'Gypsies' – or else they have the potential to become such – those English vagabonds in family-type units. Fourthly, ethnic nomads – the Irish and Gypsies – were the principal alternative societies at the time. Thus only a minority of vagrants were members of 'alternative societies'; but a majority of this minority were ethnic nomads.

Despite these important distinctions, Beier points to the overlap between the construction of vagrants and ethnic nomads. He suggests:

"Gypsies and English vagrants merged in the official view for four reasons. First, they both led itinerant and masterless lives... Secondly, some vagrants may have taken the speech and apparel of gypsies. A third reason for the merging of the two groups is that, although foreign immigrants in the previous century, by Elizabethan times most gypsies were born in England. But if they were considered natives, then governments had to develop some means of dealing with them. In the event the answer, as with vagrants, was compulsory service, thus blurring the distinction once again. Finally, gypsies were suspected of similar offences to vagrants, including larceny and cheating. They were also considered threats to the government." (1985:62)

Thus, whatever the consciousness of internal differences among members of the nomadic and vagrant communities themselves, the subtleties of these distinctions are often lost on sedentary people with the power to define the 'whole vagrant population'. I want to suggest that this continues to be the case. Although any anthropologist could identify profound differences between ethnic nomads, other 'alternative societies' and individual vagrants, these are not necessarily of immediate importance in terms of sedentarist philosophy and practice. So, while I want to confirm that sedentarism assumes specifically racist forms when it affects ethnic nomads, I also want to suggest that not all sedentarism is racist. In the case of nomadic ethnicity, sedentarism inevitably assumes racist forms. This is because nomadism is a constituent part of the ethnicity of 'ethnic nomads' - forcibly to sedentarize them is not simply to stop them travelling, it is actively to destroy their ethnicity or 'race'. Thus sedentarism has genocidal implications *vis-à-vis* ethnic nomads, like Roma and Irish Travellers, which are missing with non-ethnic nomads, however vicious or unjust the oppression of the latter. Despite this, however, it is not of the essence of sedentarism that it is racist – it can be used against any travelling person or group of persons whatever their ethnic identity or background. Thus, all sedentarism which affects ethnic nomads is *ipso facto* racist but not all sedentarism affects ethnic nomads.

In this way the structuring effects of sedentarism extend well beyond ethnic nomads. I have laboured this point but this is absolutely necessary since leaving ambiguity on the issue lends support to the sedentarist and racist. It bears emphasis that a crucial element in the operation of contemporary sedentarism is the denial of the ethnicity of *any* nomads. Although working with an exoticised fantasy of the 'true Romany', the experience of discrimination and oppression by nomads is repudiated because they are not 'real Gypsies'. This process serves to deny the authenticity of sedentary/nomadic difference. It re-invents 'Gypsies' and Travellers as 'itinerants' and explains their oppression in terms of a 'subculture of poverty'. In this way the solution to the problems of nomads becomes assimilation, they must become sedentary in order to be helped. Because of this process, the demand of groups like English Romanichals and Irish Travellers for recognition of their ethnicity is about much more than responding to liberal multiculturalism – it is a key strategy in their struggle for survival as nomads. Thus, it is important not to collapse the differences between ethnic nomads and non-ethnic nomads. That said, however, it is still possible to begin to theorise sedentarism in a way that sees it structuring the lives of ethnic nomads and non-ethnic nomads alike. Once the specificity of the experience of ethnic nomads is recognised, it is possible to make sense of the commonality between their experience and that of contemporary nomadic 'alternative societies', including the New Travellers. In this way sedentarism is seen as having a much wider structuring influence than has been previously suggested. Because of this, it is my contention that the sedentary/travelling nexus remains one of the *key* power interfaces in *every* European social formation, however few or many ethnic nomads there are in a given state.

The triumph of sedentarism: modernism and the nation-state
The final triumph of sedentarism was represented by the arrival of two distinct but related phenomena in human history – the nation-state and modernity. With the nation-state came the border – the key metonym for the sedentarist social formation. Witness Giddens (1985:49-50) on the arrival of the nation-state.

> "In distinguishing the territoriality of traditional states from nation-states, it is essential to see that the 'frontiers' of the former are significantly different from the 'borders' that exist between the latter. In all cases, 'frontier' refers to an area on the peripheral regions of a state (not necessarily adjoining another state) in which the political authority of the centre is diffuse or thinly spread. A 'border', on the other hand, is an known and geographically drawn line separating and joining two or more states. While there may be, and often are, 'mixed' social and political traits displayed by groups living in border areas, those groups are distinguishably subject to the administrative dominion of one state or the other. Borders, in my view, are only found with the emergence of nation-states."

He is correct in this. Compare his borders with the 'frontiers' which characterised early sedentary societies still permanently threatened by nomadic invasion – the Great Wall of China, the Roman *limes* in North Africa and so on (Khazanov 1984:222). Thus with the arrival of the nation-state and the notion of the *border*, space began to be occupied in a totalised way – there were fewer and fewer places for nomads to move on to.

They were increasingly problematised and controlled and repressed within nation-states intent on the centralisation and consolidation of power and surveillance. As these new states sought to copper fasten their monopoly over the legitimate means of coercion, they showed particular interest in removing nomads from their jurisdiction.

But there was also an intellectual and spiritual dimension to the drive for order and control characterised by the emergence of the nation-state. There was an elective affinity between the re-ordering of the world in the intellectual domain and the more mundane and practical imperative to do the same thing in the social and political domain. The continued existence of nomads and vagrants was a key symbol of the unfinished project of modernity and the evidence of the survival of unwanted elements from the pre-modern. Thus modernity signalled a profound change in the symbolic function of the nomad and vagrant, especially and crucially in the cityscape of modernity. Intellectual and administrator conspired to construct the nomad and vagrant as a key symbol of disorder and disorder as the bane of modernity. As Zygmunt Bauman (1992: xiv-xv) puts it in his powerful evocation of the moment of modernity:

"The vision of visionaries joined hands with the practice of practitioners: the intellectual model of an orderly universe blended with the ordering bustle of the politicians. The vision was of a hierarchical harmony reflected, as in a mirror, in the uncontested and uncontestable pronouncements of reason. The practice was about making the pronouncements adorned with badges of reason, uncontested and uncontestable. The new, modern order took off as a desperate search for structure in a world suddenly denuded of structure. Utopias that served as beacons for the long march to the rule of reason visualised a world without margins, leftovers, the unaccounted for – without dissidents and rebels; a world in which, as in the world just left behind, everyone will have a job to do and everyone will be keen to do the job he has to: the *I will* and *I must* will merge. The visualised world differed from the lost one by putting assignment where blind fate once ruled. The jobs to be done were now gleaned from an overall plan, drafted by the spokesmen of reason; in the world to come, design preceded order. People were not born into their places: they had to be trained, drilled or goaded into finding the place that fitted them and which they fitted. No wonder utopias chose architecture and urban planning as both the vehicle and the master-metaphor of the perfect world that would know of no misfits and hence of no disorder; however much they differed in detail, they all lovingly detailed the carefully segregated and strictly functional urban quarters, the straight, unpolluted geometry of streets and public squares, the hierarchy of spaces and buildings which, in their prescribed volumes and austerity of adornment, mirrored the stately sovereignty of the social order. In the city of reason, there were to be no winding roads, no cul-de-sacs and no unattended sites left to chance – and thus no vagabonds, vagrants or nomads."

"The vision of visionaries joined hands with the practice of practitioners" – the elective affinity of modernity and the nation-state. These worked symbiotically to problematise nomadism and itinerancy. If modernism was about ordering and controlling, then the nation-state became the key mechanism for securing order and control. And no-one threatened the emerging hegemony more than the nomad whose mode of existence was the very antithesis of this project. Thus sedentarism became a central motif of modernity. The persecution of 'vagrancy' developed apace from the fifthteenth century onwards; it sought to deny an existence which represented a fundamental challenge to dominant and dominating sedentary modes of production and consumption. And this aspect of sedentarism extended well beyond petty discord between nomads and sedentaries. It was most brutally manifested in the frequent attempts by European states to exterminate all 'Gypsies' within their borders. This aspect of European sedentarism reached it nadir in the *Porraimos* or great devouring – the Romani holocaust. The total annihilation of 'Gypsies' and other Travellers was attempted through sterilisation, deportation and murder (Hancock 1988a). Up to 1,500,000 European *Roma* and other Travellers were killed by *Einsatzkommando* death squads and in death camps. However, the *Porraimos* was not a terrible aberration: it was only the logical development of centuries of anti-Gypsy racism which had already become manifest in slavery and genocide (Hancock 1988b; Kenrick and Puxon 1995). Thus sedentarism has long been about more than unfocused and localised anti-nomad prejudice. It is important to remember that anti-nomad prejudice and discrimination has been (and remains potentially) a prelude to genocide.

Once again there are obvious similarities between racialised discourse about ethnic nomads and ideas about 'vagrants'. Just as anti-Semitism and anti-Gypsy racism have been dressed in the most technocratic and rational language as answers to the 'Jewish problem' and the 'Gypsy problem', so the 'vagrancy problem' can inspire 'moderate' and 'sensible' solutions with quasi-genocidal implications. Such is the tone as William Harbutt Dawson sets out his stall in his 1910 thesis *The vagrancy problem*. In his argument there is no suggestion of the atavism or irrationality with which we might dismiss contemporary racism – it is modern, mature, indeed, *sociological*, to plan for the 'rational treatment' of the 'vagrancy question':

> "The principles which underlie our [English] treatment of the social parasite afford an illustration of our national conservatism. Alone of Western nations we still treat lightly and almost frivolously this excrescence of civilisation. Other countries have their tramps and loafers but they regard and treat them as a public nuisance and as such deny to them legal recognition; only here are they deliberately tolerated and to some extent fostered. Happily we are now moving in the matter and moving rather rapidly. A few years ago it was still accepted as an axiom by all but a handful of sociologists – men for the most part regarded as amiable faddists, whose eccentric notions it was, indeed quite fashionable to listen to with a certain indulgent charity but unwise to receive seriously – that there was really only one way of dealing with the tramp and that was the way of the Poor Law. That this was also the rational way was proved by

the fact that it had been inherited from our forefathers and who were we that we should impugn the wisdom of the past? And yet nothing is more remarkable in its way than the strong public sentiment hostile to inherited precept and usage which has of late arisen on this subject. It is the object of this book to strengthen this healthy sentiment and if possible to direct it into practical channels. The leading contention here advanced is that society is justified, in its own interest, in legislating the loafer out of existence, if legislation can be shown to be equal to the task."
(Dawson 1910: viii-ix)

This approach repeats itself time and again as different modernising theorists address the problems of 'vagrancy' or 'itinerancy' or nomadism. It includes the repression of the 'travelling' or 'tramping' system which had been part of the first attempts of organised labour to resist unemployment and wage restraint (Leeson 1979). Towards the end of the nineteenth century both the state and the new unions strove to eradicate the system. The pathologisation of tramping is witnessed by the pejorative connotations which the word 'tramp' came to assume; earlier tramping was perfectly 'respectable' for craftspeople in search of employment. Whether the subject is ethnic nomads or 'tramps' or 'vagrants', whether their putative solution is cultural assimilation or physical extermination, the motif is an obsessive desire to *control*. This is the linking thread between history of nomadic/ sedentary tension and the triumph of sedentarism in modernity and the nation-state. It is the linking thread between enlightenment rationality and the social formations it inspired. In the movement towards 'modernity', we see a similar quest to eradicate difference in pursuit of the better society manifested in fascism and state socialism and the welfare state.

Theorising sedentarism
So far I have argued that the sedentary/nomadic interface is a long-standing, important and under-theorised dialectic in human history. I want to turn now, however, to the present – to a period of sedentarist hegemony – and begin to make sense of the effects that the ascendancy of sedentarism has on people's lives, nomadic and sedentary alike. It is not easy to theorise sedentarism in any simple or straightforward way. Contemporary sedentarism is rooted in the transition from nomadic to sedentary modes of existence that I sketched above. However, it has also assumed novel forms in the late twentieth century and we need to understand these in order to resist the pathologisation and repression of nomadic peoples.

Although sedentarism is not reducible to race or class, it is structured by both. We have already seen how sedentarism is racialised in the construction and treatment of Irish Travellers and English Romanichals. I want to turn now to the sense in which it is about class and property relations. The class element in sedentarism is most obvious when it reproduces and legitimises capitalist notions of ownership and control. This happens because the very existence of nomads continues to raise questions about the legitimacy of 'legal' ownership – particularly the ownership of land. If a nomad stops somewhere where nomads have always stopped (especially if this is or was 'common land') and the 'owner' raises questions about their right to be there, this in turn raises questions about the legitimacy of the owner's claim to ownership and wider questions about the legitimacy of current land-holding patterns.

This nomadic challenge to capitalist property relations is obvious because the claim to individual possession of land is itself so bogus. Unlike capital or property which can become reified in the process of commodification and reproduction, the connection between pre- and post-expropriated land is very obvious. Land stays in the same place, it often retains the same name, hence it is especially difficult to justify the process which saw landholding transformed from democratic common ownership to undemocratic individual ownership. Since this transformation was achieved by theft and violence – against the will of the vast majority of the people to which it belonged in common – it is something which is difficult to defend or disguise. Nomads, by their very existence, bear witness to this unjust and brutal transformation and underline the continued illegitimacy of contemporary property relations.

In many colonised countries the transformation from common ownership to private possession goes back to the moment of colonial confiscation. It bears emphasis that the nomadism of indigenous peoples was often the justification for a particularly vicious form of colonial expropriation. Where indigenous peoples were sedentary, prior ownership was sometimes recognised (albeit through vastly unequal and frequently broken treaties). Where indigenous peoples were nomadic, prior ownership was denied and the colonised given the status of non-people, uncivilised and incapable of civilisation. In these instances, colonies became identified as *terra nullius* – or an 'empty land' – not because they were empty but because their inhabitants were nomadic. As nomads – or so the argument went – they were inherently incapable of exploiting the land properly. This could only be done by the civilised and sedentary colonists.

In countries that were not formally colonised, the transformation from common to individual ownership goes back to the enclosures and the privatisation of common land. Thus most peoples have experienced a process of land expropriation of epochal proportions as a consequence of either capitalism or colonialism or both. Whether or not this took place in the context of imperialist expansion, it involves the sedentary colonisation of nomadic space. Ever since the simultaneous and intrinsically related expansions of capitalism and colonialism, the travelling dispossessed have threatened the established economic and political order. Their existence remains evidence of the acts of colonial and class theft which were the definitive part of the transition from free nation to colony and from feudalism to capitalism.

Ultimately, however, anti-nomadism is not simply about bourgeois or colonial hegemony – it is not reducible to class or colonialism. This is because nomads do not just threaten current property relations which benefit a particular sedentary class: they also threaten the sedentary identity which has been adopted by *every* non-nomadic class. The affinity of sedentary peoples to particular places and localities contrasts with the more general relationship to land and environment which exists with nomads. More specifically, sedentary peoples possess and exploit land in an individualised, privatised and capitalised way which is impossible among nomads. Because of this difference, the nomad occupies a central position as a symbolic other within sedentary cultures. The cultural and social identity of nomadic communities continues to undermine hegemonic sedentary notions about work and property. The resistance of nomads to proletarianisation (or more likely now 'lumpenproletarianisation') has been and remains an example of the possibility of alternatives to this process. In addition, nomadism illustrates alternatives to the order and control exercised through settlement and individual property rights. Thus, the political and cultural resistance of nomads continues to subvert deep-seated beliefs about the normalcy of settlement and wage labour and private property which pervade the *whole* of sedentary society. This is precisely what New Travellers have achieved. In a period of Thatcherite/ Blairite hegemony they represent the continued possibility of alternatives; indeed the continued possibility of *resistance*.

Nomadic/sedentary tension is therefore about something more than class location. Nomads *qua* nomads and sedentaries *qua* sedentaries stand in a contradictory relationship because they occupy the same social space in a profoundly different way. If there are nomads and sedentaries in a given social formation, they share an environment but relate to it in very different – and sometimes contradictory – ways. This is not dependent on whether the sedentary or nomadic social relationships involved are primarily capitalistic or communistic. When nomads and sedentaries coexist, the pre-conditions for nomadic/sedentary tensions also exist; *whatever the social relations of production predominating in the two groups.* This is not to suggest that these tensions cannot be accommodated or even transcended. But it is to suggest that the contradictions are *real*. They are more than the false consciousness of a sedentary working class who have failed to see that their true interests lie in solidarity with nomads rather than with those of a repressive sedentary state. Nomads receive immediate and oppressive policing by the state in the interest of all sedentary people, not because of what they *do* but because of what they *are*. Their very existence threatens, undermines, 'invades' sedentary identity. In consequence, the repression of nomads is supported because it is in the interests of a sedentary population which has internalised the dominant ideology of sedentarised identity and individual property rights.

The continued criminalisation of nomadism seeks to deny an existence which – symbolically and practically – challenges a sedentarist hegemony. This aspect of sedentarism is about much more than localised tensions between nomadic and sedentary populations. Sedentarism is more properly seen as a specific form of oppression – like racism or sexism – which developed historically out of the interface between nomadic and sedentary modes of existence. A crucial point is that the logic of much of its practice is not simply to repress or discriminate against nomads but to get rid of them altogether. Thus both 'liberal' and 'reactionary' sedentarisms have posited 'final solutions' to the 'problem of nomads' which actively seek their annihilation. Because of this the historical and contemporary treatment of nomads should not be dichotomised as repressive extermination versus sympathetic assimilation. Rather both approaches have been part of a complex dialectic committed to a 'final solution' to the 'problem of nomads'.

Bearing this in mind, it seems likely that the moral panic around New Travellers will soon enter a new phase. Words like 'plague' and 'blight' will disappear – at least in official discourse. Liberal experts will appear to answer the question, "What can we do for these people?" And a whole series of measures to 're-integrate them into society' will be suggested. But this discourse is itself inherently problematic and it is hardly new. For years ethnic nomads have been harassed by 'sympathetic' organisations who insist that assimilation – *sedentarisation* – is the answer to their problems. Earlier I mentioned how the denial of ethnicity becomes a central means of supporting liberal assimilationist strategies. It is necessary to draw out the implications of these strategies since they are often contrasted benignly with the kind of overtly genocidal policies which reached their terrible nadir in the Nazi holocaust. When people begin to speak of assimilation, it seems that, at last, somebody is doing something *for* the nomad. While previous policy alternated between expulsion and extermination, both unambiguously premised on the notion that the nomads were inherently undesirable, now the assimilationists promise a more sympathetic ear – the assimilationists are actually doing something in the nomads' interests. (This is not to suggest that assimilationism arrived from nowhere in the 1960s. Much earlier and more overtly violent assimilationist strategies had been applied in Austria and Spain where nomads became, respectively, 'New Hungarians' and 'neo-Castillians'. Assimilationism was also actively applied within the Communist states of Eastern Europe.)

It is true that assimilationism signals a change at the level of discourse – extermination and expulsion are solely concerned with the interests of sedentaries while assimilation is *presented* as being in the interests of sedentaries *and* nomads. But the logic of assimilation is the logic of 'final solution' – after the nomad is sedentarised, the 'Gypsy problem', the 'New Age Traveller problem' and the 'itinerant problem' all disappear. In this sense, the aim of assimilation – 'getting rid' of nomads - is little different from extermination. The efforts of well-meaning politicians, social workers and educationalists and health workers who adopt a sedentarist and assimilationist paradigm *vis-à-vis* Travellers and other nomads is equally genocidal in effect. Forcing nomads into houses is – at a social, cultural and spiritual level – no different from forcing nomads into gas chambers. Whether the rhetoric is couched in terms of kindness to the nomad or sedentary necessity, the solution is always the termination of nomadism: genocide and assimilation are simply variations on the theme of the 'final solution'. The nomad is increasingly caught in this genocidal dialectic between sympathetic incorporation and unsympathetic repression. Repression ranges from forcible moving on to attempted genocide – both equally intent in removing the nomad and 'itinerant' from society. But benevolent assimilationism has had just the same intent. Indeed, perversely, it has sometimes been the case that sympathetic welfarism has proved *more* successful in the obliteration of nomadic people. Repression may simply lead to the expulsion of nomads from an area with their identity intact while assimilation insists on their absorption. In the end, however, repression and assimilation are complementary sedentary projects. Genocide and assimilation carry with the same ruthless imperative – the relentless sedentary colonisation of nomadic space.

Coda

Human rights activists and anti-racists must begin to actively oppose sedentarism – not only because it is oppressive to different nomadic peoples but also because it has much wider implications. Sedentarism is already being employed to strengthen a coercive and repressive apparatus that will be used against sedentary people as well as nomads. To begin with, anti-nomad stereotypes must be challenged and inverted. The myth that nomads are pathologically anti-social and criminal must be repudiated. The reality of sedentary colonisation of nomadic space must be traced and exposed. This process begins with the removal of access to traditional nomadic sites. It continues with the refusal of the sedentary state to provide alternative legal, serviced sites for nomads. In the absence of legal sites, nomadism is rendered illegal *whatever individual nomads do*. Thus sedentary colonisation ends up with nomads criminalised not for their acts but for their *existence*. Through this kind of sedentary incursion, nomads are forced into illegality by the logic of sedentarism rather than the 'nature' of nomadism.

We must also address anti-nomadism in a way which encourages the development of a partnership between nomads and sedentaries which is emancipatory for both. This is no easy task. We have looked at the long-standing basis of nomadic/sedentary conflict – this will not disappear overnight. Tensions associated with the different nomadic and sedentary 'modes of existence' need to be engaged with imaginatively. But the recognition of nomadic rights – most importantly an unambiguous acceptance of the right to travel – will transform this situation. Many anti-nomad stereotypes are reproduced because of the state's refusal to provide even the most basic services for nomads. If services were provided with the active participation of nomads (and in a nomad-specific way where necessary), many of the immediate causes of sedentary/nomadic friction would disappear. Most crucially, the provision of an adequate network of legal and properly serviced sites would undermine much sedentary prejudice. It would begin to allow the opening up of nomad/sedentary dialogue on a more equal footing and encourage nomads and sedentaries alike to think about ways in which the genuine differences between them can be accommodated.

We also need to think seriously about *difference*. We must move away from a position of assuming that equality will obliterate difference towards thinking about how we can actively create societies in which people are genuinely 'equal but different'. This is palpable in the case of nomads when it becomes reactionary – and sometimes genocidal – to support sedentarisation. We must begin to think creatively about ways in which the continued difference between sedentary and nomad can be rendered less antagonistic. It is true that the otherness of nomads *vis-à-vis* settled society often appears more stark and absolute than any other difference. (At times every category of sedentary has united against the nomad across gender, race and class.) But there are ways of subverting this sedentary consensus without supporting assimilation. Here the importance of theorising – and celebrating – difference becomes apparent. The aim of public policy should not be to get rid of nomads, nor indeed to 'tolerate' them. Rather, we should accept that it is a 'good thing' - economically, politically, and spiritually - to live in societies, locally and globally, which include nomads *and* sedentaries. This is the first step towards dismantling contemporary sedentarism and challenging the reactionary and oppressive consequences it has for sedentary and nomad alike.

References

ACTON T 1974 *Gypsy politics and social change: The development of ethnic ideology and pressure politics among British Gypsies from Victorian reformism to Romany nationalism* Routledge and Kegan Paul, London

BAUMAN Z 1992 *Intimations of Postmodernity* Routledge, London

BEIER A L 1985 Masterless Men, the vagrancy problem in England 1560-1640 Methuen, London

CALLANAN H 1995 "Just Opt-outs with bare feet and beautiful handwriting: Helen Callanan visits the New Age travellers at the centre of the rumpus in Fermoy" *Sunday Business Post* 3 September

DAWSON W H 1910 *The Vagrancy Problem: The case for measures of restraint for tramps, loafers and unemployables: With a study of Continental Detention Colonies and Labour houses* King, London

DELEUZE G and GUATTARI F 1988 *A Thousand Plateaus: Capitalism and Schizophrenia,* trans B Massumi, Athlone, London

DUBLIN TRAVELLERS EDUCATION AND DEVELOPMENT GROUP 1992 *Anti-Racist Law and the Travellers* DTEDG, Dublin

GIDDENS A 1985 *The Nation State and Violence* Polity, London

HANCOCK I 1988a " 'Uniqueness' of the Victims: Gypsies, Jews and the Holocaust" *Without Prejudice: International Review of Racial Discrimination* vol. 1, no. 2, pp.45-67

HANCOCK I 1988b *The Pariah Syndrome: An account of Gypsy Slavery and persecution* Karoma, Ann Arbor

IBN KHALDUN 1980 [1377] *The Muqaddimah: An introduction to history* trans. Franz Rosenthal, Princeton University Press, NY

KENRICK D and PUXON G 1995 *Gypsies under the Swastika* University of Hertfordshire Press, Hatfield

KHAZANOV A M 1984 *Nomads and the outside world* Cambridge University Press, Cambridge

LEESON R A 1979 *Travelling Brothers: The six centuries' road from craft fellowship to trade unionism* Granada, London

LIÉGEOIS J P 1995 *Roma, Gypsies, Travellers* Council of Europe, Strasbourg

McCANN M, SIOCHAIN O and RUANE J 1994 *Irish Travellers: Culture and Ethnicity* Institute of Irish Studies, Belfast

McDONAGH M 1994 "Nomadism in Irish Travellers' Identity" in McCann et al 1994

NÍ SHUINÉAR S 1994. "Irish Travellers, Ethnicity and the Origins Question" in McCann et al. *1994*

OKELY J 1983 *The Traveller-Gypsies* Cambridge University Press, Cambridge

Chapter 2 Why do Gaujos hate Gypsies so much, anyway? A case study

Sinéad ní Shuinéar, Researcher and Translator, Dublin

Robbie McVeigh's chapter in this book looks into why people whose lifestyle keeps them more or less tied to one place (sedentary people) feel so much hatred and mistrust towards those whose lifestyle does not (nomadic people). This is an extremely complicated question and so basic that it has almost never been tackled head-on. This chapter tries to build on his work.

McVeigh goes deep into the social and psychological roots of this hatred and mistrust but does not touch upon three other related issues, all of them of direct interest in the real world:

1 Why do New Age Travellers inspire such fanatical hatred? Why single them out instead of simply lumping them in together with other Travelling groups? This question has intrigued me since I first saw a British documentary on the subject, in which 'local residents' claimed over and over again that they had no objection to 'genuine Romanies' (nothing new there), *nor* to 'Irish Tinkers' (a first!), but only to New Age Travellers.

2 If it really is nomadism they object to, then why do settled people always insist that they have nothing against what they call 'genuine Romanies', a sort of fairy-tale idea of a super-nomad? Wouldn't it make more sense for their strongest hatred to be aimed at the most nomadic of the lot?

3 Why do settled people everywhere block the exact same thing that they demand': that is, that nomads should settle down and become part of the community? And how is it that, where nomads *have* settled down (sometimes over many

generations, as with the Roma of Central Europe) the hatred
is still there, as strong as ever?

These are huge questions and very, very complicated ones; every time
we think we've made sense of something, we find we've opened yet another
can of worms. This short chapter, the work of months rather than years,
cannot answer all the questions. It can make a start, although, in the
interests of getting that bit closer to the root question, 'Why?' In doing this,
I will be focussing on Traveller/Buffer relations in Ireland. ('Buffer' is the
Irish Traveller word for 'Gaujo'. It is used here to describe the non-Traveller
Irish. 'Irish' will cover both Irish Travellers and Buffers. 'Gypsy' and 'Gaujo'
(the Romani word for non-Gypsy) respectively will be used to describe
Travellers and non-Travellers generally, and 'English' will mean British
Gaujos, including the Anglo-Irish). Traveller/Buffer relations in Ireland
have enough in common with Gypsy/Gaujo relations in other places to
suggest that what we learn from them may help us to understand things
much further afield.

Gaujo images, Gypsy screen
Many before me have suggested that Gaujos *need* Gypsies, an idea
beautifully summarised by Jean-Pierre Liégeois (1994:199):

> "The image of the stranger and of the strange, updated every few
> years, exposes the fears and worries of those who create it, by
> giving shape to the group's idea of its 'opposite'; this idea is then –
> like a film – projected away from the group, so they can see it
> clearly and distance themselves from it. Just as a tent is held up
> by the guy ropes holding it down, the group needs a
> counterbalance to stand upright. The worries projected onto this
> image are the worries on the mind of the group at any given time.
> Therefore, whenever we look at how Gypsies and Travellers are
> treated, we are at the same time looking at the social history, the
> politics and the psychology of those who are reacting to them."

I want to put it even more precisely: just as Santa Claus is the idea of
Christmas cheer and giving all rolled into one fairytale person – their
personification – Gaujos need Gypsies to *personify* their own faults and
fears, thus lifting away the burden of them.

This need is so overpowering that time after time, in place after place,
Gaujos create situations forcing Gypsies to fill this role.

It is important to remember that what we're talking about here are
not 'alien' faults and problems but *Gaujos' own;* therefore, the people onto
whom these are projected must be clearly distinct from the Gaujo
mainstream, but not utterly foreign to it: just as in a cinema, the screen
must be neither too close nor too distant if the image projected onto it is to
remain sharply focused.

This insight already suggests answers to our first two questions. The
fairytale 'ultra nomad' would be too different – too distant – to serve as a
focus for Gaujo problems. Unlike the Gaujo's 'genuine Romanies' (quietly
carving clothes pegs and snaring rabbits in a forest somewhere), however,
New Age Travellers actually exist and can be seen to exist. What makes

them even more terrifying than Gypsies is that, while it is easy to tar them all with the one brush and claim that everyone living on the road does the same horrible things, the fact that there is no clear dividing line between New Age Travellers and Gaujo society spoils the illusion that these negative characteristics exist only among nomads and are foreign to the majority. New Age Travellers are too close to other Gaujos to function as a projection screen. Indeed, they are a spanner in the works of the whole projection process since they force those trying to distance themselves from the faults they despise to face the uncomfortable truth that, much as they try to fool themselves, these problems are in fact at least as much their own as anybody else's.

It also explains why – from Ireland to Russia and from Finland to Spain – the overwhelming evidence of Gypsies' own history, language, culture and so on is systematically ignored and denied and Gypsies defined as criminal, backward, deprived, etc: that is, as being just far enough from the mainstream to sharply focus what Gaujos fear and dislike about themselves.

Good traditions and good changes, bad traditions and bad changes
In any society some things change while others do not; some of the changes are seen as improvements, others as deterioration, while some of the constants are cherished and others rejected as old-fashioned and due for the scrap-heap.

Obviously, there is never 100 per cent agreement within the society as to which is which: for example, the fact that the Catholic Church controls less and less of Irish life is seen by some as painfully slow positive change to something that should have gone long ago and by others as disastrous negative change to a positive core element.

This kind of disagreement might lead to real problems. Conflict within the group, and the bad feelings it gives rise to, must be channelled outwards for the group to function smoothly. The tried and tested method for achieving this is the presence of an outside threat, which is why Londoners look back to the 'good old days' of the Blitz, a time when everything that divided them became meaningless compared with the danger they faced together.

Who we are not shows us who we are
It is also true that 'we' can only really see ourselves and figure ourselves out, when there is a 'them' with whom to compare ourselves. It is only by seeing what we are *not*, that we realise what we hold in common.

This broadens out how we see society. It's not quite as simple as 'us' and 'them' because people and ideas change over time. Both groups have some traditions seen as good and others seen as bad; both groups change with the times and some of these changes are seen as good (throwing out old fashioned bad traditions) while others are seen as bad (throwing out honoured good traditions). 'We' measure 'them' by our ideas of right and wrong; more important, 'we' measure *ourselves* against what we imagine 'they' are up to.

Travellers, as the only minority group native to the island of Ireland, were the only candidates for this 'yardstick of otherness' post, although societies with far broader options likewise chose the nomads, or the descendants of nomads, among them to play this role, for all the reasons identified by McVeigh. Sedentarism – living in one place – is so taken-for-granted that it isn't even recognised as something that unites the sedentary until they see that some people somehow manage without it. The non-sedentary group is so tiny that almost everybody in the society, regardless of class, religion, even language and race, can use it as a shared 'them', compared to which people from all these classes, religions, languages and races can see themselves as forming a single, united 'us'. In the everyday world, Gypsies help to bring everybody else together, much as German bombs did.

But the Irish situation involves more than two players. Our society was formed under centuries of colonial occupation and this has shaped both how Buffers see themselves and how Buffers see Travellers. There are two 'thems' against which Buffers measure and define themselves:

English	**Buffers**	**Travellers**
('them')	('us')	('them')
foreign	native	native
minority	majority	minority
powerful	powerless/powerful	powerless

Clearly, Irish Buffers are in the middle: 'not English' and 'not Traveller'. For centuries they themselves served as a yardstick of otherness for the English, as a powerless 'minority group' in their own homeland where they unlike equally powerless Travellers – are the majority in terms of numbers. Caught in the middle like this, Buffers (unlike, say, the English or French) cannot ever see their ways as the only possible ones; instead, they see themselves as a happy medium somewhere between two different groups, both of which go too far in opposite directions. We must also remember that the powerful 'them' (the English) shaped not only how Buffers see themselves but also how Buffers see the other, powerless 'them' – Travellers. Yet another can of worms is the idea that the Travellers may be the descendants of a pre-Celtic people conquered by the ancestors of today's Buffers, in which case the two relationships (English/Irish, Buffer/Traveller as coloniser and colonised) are even more alike.

The English/Buffer/Traveller relationship is one which has grown and changed over time and which is very, very complicated. It is even more complicated by the fact that, after hundreds of years of direct political control of Irish affairs, the role of the English has, in the Republic of Ireland, changed to one of indirect but ever-present social and cultural influence – a direct continuation of the historic past – over the last fifty years.

Since I want to see if my idea – of Travellers as a projection-screen for the things Buffers hate and fear within themselves – holds true over time, I will have to look at the English dimension but, both because Ireland is now independent and to keep things clear, I will concentrate on the two-player 'them' and 'us' situation and limit reference to the third party (England) to the time when they were in direct control of – and defined – *both* Irish groups. Concentrating on two players should also make it easier to take the lessons learned from the Irish situation and see if they apply in Gaujo/Gypsy relations in other places.

The yardstick of otherness

The point is that 'we' are defined, not by who 'we' *are* but by who 'we' are *not*. We understand only what makes us us when we have something with which to contrast ourselves. Even so, we do not approach the problem directly, as one of figuring out what makes ourselves tick. Instead, we do it by figuring out the other group and what they are like. The less powerful that group is the freer 'we' become not only to believe whatever we like about them but also to control conditions in such a way that 'they' must behave as we need them to, to be whatever it is that we need them to be. This is how we see it:

'Us'	**'Them'**
Good traditions	*Good traditions*
The time-honoured core values, beyond questioning.	These basic values are so taken for granted that, where they are shared neither side even notices. Values that are not shared, are not recognised as positive.
Good changes	*Good changes*
In general 'our' changes are advances; 'new' = 'improved'.	Any change 'they' make which brings them closer into line with 'us' is a good thing.
Bad traditions	*Bad traditions*
Hangovers from the past. Changing slowly – but changing.	Anything which 'they' do but 'we' do not or which 'we' used to do but don't any more.
Bad changes	*Bad changes*
The side-effects of progress; we'd rather avoid them but they're a fact of life (apologetic/passive attitude).	'They' are changing in far worse ways than 'we' are (alarmist/activist attitude).

Ideas and ways of doing things that have been around for a long time tend – whether the people concerned are happy with them or not – to be seen as 'natural'. In fact Travellers and Buffers share so many of these that people who are not part of either group – in particular the American anthropologists George and Sharon Gmelch, who wrote a number of books about Irish Travellers – may fail to see any meaningful differences between them at all. Most of these ideas are so basic that neither group can imagine any other way of doing things: having only one husband or wife, the fact that women do most of the childcare, different rules for men and women. Others are more particularly Irish: being Roman Catholic, the kinds of foods people like to eat, putting a lot of value on being able to use language in creative and colourful ways. Since the whole function of 'them' is to be different from 'us' so we can see ourselves in comparison, neither group notices core values shared by both: these are not recognised as the cultural common ground they are.

On the other hand, long-term elements which the groups do not share stand out very clearly. They take two different forms: things which have 'always' been seen as belonging only or mostly, to Travellers (nomadism being the most basic of these) and things which the two groups used to share but which 'we' have changed while Travellers haven't: arranged marriages, large numbers of children, violent feuding between different groups of families. These traits that used to be shared by both groups are a particularly sore point, not least because they were exactly what the English pointed to when drawing the lines between themselves and the Irish in general. When Buffers see Travellers still doing these things, they go on and on in just the same way as someone who's finally given up smoking and won't rest until they've converted the rest of the world. Their message to Travellers is "It wasn't easy but *we* did it – *we* gave them up – why can't *you*?" Ideas and customs that Travellers have held on to but Buffers have got rid of, are seen by Buffers as backwardness, superstition, and old-fashioned or, in the language of political correctness, as internalised oppression. Buffers can't help having very strong, uncomfortable feelings about them because they're a reminder of who and what they themselves used to be.

Because it is new, people *do* notice change, even without another group with which to compare themselves since they can use their memories of 'the way we were' as a measuring-stick. Any changes 'they' make that bring them more into line with things 'we' approve of, are noticed and give 'us' a feeling of satisfaction, since this just proves that we were right all along and the others are finally seeing the light. This is true whether the changeover is towards something which 'we' have been doing for so long that we're convinced it's simply natural (for example, more Traveller children going to school, more Traveller families moving into houses) or is new for both groups (greater freedom for women, for example). *'We' do not notice any of the positive things we share with 'them', unless 'they' are only just taking them on.*

But what I want to focus on here is the kind of change that people feel bad about and would rather put a stop to if they could. It's impossible to pretend that something bad is natural if you can remember a time when things were different.

Other people's problems take your mind off your own
Buffers, like any other people forced to live under a foreign power, know all too well what it is to feel angry and helpless. But now that the English have gone, Buffers are still not fully in control of their fate. On the contrary, bad change is happening so fast and going so deep, that people get dizzy just thinking about it: unemployment, violent crime, drug addiction, AIDS. These problems are huge, complicated and seemingly impossible to halt. They are so big that it's difficult to even figure out what's causing them, let alone do something about them. This adds an unbearable helplessness to an already desperate atmosphere of personal threat and the awful feeling that everything is falling apart. Now as in the past, these problems must be made to seem *relatively* small by inventing *even worse* versions of them and projecting these onto a *small* group of outsiders so that the majority can feel it can do something about solving them. Of course, since the outsiders' problems are supposedly so much worse and so much more urgent, than 'ours', it makes sense to put our energy into solving 'their' problems first.

The theory I want to consider is that Gaujos use Gypsies to personify *whatever it is that they are unhappy or worried about in themselves and their own society* at any given moment. If I am right, then we will see that Gaujos have been doing this for a long time but that at least some of the things they accuse Gypsies of will have changed over the years.

Gypsies play along
Before going on to look at the historical evidence I would like to point out that Gypsies themselves are not entirely passive victims in this process. On the contrary, they know all about it and make it work to their advantage. There are two reasons for this, both of them perfectly practical. Firstly, a tiny minority group, always scattered in even tinier units of a couple of families at most, living in among a huge majority who make no secret of their hatred, must use every possible means to prevent physical attack. The best way of achieving this is by making the majority afraid to do so.

Gypsies work on Gaujo fears. Whenever Gypsies publicly display themselves as 'insanely' violent, they are effectively warning Gaujos not to mess with them. Every Gypsy association with fortune-telling, curses, mysterious powers and all the rest of it sends the same message. These are long-term strategies.

Second, since Gaujos are going to believe the worst of Gypsies anyway, it makes sense to plug into this belief in the short term as well. This is why Gypsy women begging are only too happy to tell Gaujos exactly what they want to hear about how their drunken, violent husbands refuse to work, leaving them and the children, desperately short of food, clothing and anything else that might be going. Families trying to get a place on a legal site tell Gaujo authorities piteous tales of the dreadful hardships of life on the road. The Gaujo belief that all Gypsies are poor comes in handy for getting food, clothing and other things at a good discount; when looking for this kind of special treatment, Gypsies dress and speak in ways that make their Gypsy identity very clear.

Books written about Gypsies give loads of examples of how this works. For example Ann Sutherland (1975) describes how Gypsies in California made a hilarious game out of failing intelligence tests, in order to qualify for disability payments. Jan Yoors (1967) tells stories of Gypsy children scratching themselves as if they had lice or some horrible disease, in order to clear a train compartment of Gaujos and to get meat that they had made a point of pawing, at reduced price. In the early nineteenth century George Borrow came across Gypsies using a special kind of poison that kills cattle without affecting the flesh – they could then get the carcasses for little or nothing by assuring the Gaujo farmer that Gypsies enjoy eating carrion (Borrow 1874, cited in Okely 1983:98). And so on and so forth. In other words, Gaujos – be it in Ireland or anywhere else – do not act alone when they form their picture of who and what Gypsies are. Convincing them of just how right they are when they believe the worst, is a highly-developed Gypsy art form. We should bear this in mind when trying to figure out the real meaning of whatever information comes our way, whether it is from a hundred years ago or in today's newspaper.

Examining the evidence
To write this paper, I needed to find out, not what language experts,

folklorists and the like had to say but rather how the ordinary grassroots Buffer or Gaujo has seen Travellers down through the years. I found the information I needed in the Irish Traveller Resource Collection assembled by Aileen L'Amie at the University of Ulster at Jordanstown, just outside Belfast: over 200 years' worth of sources as varied as *The North British Advertiser and Ladies' Journal, Ireland's Own, Ireland of the Welcomes,* collections, novels, tourists' diaries, newspaper cuttings, residents' association newsletters and so on. I also looked at dozens of questionnaires about Travellers issued by the Irish Folklore Commission and filled in by Buffer contacts in every county north and south, back in 1952, which gave a very broad picture of Buffer thinking at that particular time. I read dozens of official policy statements from government departments, county councils and the like and checked out hundreds of more recent (late 1960s onwards) Traveller-related newspaper cuttings in both the *Irish Times* and Pavee Point archives.

My basic idea is that Gaujos project their own badness and fears onto Gypsies. If I am right, then we should find a sort of hard core of anti-Traveller ideas that stays the same over long periods, as well as a number of accusations that come and go and perhaps come back again as the things that Buffers worry about change over time.

Changing times
As we look at the information I have put together here, I would like to remind the reader of three hugely important developments that have happened in Ireland over the past 150 years and which have affected everyone, Buffer and Traveller, living on this island. The Famine, in the mid-1840s, exactly 150 years ago, marks the time when we were completely powerless under English rule. Gaining our independence was a long process – the British army left Southern Ireland in the 1920s but Éire only became a fully independent republic in 1949. This was when Buffers began to take responsibility for running their own affairs and as they did so asked themselves a lot of hard questions about who they were and what kind of country they wanted. They didn't turn their attentions to Travellers until the mid-1960's, when the 'itinerant settlement' industry got started and has got bigger and bigger, under various names, ever since. This new way of treating Travellers, essentially exactly the same as Buffers themselves were treated by the English, came about when Buffers felt more sure about who and what they were.

Before the Famine

> I see a column of slow rising smoke
> O'ertop the lofty wood that skirts the wild.
> A vagabond and useless tribe there eat
> Their miserable meal. A kettle flung
> Between two poles upon a stick transverse
> Receives the morsel, flesh obscene of dog
> Or vermin; or at best of cock purloin'd
> From his accustomed perch. Hard faring race!
> They pick their fuel out of ev'ry hedge,
> Which kindled with dry leaves, just saves unquench'd

The spark of life. The sportive wind blows wide
Their fluttering rags, and shows a tawny skin
The vellum of the pedigree they claim.
Great skill they have in palmistry, and more
To conjure clean away the gold they touch,
Conveying worthless dross in its place.
Loud when they beg, dumb only when they steal.
Strange! that a creature rational and cast
In human mould, shou'd brutalise by choice
His nature! and tho' capable of arts
By which the world might profit and himself
Self-banish'd from society, prefer
Such squalid sloth to honourable toil.
Yet even these, tho' feigning sickness oft
They swathe the forehead, drag the limping limb
And vex their flesh with artificial sores,
Can change their whine into a mirthful sound
When safe occasion offers, and with dance
And music of the bladder and the bag,
Beguile their woes and makes the woods resound.

This poem (Anon. in *Belfast News-Letter*, 1785, from Cowper 1785) is a sort of shopping-list of stereotypes and includes just about everything imaginable: eating carrion and the famous stolen chicken, fortune-telling, trickery, refusal to work, miserable poverty, pretending to be ill or crippled to get money by begging – and the awful suspicion that, whenever they're on their own, Travellers are laughing their heads off at the stupid Buffers. It was published in the *Belfast News-Letter* in 1785. Although English in origin it wouldn't have been printed in Belfast unless readers there would recognise the ideas in it. Fifty years later, The Reverend Mr. Burke (1835) in an article in *The Westmeath Chronicle and Longford News-Letter* on the widespread practice of begging explains how:

"Able-bodied men sometimes put forward the *plea of fruitless search for labour, and* women say it of their husbands, and vagrants often *foster rags, dirt, and the appearance of disease,* for the purpose of exciting sympathy ... they have been detected using forged recommendations, & co., and thus evince a state of mind *incompatible with morality.* They sometimes, too, *by their exhibition of sores, have done injury to women in the family way* ... The habits of those who live by begging are frequently *dissolute, and* the town beggars drink and smoke ... the number of *thefts* committed by them is very great ... The *earnings of the beggar increase according to the number of family* ... they have in general from 3-7 children, and a great [sic] number of *illegitimate children* than the other [sic] class ....The effects of vagrancy are agreed on by the witnesses to be: the *spreading of diseases, the contamination of morals,* and the mischievous effects of spreading and inventing stories ..." The iItalics in this and, unless otherwise stated, every other quotation are mine, just to draw attention to things.]

The author goes on to explain how beggars collect such vast amounts of potatoes that they sell the extras to buy – surprise, surprise – "whiskey, tobacco, tea, & co". He claims one shopkeeper had recently resold 300 *stone* of potatoes bought from beggars. He finishes off by saying that "religious feelings at present exist in some degree on the subject; but if an institution were on hand to relieve the beggar, the priest said it would be looked on as a sin to give him anything," also claiming that "the dislike of the peasantry to prosecute for petty offences was chiefly owing to sympathy for their poverty ... but if [public] provision was made, that repugnance would certainly cease."

The interesting thing about this piece is that it was written, not by a Buffer but by a member of the other 'them', an English vicar. Not only are all of the familiar Traveller stereotypes – including supernatural power, in this case to harm babies in the womb – to be found here; so too are English middle class perceptions of the Buffer peasantry, since the author says that: "There are a good many who have always been beggars from childhood, but the majority are reduced persons ..." in other words, drop-outs. Since as far as the writer is concerned, the people in question are mostly Buffers, then the bad qualities he sees in them are clearly concentrated versions of general *Irish* (Buffer *and* Traveller) traits: avoiding honest labour, loose, drunken living, irresponsibly (not to mention immorally) breeding large numbers of children on purpose just to get people to feel sorry for them.

I have copied out quite a lot of this piece, both because it is the longest one I've come across that was written before the Famine, and because it clearly shows us how the powerful 'they' – the English – shaped the way Buffers see themselves, the way they see Travellers and the way the two groups relate to each other – not to mention taking on the power to decide who and what Travellers are, by deciding how they came into being. It is especially interesting to note that the author feels there is a common bond of sympathy between the two (the peasants, and the 'vagabonds' who, he says, are basically peasant drop-outs themselves), which he says should be broken by state (English) intervention. At the time that this English vicar was defining Travellers as the dregs and dropouts of the lowest part of Irish society, that is, the peasantry, the peasants themselves believed the exact opposite: that Travellers were the descendants of the old Gaelic aristocracy – the very highest part of Irish society before it was conquered and brought low by the English.

From the Famine to Independence
Between the time of the Famine and Independence, English sources outnumber Buffer ones by about three to one and as we read their words, we must bear in mind where these writers are coming from: the English, after all, saw Travellers as an even more alien, exotic extension of the already alien and exotic Irish peasantry. The (unfavourable) contrast with British Gypsies must always be there and was sometimes put into words.

George Borrow (1862, 1969:31) gives a description of some Irish Travellers met in Wales in 1854: they "had nothing of the appearance of the children of the Egyptian race, their locks not being dark, but either of a flaxen or red hue, and their features not delicate and regular, but coarse and uncouth, and their complexions not olive, but inclining to be fair". Later (p.34) he gives us a portrait of two Irish Traveller women "both were ugly. The younger was a *rude, stupid-looking* creature, with *red cheeks and redder hair*, but there was a dash of intelligence and likewise of *wildness* in the countenance of the elder female, whose *complexion and hair were rather dark"*. Here racial characteristics are clearly associated with ethnic characteristics: while "the children of the Egyptian race" have dark hair and skin, and delicate regular features – which he associates with intelligence and wildness – the Irish are not only fair or red in skin and hair but ugly, coarse, uncouth, rude and stupid-looking.

Many of today's familiar themes are already to be found from the mid-1800s on: nomadism or "the mania for vagrancy" (Bulfin, 1907, 1981), untidy appearance or "a number of mutilated garments of various structures and colours oddly patched together, the whole giving no indication whatever of the sex of the wearer" (Finlay 1873 – notice how horrified the writer is at the idea of clothing that is not completely different for men and women). They are accused of dirt, persistent begging and general trickery, particularly in connection with horse/donkey dealing. This last has since been updated to cover more current trades: scrap, tarmacadaming.

Another striking preoccupation of the time is the religious question: they are bad Catholics or none (Bulfin, 1907). The *Ulster Journal of Archaeology* devoted a long article to Travellers' keeping on pre-Christian ("idolatrous") beliefs and practices and comments: " ... they can scarcely be called Christians, notwithstanding their outward pretensions to devotion and their constant attendance at places of prayer. They are always conspicuous *outside* the gates .... They never attend or receive the sacraments of any church ..." (Hackett 1862, original italics). Borrow himself (1862, 1969, pp.35-6) was treated to a virtuoso performance by Irish Travellers who took him for a man of the cloth:

> "Oh it was kind in your honour to come to us here in the Sabbath evening, in order that you might bring us God. Oh, your Reverence! Give us God! Pull out the crucifix from your bosom, and let us kiss the face of God! Oh, Sir, do give us God; we need him, Sir, for we are sinful people ... we do many things beside tinkering, sinful things.. Give us God! Give us God!"

As far as the English are concerned, Travellers *cannot* be Gypsies because Gypsies are the projection screen of the English; instead, Travellers personify everything the English see as typically Irish.

Accusing Travellers of sexual conduct outrageous by the standards of the time is a theme that crops up over and over again. Many sources mention casual wife-swapping, couples agreeing to stay together for a fixed period before going their separate ways, men having several wives at the one time and divorce. Just about everybody – well into the present century – mentions 'jumping the budget' (a Traveller, non-Church wedding ceremony).

Most remarkable of all is the way Gaujos see Travellers as being at one with nature (which, of course, means that they have more in common with animals than with people). The following quotation is typical:

> "They seem to be proof against chills and aches which afflict

many of the well-cared members of society ... They sleep comfortably on the ground on the wettest night with only an old sack thrown over them." (O'Connor 1918)

Once in a while this is put directly into words as in this account from Simson (1865) in which a Gaujo describes seeing,

" ... outside one of the tents, in the open air, with nothing but the canopy of heaven above her and the greensward beneath her, one of the females, *like the deer in the forest*, brought forth a child, without either the infant or mother receiving the slightest injury". (In fact, the picture is not quite so idyllic as the author insists, since the reason the birth took place "on the greensward" was because the midwife in attendance "said these Irish Gipsies are so covered in filth and vermin that she durst not enter one of their tents, to assist the female in labour".

Despite being "of nature", Travellers are not 'natural'; after all, they breed children just so they'll be given more when begging, "as auxiliaries and profitable appendages" (Hackett, 1862). In this way, Travellers are *below* nature but in other – threatening – ways, they are above it: they are closely and firmly associated with the *super*-natural and this is repeated and confirmed on the flimsiest of evidence. Synge (1906, 1980), an Irish author who studied country folk and their beliefs around the turn of the century, comments that "tinkers have a curious reputation for witching and unnatural powers" and relates the following story in which a Traveller woman enters a home where her husband is carrying out repairs to the tinwork, making polite conversation by complimenting the baby:

" 'That's a fine boy, God bless him.'
'How do you know it's a boy,' says my woman, 'when it's only the head of him you see?'
'I know rightly, and it's the first too.'
Then my wife was going to slate me for bringing in people to bewitch her child, and I had to turn the lot of them out to finish the job in the lane." (Notice that the Travelling woman used the phrase used by both sets of Irish to this day to *protect* the child from evil, by adding "God bless him.")

Independence: Buffers finding their feet
These well-established ideas live on after Independence – and some new ones make an appearance. A piece with the interesting title, *Parasites without power* (Daiken 1947), introduces a new way of looking at what it calls "this pariah of the new democracy in Éire." Note that the Travellers are seen as predatory despite arriving at harvest time, presumably to work:

"To see tinkers converging on a fat parish, in a single large family, or a winding procession of wagons, carts, and trotting foals, the women and girls hardy and bright-eyed, holding infants, the men independent, if ragged, with glances full of that 'separateness' you sense in the eyes of the outcast and the underprivileged, the

teeming kids, wild as fox cubs and as untamable – is to witness
resentment crossing the faces of the propertied, the comfortable,
the snug. Bitterly do they inspect this parcel of human
grasshoppers and bluebottles commandeering the public road at
harvest time – and they feel uncomfortable."

There is nothing new about classing Travellers as belonging to nature
but openly contrasting them to the Buffer peasantry is something we had
not seen before. The author goes on to outline how 'tinkers' had prospered
in the ass trade during the recent war, much to the resentment of farmers
whose children had to emigrate to Britain to find work to keep themselves,
and their families at home, going. For the first time, the catalogue of
resentment of "No taxes, no commitments, no ground rent, no stabling
expenses, no overhead fees, church dues, nor liabilities other than bad
debts" is outlined. Yet the author cannot resist making digs that show how
he feels towards *both* groups:

"Private wars are commonplace and fighting – savage and foul
fighting at that – is, I should think, the primitive animal force
that keeps them alive at all ... At a pub I knew on the fringe of the
Coombe [inner-city Dublin working class community], tinker
brawls, which at closing time frequently rent the weekend
asunder, cost so much in glass and blood that the publican had to
call in a force of Civic Guards [police] to protect his *civilised
customers – who fought only for the best patriotic motives and for
freedom.*"

Another source (Duff 1952) a few years later introduces a few more
new stereotypes:

"In the old days, the tinkers did much useful work mending pots
and pans ... Carefree, colourful existence ... seldom committed any
crime worse than an occasional stroke of violence ... they were not
regarded as a bad nuisance ... they were nearly all poor ...How
different are the tinkers today! ... Real poverty among them is
rare...[they are] rich dealers in cattle, horses, and the bigger
things of life... The main characteristic of the tinker we now meet
is his aptness to 'fly off the handle' ... and then he can be a
dangerous and very violent creature."

That quote dates from 1952, the very year of the Irish Folklore
Commission's all-Ireland (Republic and Northern Ireland) survey on
Travelling People, a questionnaire covering factual questions like numbers,
types of work, surnames and so on, as well as what Buffers knew or
believed about them. It was answered by educated individuals
(schoolteachers and clergy) living in the countryside and gives us our first
real insight into popular Buffer attitudes. I studied twenty five of these in
detail. They carried – in order of frequency – the following accusations:
fighting, straying/trespassing animals, drinking, cheating, stealing,
inspiring fear, destruction, idleness, placing curses on people and animals
and dirt. The meaningful 'new' element here is the direct threat Travellers

are universally felt to pose to the property of the Buffer peasantry – although there is no way of knowing how long Buffers had felt this way since this was the first time the views of the 'plain people' were recorded. Questionnaire after questionnaire repeats farmers' complaints of Travellers loosing their horses into fields (including fields under cultivation) at night, leaving gates open and damaging fences (allowing livestock to stray), damaging potato clamps, etc.

Another point worth mentioning is the cast-iron dividing line believed to separate 'Tinkers' and 'Gypsies': the latter practise different trades (lace, artificial flowers and three-legged tables, in addition to horse and donkey dealing on a vast scale) and are noticeably distinct both physically and by clothing. Yet virtually all of these sources identify these models of respectability as the Munster-based Sheridans – to this day remarkably successful but staunchly insistent on their identity as Irish Travellers (with Gammon, not Romani, as their ethnic language). Going over the sources from the early 1950s, I was also struck by a *Beano*-like obsession with 'grub': statements like "they look well fed", "good food and plenty of it" crop up over and over again. More directly linked with the question this chapter is looking at, is the following extract that I found in one of the original responses to the Irish Folklore Commission survey, by a man aged eighty-six at time of writing:

> "I think that while not endeavouring to wipe out completely the tinker tribe, an effort should be made to control the whole class and make them do more work for the nation at large. Ancestrally tinkers may claim a sort of protection but when one sees them as a class they will become a damned nuisance. Unless some steps are taken to put a limit to their number we shall soon have such an increase to their ranks as will cripple the present efforts of our rulers to make our people into workers for the country's good. Tinkers are, as you know, idlers, and we want no idlers at this juncture in our efforts to advance our nation. I do not know if you notice that our workers now do as little as possible to speed up any kind of work they happen to engage in ... somehow I fancy they say to themselves, 'Why should we work hard when we see so many of the tinker class idling about and having a good time?'" [He goes on to tell a long story about watching builders' labourers combing their hair, chatting up passing girls, etc. while keeping a lookout for the boss] "I have come to the conclusion that we are fast becoming a nation of slackers."

It would be hard to spell it out more clearly: the borderline between "their" undesirable characteristics and 'ours' is blurred indeed. The writer claims both that 'our rulers' are trying to *cure* the Buffer population of idleness and that the same population is *"becoming* a nation of slackers". In either case, Travellers personify this 'idleness' and so must – despite their 'ancestral claims' which the writer clearly feels positive about although he does not explain exactly what they are (probably because Buffers in general shared this positive image at the time) – be 'controlled', their numbers limited. He does not go into detail as to how this should be done; a decade later this had become a growth industry.

Solving the itinerant problem: we're okay and you can be, too
"The Commission on Itinerancy was established by the government in June 1960 with the following terms of reference:

1 to enquire into the problems arising from the presence in the country of itinerants in considerable numbers,

2 to examine the economic, educational, health and social problems inherent in their way of life,

3 to consider what steps might be taken –

a to provide opportunities for a better way of life for itinerants,

b to promote their absorption into the general community,

c pending such absorption, to reduce to a minimum the disadvantages to themselves and to the community resulting from their itinerant habits, and

4 to make recommendations." (Commission on Itinerancy, 1963:1).

The Commission itself was a made up of a cross-section of broad Buffer interests comprising representatives of the health services (three), local authorities (two), the law (two), agriculture (two) and education (two). In addition to general appeals through the mass media, direct approaches were made to various religious leaders, government departments and fifteen charitable/voluntary organisations – six of which were connected with agriculture! The purpose of the exercise is "the solution of the itinerant problem" and the *Report* makes detailed recommendations with a view to achieving this goal. For example, state benefits to caravan-dwelling "itinerants" are to take the form of vouchers rather than cash, "so as to overcome abuse by dissipation on intoxicating liquor"; scrap collection should require a licence valid only within a "clearly defined" area, so as to "discourage" nomadism; "education" for "the children of itinerants" is deemed "urgently necessary", not as their right, but "as a means of providing opportunities for a better way of life and of promoting their absorption into the settled community" (Commission on Itinerancy, 1963:92-3, 74, 67). The colonised had become colonisers.

It is important to understand that Buffers acted this way out of feelings of charity and kindness: "itinerant settlement" was a 'liberal' cause, as we see in this 1964 reader's letter to *The Evening Press*, published under the heading, *Homes for itinerants*. Notice that Buffer (as opposed to English) society is now not only seen as 'normal' but 'industrious and self-respecting' in contrast to a group who (unlike 'us') "have no sense of their own worth as human beings":

"Nenagh guild Muintir na Tire [a farmers' community organisation, literally, "The People of the Country(side)"] is to be congratulated on the constructive way in which it has set about helping the itinerants. It is only by offering homes and the opportunities of leading a normal life that there is any chance of the itinerants becoming normal members of society. Time and again we hear people piously stating that the itinerants would not be happy in houses. Very often these people are afraid that, should the itinerants be put living next door to them, it would lower the tone of the district. These selfish people are all for herding the itinerants together in encampments and then conveniently forgetting about them. It is only by settling one family of itinerants in each town or district that they will become industrious, self-respecting members of society. The itinerants have no sense of their own worth as human beings but it is up to us to treat them as we would have others treat us."

The *Report* inspired a rush of voluntary activity nationwide.

"I remember it well – the day the penny dropped ... Of course, I had seen people like this before, sometimes *drinking and fighting* in the market-places, being hunted out of town ... All over Ireland, and particularly in the vicinity of the larger towns and cities, human beings are living in *abject distress*, sometimes *hungry*, always *cold* and *miserable*, completely *cut off* from the amenities which the normal individual takes for granted. These are the *untouchables*, the *leper colonies* of Ireland. They are existing in caravans – if they are lucky – otherwise under canvas, without heating, cooking or toilet facilities ... Is it any wonder that they grow up without any of the social graces and very often with a confirmed distrust towards society? ... You will be glad to hear that an opportunity now exists in our town to *wipe out this cancer* which is *eating into our inner lives* and is a terrible reflection on our sense of justice and charity. An association is now in existence, willing to *solve the itinerant problem*." (Keane, 1989).

In March 1969 local bodies like this one came together under the clear title of The Irish Council for Itinerant Settlement. Just over a year later, the first issue of their organ, *Settlement News*, gives a detailed report of developments in Killarney, Co. Kerry:

"The committee decided that the only permanent solution to the problem was to house the eleven families they thought belonged to Killarney ... There were a lot of hurdles to jump before the ultimate goal was reached – the first of these was to get them off the road." [local opposition, influx from outside, "a bit of a flare-up", but] "at least the itinerants from other counties left, while the indigenous members remained."

This introduces themes which were to become universal: moving Travellers about like pawns on a chessboard, the claim that provision acts as a magnet, bitter local opposition to provision of any kind and, perhaps most tellingly, "A new type of 'foreigner' was thus created: not one from another land, but one who had crossed a Gorgio [sic] administrative boundary" (Okely 1983:77).

Two years later, a local fundraising booklet (Ennis Itinerants Settlement Committee 1972a) spelled it all out:

What itinerancy is

To 'us'
Unsanitary and ugly roadside camps
Begging in streets and shops
Drunkenness, fighting, and anti-social behaviour
Trespass
Laziness and idleness

Simple – isn't it?

To "Them"
Ditches are cold and hostile but they must do – there is no home, no open door
Plagued by ignorance and years of isolation there is no method or know-how. Money is wasted or in the vicious circle of things demanded in fines
No regular or proper meals plus lack of self restraint
No education, discipline, proper feeding, clothing, or shelter ...

Not so simple – is it?"

Among the listed needs:

"A COMMUNITY HALL where travellers can come together and learn in security to grasp the new life. If they do not grasp, adapt and relate they will slip down the ladder of society becoming spiritually impoverished people devoid of culture and character – the body and soul of living. [sic]

A SCHOOL – it is recognised that all of them need some special education.

ENTERTAINMENT & CHILDHOOD for the children. It has been discovered that most traveller children don't even know how to play! Weird – isn't it?"

A few months later, the same body issued a special report on progress in education, with the following newly identified 'need':

"THE CHILDREN need to be dressed *like all other children*. Harmonious integration will not be helped if one set of children wear *distinctive* or inadequate clothing (Ennis Itinerants Settlement Committee 1972b).

By now, clearly, the very fact that Travellers exist at all has become objectionable and seen as an absolute reversal of normality. Who could fail to be moved by the plight of distinctively dressed children who don't even know how to play, in danger of becoming spiritually impoverished, devoid of culture and character?

Yet new problems were quickly identified. In 1974 a social worker (cited in Dublin Committee for Travelling People 1977) reported:

> "The children from these families constitute the biggest single social work problem in this area ... begging and stealing ... The worst aspect of the problem is that the children spend so much of their lives on the streets, even at night, that they have now picked up all the vices that one would expect in an urban area."

The 5th Report of the National Council for Travelling People (1974) noted:

> "Many committees are worried about increasing incidence of prostitution among newly housed teenage girls. These girls are ill-equipped to meet the social and economic pressures of their new surroundings, which urge them to shake off parental discipline and old *tribal* conventions. Social activities and employment must be made available to these girls, to offset this trend. Early marriage is *not* the solution. ... Early marriage often takes place because of fear of pregnancy outside marriage. *Small families should be encouraged and the teaching of some form of family planning is desirable.*"

Note that promoting contraception was a radical position at the time, when the pill was only just becoming available, *not* as a contraceptive (which, like every other artificial means of birth control, was still illegal) but supposedly as a cycle regulator to help married women whose unpredictable fertility made it difficult to practise the church-approved rhythm method.

Another pamphlet (Sligo Committee for Travelling People, n.d.) of about that time spells it out even more clearly, starting with the alarming statistic of:

> "...a natural increase in the [Traveller] population [of Co. Sligo] of about 5 per cent per annum ... This indicates that if emigration stopped, the problem facing the authorities in integrating this community would grow at a startling rate and this does appear to be now happening.

> The people [sic] of Sligo are, therefore, faced with three choices:

> **a** ensuring that emigration of itinerants to Britain continues, banishing our social problem
> **b** tolerating a very fast-growing itinerant population, especially around the town
> **c** integrating the present travelling community quickly."

Unlike most other publications of the time, with their 'Christian charity' lines, this publication is refreshingly honest and practical:

"...This tendency for the whole Travelling Community to avoid full-time work costs the state unemployment assistance alone in the Sligo area £646 per week. Now the Travellers have to a large extent settled within localities and the payment of unemployment assistance is hindering their integration because it reduces their incentive to work ... At the moment this community is contributing the minimum to society and taking the maximum in the form of social welfare and other benefits. Our economy is too poor to allow this situation to continue."

"Where do they come from?"

"Where do you come from?" is the Gaujo way of asking "Who are you?" and so, as Buffers transformed 'tinkers' into the 'itinerant problem', they also had to change their ideas about how Travellers came into being. The Commission on Itinerancy (see list of membership above for an idea about how well-qualified its members were to make pronouncements about Traveller history), while stating that it had not been asked to do any research into Traveller origins, was not shy about spelling out its understanding that itinerants are the "...descendants of the remnants of Irish tribes dispossessed in the various plantations ... the descendants of those who were driven to a wandering way of life because of the poverty and distress caused by the famines of the last century, the oppressions of the penal law era and earlier ..." (Commission on Itinerancy, 1963:34) Travellers, then, are (like 'us'), the victims of colonialism but (unlike 'us') were crushed by it: there but for the grace of God we go, with "no sense of our own worth as human beings" and "spiritually impoverished, devoid of culture and character".

By 1971 the redefinition process was complete, thanks to an unusually well-researched and clearly written master's thesis, (McCarthy 1971) the very title of which, *Itinerancy and Poverty,* makes it clear that these two go hand-in-hand. Surely the most widely circulated and quoted unpublished work in Irish history, its key concepts are outlined in firm detail:

"It is a basic assumption of this study that the Irish travellers are not gypsies [sic] and do not constitute a separate ethnic group with an entirely separate tradition and culture. Poverty is considered to be basic to the problem of itinerancy in this study."

The author addresses policy questions head on:

"It is legitimate to ask why the travellers have been defined as a social problem to the extent that a government commission was set up to investigate their way of life and make recommendations to improve it. Such factors as increased social consciousness, increased affluence and thus the ability to do something about it, fear of trouble from the deprived sector and damage to property, adverse effect on the tourist industry, increasing lack of tolerance for nuisance and dependent behaviour, all play a part in the definition of itinerancy as a social problem."

Moreover,

"It appeared in many ways as if the folkways of the travellers had been frozen at some point around the end of the last century, possibly coinciding with a breakdown in any reciprocal relationships with the settled population. The symbols of poverty are retained by the travellers and this is undoubtedly a factor in the prejudice against them. The donkey, the pony and cart, the barefoot children, the dress of the women, the squalid living conditions, all have a negative value *now* for Irish people because of their association with poverty. Often these folkways are just rituals retained from the past which may lead the scholar to believe that they are part of a functioning and satisfying total culture. The travellers may indeed speak with the voice of tradition, but they are forced to act with the logic of inherited poverty." (McCarthy 1972 pp 6, 8, 13, 14).

Note that, despite the fact that McCarthy completely changed her ideas within a couple of years, her efforts to take back what she wrote in the early 1970s have been completely ignored by the establishment (cf McCarthy 1994) which continues to quote *Itinerancy and Poverty* as convenient scientific back-up.

On the ground McCarthy (1972) was translated as:

"The policy makers believe that the differences in culture have been brought about by poverty and social isolation and that these cultural differences are therefore not worth preserving." (Sligo Committee for Travelling People n.d.).

Key words at this period were *re*housing, *re*settlement and even *re*habilitation: the official line was one of righting an ancient wrong, done not to 'them' but to 'us' from whose ranks 'they' were unwillingly driven. Everything distinguishing Travellers from Buffers was seen as a legacy of colonial oppression, backwardness clinging to characteristics proper to the Buffers of yesteryear and/or a direct result of poverty.

Political correctness: words change, ideas don't

The original key words, 'itinerant settlement', quickly became politically incorrect: within four years of its foundation, the committee renamed itself 'The National Council for Travelling People', although 'itinerant', a term invented back in the 1960s, is even now to be heard in the general media and particularly from individual Buffers wishing to demonstrate how liberal they are (by not using the more popular terms, all of which are meant to be insulting). The hysterical language of the early days (see above) was replaced by sweet reasonableness,with more and more lip service to respecting Travellers' own wishes. Twenty years on, in 1983, a follow-up *Report of the Travelling People Review Body* published the lessons learned and updated recommendations:

"The Review Body considers that in the light of experience and current knowledge the concept of absorption is unacceptable, implying as it does the swallowing up of the minority traveller group by the dominant settled community and the subsequent loss of traveller identity. It is suggested that it is better to think in terms of integration ..."

"Objectives: To provide within a relatively short number of years, a house for all traveller families who desire to be housed ... Nevertheless, the wishes of those travellers who choose to remain on the road must be respected and serviced sites must be provided to allow them to continue that form of life with such dignity and comfort as it allows."

Only occasionally does the mask slip to reveal the familiar attitudes:

"Newly-wed couples who have to occupy caravans following their marriage should be considered extra sympathetically for housing to *lessen the risks of regression to a travelling way of life and consequential negativing [sic] of the benefits of permanent accommodation and education.*" (Travelling People Review Body 1983:6, 15, 45).

The 1983 Report confirms the findings of the one twenty years earlier with the core accusations and their link with nomadism unchanged, quoting:

" 'Itinerants as a body do not constitute a criminal element in the population and they have not a predisposition to crime. Many of the crimes which they commit are incidental to their daily life, and facilitated by its circumstances.' This assessment is, in most areas, as true now as twenty years ago. The law-breaking which most frequently receives publicity is not of a serious nature. *Petty theft, brawling, trespass, minor traffic offences, erection of temporary dwellings* – these are the most usual and are, indeed, incidental to the kind of life they lead. It must be admitted, however, that a higher level of more serious and organised crime has been encountered among travellers in recent times. *Some of those who have been left on the roadside without hope of improvement in their living conditions have been known to develop serious criminal tendencies.*" (Travelling People Review Body 1983:29)

Meanwhile, back on the ground ...

While all of this soul-searching and striving for justice has been going on in liberal circles, with government backing, we have only to look at Traveller/ Buffer relations on the ground, as portrayed in the popular press, to see that tension between the two is as high as ever. The press archives of the *Irish Times* and at Pavee Point, Dublin, house literally hundreds of articles from both the national and regional/local press, at least 90 per cent of which focus on accommodation-related issues: evictions, residents' protests, site plans, intimidation of Traveller families assigned standard local authority housing: Buffers refuse absolutely to allow Travellers live anywhere near them. In line with the demands of political correctness, this is *never* done out of anti-Traveller feeling; support for Travellers and for their right to decent accommodation, is automatically voiced alongside or even as part of, the objection. Opposition is always for some *other* reason: the site is more suitable for a bird sanctuary, for example (*Irish Times*, 28/5/91) or has been zoned low-density (Irish Times, 8/3/91) or is dangerously near a main road.

What's more, a frightening new dimension has crept into the objections: at a time when all political parties officially supported Traveller accommodation developed in consultation with Travellers, the Minister of State at the Department of Industry and Commerce voted against building *one* house for *one* Travelling family in his native town (where he was also a County Councillor) "because of the adverse effect this might have in attracting investment to the community" (*Irish Times*, "Jekyll and Hyde Politics", 11/4/91). This has been stated even more openly elsewhere, for example:

> "The creation of employment for several hundred people on a proposed industrial estate at Walkinstown, Dublin [a high unemployment urban area] was being hindered by an itinerant encampment of 36 caravans, a Dublin County Council official told the High Court yesterday. ... The encampment constituted a serious health danger and was preventing the marketing of lands for industrial development and job provision." (*Irish Times*, 3/12/92)

The "employment for several hundred people" being spitefully blocked by the itinerant encampment is a daydream: clearly, the site in question is unused waste ground with industrial zoning and no buyers. This is as clear an example of magical thinking as one is likely to come across in Western Europe: the reason why the industrialists do not come, bringing "hundreds" of jobs, is because the land where they would build their factories is occupied by Travellers.

Buffers' demons, Traveller devils
Not only are Travellers the cause of mass unemployment, they embody every demon of the day: a seventy-four-year-old nun attempting to set up a European Travellers' Centre in a secluded big house outside a Co. Galway village was physically threatened ("We have guns, you know"). Eighty families withdrew their children from the (136-pupil) primary school elsewhere on the grounds, 500 marched in protest, 800 attended a protest meeting:

> "All sorts of false rumours were spread about this project, including suggestions that *people with criminal records, drug addicts and victims of AIDS* would be brought into the centre. It was all lies, reflecting on innocent travellers who want nothing more than to better themselves in life." (*Irish Times*, 30/8/91)

Other issues of concern come and go: in the early 1980s, as heroin addiction in Dublin's inner city soared higher than in Harlem, media hysteria spotlighted the (highly visible) handful of of Traveller children openly sniffing glue in the streets. More recently, as AIDS – a disease which, to the best of my knowledge, has not affected the Traveller population at all to date – has become a cause of panic within the buffer population, public attention and concern are being directed towards an alarming problem particular to the Travelling community:

> "A study in the west of Ireland suggests that genetic disorders among travellers are more common than among the settled population, because of the marriage of close blood relatives ... many serious genetic disorders that are causing the children of travellers to *die in infancy* or to *suffer chronic disabilities* throughout their lives: a traveller child is 20 times more likely than a settled child to have *profound deafness*, and 8 times more likely to need *mental handicap* services. In many cases, the causes could be directly related to in-breeding ... There is evidence that the incidence of first cousin marriage [among Travellers] is as high as 30 per cent ... Most Irish travellers get married within the Catholic Church. Accordingly, the Church bishops and clergy could play a very important role in discouraging – and if possible *preventing* – first cousin marriage *among travellers*." (*Irish Times*, 15/12/92)

Such an accusation tickles the reader's imagination with a suggestion of incest and subtly defines the entire Traveller population as flawed, as genetically – *racially* – inferior. Just as importantly, it also suggests that this (unlike the AIDS raging through the Buffer community) is a problem 'we' can handle – out of our kindhearted concern for their poor little children, of course.

Full circle ... ?
This is not the whole picture. There is press coverage of positive events, including a number in which President Robinson has been enthusiastically involved and interviews with articulate Traveller spokespersons. A certain number of Buffers even seem to have come full circle as regards colonialism, now defining their own culture as colonialist and encouraging Travellers to stand up for the things that are special to them:

> "'For Travellers to move forward, they must have a healthy sense of who they are,'" [says a Buffer spokesperson for a Travellers' cultural centre, which will be] "like a mirror"[in which Travellers will] "see that there is a separateness there and something worth celebrating." (*Irish Times*, 21/4/91)

But looking into this new development will be another day's work.

The picture takes shape
English anti-Irish stereotypes are depressingly familiar: drunken, lazy, stupid, ignorant, violent and superstitious. These are also the core Buffer anti-Traveller stereotypes, stable over time. Others come and go. To illustrate, here is a comparative chart of Buffer worries and problems as they appeared to me in 1993, alongside what Buffers see as the Traveller versions of same:

Buffer	Traveller
deteriorating health services	infant mortality, low life expectancy
deteriorating housing provision	self-created squalor; ungratefully leaving local authority housing when provided
deteriorating education service	Traveller children 'backward'; would hold back the class if allowed in
unemployment	dole scroungers; actively *cause* Buffer unemployment
forced dependence on state aid	begging (despite welfare scrounging and black market prosperity)
violent crime	rob and abuse the most vulnerable Buffers (old people in isolated farmhouses)
women still not equal	Traveller women brutally exploited by Traveller patriarchy, including by being forced to have too many children and regularly beaten
families falling apart	Traveller families stick together *too* much: factionalism
teenage drug addiction	glue-sniffing among pre-teens
AIDS (which comes from the outside!)	genetic disorders (carried within the group itself!)
a feeling that nothing makes sense, everything is impersonal and changing too fast	the myth of a golden past when Travellers were welcomed because they were useful, contrasted with what is seen as total loss of economic function and identity; everything good and special about Travellers (music, storytelling and crafts) has been lost; everything traditional that remains is seen as negative.

As Buffer society changes, it must redefine who 'we' are; this is done by focussing on 'otherness' (who 'we' are *not*) which must in turn be controlled to make certain it goes on fulfilling this vital function. For example, to prove that 'we' are clean, 'they' must be seen to be a lot dirtier than we are; this is done by refusing to provide rubbish collection, toilet facilities, hard standing, running water etc. or, even better, through *pretending to* provide these (skips that are never emptied, toilet/washing facilities that so offend Traveller ideas of decency that they will never be used) so that 'we' can claim to have (at vast expense) done our very best for a bloody-minded 'them' that simply refuse to be helped. (This is made worse by the widespread practice, among individual Buffers, of dumping household waste wherever Travellers are to be found whether legal or illegal sites or houses.) This manipulation is part of a vital *political* function: since Travellers tend to live alongside the least advantaged and therefore most discontented, groups in Buffer society, the latter's loyalty to the middle-class institutions that control so many aspects of their lives is gained through showing that, when push comes to shove, 'we' are all on the same side: "the pigs" earn under-class support when they 'get tough' with Travellers, while politicians know exactly what they're doing when they seek out and act upon, slum-dwellers' objections to Traveller neighbours (cf. Liégeois, 1994:174).

As 'we' change, so too must 'they' or the way we see them, for example, the English, with their Protestant ethic, have long looked down on family size here as a sign that the Irish are irresponsible and let priests bully them, while the Irish felt that children were literally sent from God. Over the last twenty years or so Buffers of all social classes have switched over to more 'English' models of family size while Travellers have, by and large, not done so or done so to a lesser degree. Therefore, now that large numbers of children are a *peculiarly* Traveller trait, they are also perceived as a *typically* Traveller trait and condemned as a sign of Traveller irresponsibility and religious superstition, whereas, when the trait was shared, Buffers didn't notice it at all.

Some Buffer concerns continue over time, changing shape as they go along. Traveller marriage is a good example. A century ago, Buffer observers condemned Travellers for their supposedly loose sexual morals: Traveller marriage was seen as taking place outside the blessings of the Church, by agreement of the two individuals involved and easy to get out of if one or both partners wanted to go their own way. This was the exact opposite of the Gaujo (Buffer/English) code at the time, of Church marriage "till death do us part", arranged by parents for the good of their offspring. By the late twentieth century Gaujo ideas have come full circle and now Travellers are condemned both for their arranged marriages and for staying with drunken, violent spouses. This is closely tied in with changing religious views: the nineteenth century Buffer condemned the Traveller as a bad Catholic or none, if not out and out idolatrous, while today's Buffer marvels at his superstitious attachment to saints, pilgrimages, curing priests and all the rest.

The way that Buffers see Travellers in relation to 'nature' has changed a great deal over the past two centuries. To the English observer, Travellers and nature are one and the same: fawns, bluebottles, grasshoppers. To the pre-Independence Buffer, the Traveller is both *above* 'nature' (that is, supernatural) and a *personification* of the threat that nature poses to culture, as in agri*culture* and *culti*vation: it is the Traveller who steals the hen, who sets the horse into the ripening corn, who tears down the fence thus letting loose the cattle. This popular association has entirely died away among today's city-dwelling Buffer population, with only a hint of it surviving in 'knacker', the insult that has replaced yesterday's term, 'tinker' – though wandering piebalds are a continuing cause of friction in the countryside and especially in and around housing estates. Today, Buffers are more likely to see Travellers as being *victims* of nature ("sometimes hungry, always cold and miserable") and at the same time as *below* it as they show by allowing their children to run 'wild', unschooled and unwashed, seemingly choosing to live in filth and the vicious and unpredictable violence they inflict on each other: the sort of animal images you're likely to hear today run along the lines of "I wouldn't treat a dog like ..." or "you wouldn't put a pig into ..." 'typically' Traveller scenarios.

Solving the Buffer problem(s)

The settlement movement did a lot more for Buffers than it did for Travellers. After all, the number of Travellers 'on the side of the road' was greater in 1993 than it was in 1963 and blocking of unofficial sites has meant dense concentrations in atrocious conditions. The settlement movement was the expression of a hidden agenda, namely the coming of age of Buffer identity. Shaking off hundreds of years of seeing themselves first and foremost as not English, Buffers declared themselves the norm, at the same time freeing themselves of time-honoured English anti-Irish stereotypes by projecting them onto Travellers and redeeming their own identity by pronouncing these traits curable – and they could prove it since they themselves had been 'cured' of precisely these traits. *The settlement movement was Buffers' way of freeing themselves from the colonial past by spelling out exactly who they were and who they were not. They exorcised their demons by casting them onto the Travelling People.*

The settlement movement, by insisting that Travellers were 'not-other', reinforced that very otherness by highlighting and defining it. One of the most important aspects in this process is the manipulation of Traveller *identity*, which is done by changing the story of Traveller *origin*, since the relationship of Travellers to Buffers defines the all-important distance which must be changed whenever necessary in order to keep the projections focused. When *both* Irish groups were oppressed by a common 'them', Travellers were seen as Buffers' *most* noble selves (the native aristocracy, robbed of their lands and privilege); later on, they were redefined as Buffers' *least* noble selves, evicted landless peasants, plus a ragbag of individual social misfits recruited through "Personal problems ... illegitimacy or alcoholism ... 'strolling women' ..." (Gmelch, 1977:10).

"Where do you come from?" is a question formulated by, and meaningful to, *sedentary* people. Behind it lies the understanding that identity is something that took shape in the *past*, formed by *one particular place*. It is a Gaujo question and answering it is a Gaujo need. (The Gypsy question, by contrast, is "Who are you?" expressing an understanding that identity is shaped in the *present* by one's *relationships to other people*.) That Gypsies in general, and Irish Travellers in particular, are often willing to humour the Gaujo obsession with origins (whether as Egyptians or medieval penitents or victims of clearances or descendants of dispossessed nobility) can be seen as yet another 'good or service', this time psychological in nature, supplied by the former to the latter – for a price.

Conclusion

"The figure of the witch, clearly enough, embodies those characteristics that society specially disapproves. The values of the witch directly negate the values of society. The witch myth then recognises the opposition of moral values; an opposition of good and bad, right and wrong, proper and improper, sinful and righteous. The witch is always on the wrong side of the moral line, he is a figure of sin incarnate. Witch-hunting, then, goes together with a feeling that basic sentiments, values and interests are being endangered. A society in order to feel secure must feel that not only its material interests but also its way of life, its fundamental values, are safe. Events are creating a special anxiety when they are termed unnatural or uncanny. They are seeming to run counter to the ordinary course of things. The anxiety fastens on to the question of what deeper causation can have underlain the observed event. [Identifying and purging the witch] was cathartic; it purged the whole community of certain anxieties for the time-being. They had found the public enemy who made things go wrong for all of them; they had destroyed him; they could all breathe more freely" (Mayer, 1970).

The Gypsy is the 'witch' in European society today.

Gaujos not only (consciously, deliberately) *scapegoat* the Gypsy, they also (subconsciously) *project onto* him, thus distancing themselves from things they dislike about themselves.

Anti-Gypsyism is a moral crusade – and seen as such by those who are active in it. To accept the Gypsy would be to accept everything that decent people reject.

Gaujos *need* a screen onto which to project their own negativity; if they were to give up the screen, they would have no choice but to own up to this evil. That is why Gaujos everywhere manipulate Gypsies into conformity with Gaujo expectations. Individual Travellers, in small numbers, may be readily accepted into the fold since their 'conversion' is living proof of the correctness of 'our' model and at the same time seems to show that our objections to other members of the group are not racist in nature. But Gypsies as a group cannot be *permitted* to merge into the mainstream, despite universal Gaujo demands that they do so.

References

ANON. 1785 "I see a column" *The Belfast News-Letter* 9th December, from Cowper (1785)

DUFF C 1952 *Ireland and the Irish* T V Boardman, London

BORROW G 1851 *Lavengro* J Murray, London

BORROW G 1862 *Wild Wales* J Murray, London, repr. 1969, Collins, London

BORROW G 1874 *Romano-Lavo-Lil* J Murray, London

BULFIN W 1907, repr. in 2 vols, 1981 *Rambles in Eirinn* Sphere Books, London Vol.2 pp.204-8

BURKE Rev. Mr.1835 Communication in *The Westmeath Chroncle and Longford Newsletter* 26 November

COMMISSION ON ITINERANCY 1963 *Report of the Commission on Itinerancy* The Stationery Office, Dublin

COWPER W 1785 "The Sofa" *The Task* I, cited in Sampson J ed. 1930 *The Wind on the Heath* Chatto and Windus, London p.30 (and plagiarised anonymously in *The Belfast News-Letter* 9th December 1785)

DAIKEN L 1947 "Parasites without Power" in J Lindsay ed. *Anvil: Life and the Arts: Book One* Meridian Books, London

DUBLIN COMMITTEE FOR TRAVELLING PEOPLE 1977 *Annual Report* Private, Dublin

ENNIS ITINERANTS SETTLEMENT COMMITTEE 1972a *Excursion* Private, Ennis

ENNIS ITINERANTS SETTLEMENT COMMITTEE 1972b "Report on Progress in Education" *Bulletin of Cumann Dúiseachta na hInse,* No.1, (Education Special) October

FINLAY Rev. T A 1873 "The Vagrant" *Irish Monthly* August

GMELCH G 1977 *The Irish Tinkers – The Urbanization of an Itinerant People* Cummings, Menlo Park, California

HACKETT W 1862 "The Irish Bacach or professional beggar, viewed archaeologically" *Ulster Journal of Archaeology* Vol.9, pp.256-71

IRISH FOLKORE COMMISSION 1952 All-Ireland Survey on Travelling People, unpublished questionnaire responses from non-Traveller informants

KEANE H 1989 *The National Council for Travelling People: A Short History 1969-1989* Private, Dublin

LIÉGEOIS J-P ed. 1994 *Roma, Gypsies, Travellers* Council of Europe, Strasbourg

McCARTHY P 1972 *Itinerancy and Poverty* M.SocSc thesis, University College, Dublin

McCARTHY P 1994 "The sub-culture of poverty reconsidered" in M McCann, S Ó Síocháin and Ruane J *Irish Travellers* Queen's University of Belfast Institute of Irish Studies, Belfast

MAYER P 1970 "Witches" in Marwick M ed. 1970 *Witchcraft and Sorcery* Penguin, Harmondsworth

NATIONAL COUNCIL FOR TRAVELLING PEOPLE 1974 *5th Annual Report* Private, Dublin

O'CONNOR D J 1918 "A fast-disappearing clan: the Irish Tinkers" *Ireland's Own* 27 August p.5

OKELY J 1983 *The Traveller-Gypsies* Cambridge University Press, London

SIMSON W 1865 *A History of the Gipsies* (ed. J Simson) Low, London

SLIGO COMMITTEE FOR TRAVELLING PEOPLE n.d. (but pre-1979 when known to author of this paper) *Social Contract* Private, Sligo

SUTHERLAND A 1975 *Gypsies, the Hidden Americans* Tavistock, London

SYNGE J M 1906 "The Vagrants of Wicklow" *The Seanachie* pp 93-98, repr. in Synge J M 1980 *J M Synge's Ireland: In Wicklow, West Kerry and Connemara* O'Brien Press, Dublin

TRAVELLING PEOPLE REVIEW BODY 1983 *Report of the Travelling People Review Body* The Stationery Office, Dublin

YOORS J 1967 *The Gypsies* Allen and Unwin, London

Chapter 3 Somebody like you: images of Gypsies and Yoroks among Pomaks (Bulgarian Muslims)

Ilia Iliev, Researcher, Universities of Sofia and Greenwich

Editorial introduction

Within Romani studies we have to reconstruct for ourselves both the theory of ethnic identity and the theory of political identity before we can theorise with any confidence about the connection between the two. Ilia Iliev's earlier work on ethnic identity and political identity among Bulgarian Gypsies presented the beginnings of an explanation of political diversity among Roma in terms of informal networking and, in particular, of patron-client relationships. Debates which followed started him on a still incomplete broader process of theorising, about 'vraski' or informal networks of mutual, but not necessarily equal, protection. Here, therefore, Iliev draws again on his fieldwork to present a another codicil to the notion of sedentarism presented by Robbie McVeigh in this volume, by presenting a detailed account of one instance in which sedentarism might be presented as transcending ethnic difference in the social construction of ethnic identity – but not inevitably so.

The Pomaks are those Bulgarian-speakers who are Muslim in religion. Until 1878, Bulgaria was part of the Ottoman empire, and some parts of the country remained so until 1912. The ruling monarch, the sultan, was at the same time *khalif*, the supposed spiritual leader of all the Sunni Muslims throughout the world. The population of the empire was divided on confessional criteria. For example, all Eastern Orthodox Christians were one *millet* (Rum millet), all Sunni Muslims formed another *millet*, etc. These were settled in different urban districts (*makhala*), paid different taxes and so on according to the *millet*. The lines of division were formed by religion, not by language or ethnicity.

When the idea of nation began to grow in the Balkan peninsula there was an important cultural legacy of regarding religion as one of the strongest markers of nationality – certainly stronger than language (Hupchick 1993). The divisions between Serbs, Croats and Muslims in Bosnia are an example of this.

If the Ottoman empire has an heir, it is Turkey, and different Muslim peoples often consider themselves as a part of the Turkish nation. In Bulgaria a large part of Turkish-speaking Muslim Khorokhane Roma, as well as Muslim Bulgarians, Pomaks, prefer to consider themselves as Turkish.

During my fieldwork among the Pomaks, however, I have often been told that it is better to give your daughter to a Christian Bulgarian, than to a Muslim Gypsy. The identity of Pomaks is so strongly influenced by their religion that a large number consider themselves a separate ethnic group and some even feel themselves an integral part of the Turkish nation. Their language and traditions are Bulgarian, their neighbours are Bulgarians and, in some cases, when their family had converted to Islam comparatively recently, they even have some Christian kinsfolk; but religion often turns out to be a more decisive criterion of identity – except for Gypsies.

An unpublished survey of the prestige of ethnic minorities and groups in Bulgaria showed that at the top of the scale were either Christian Bulgarians or Turks, depending on whether the answers were from Christians or Muslims. Then followed Vlachs (Rumanian speaking, sedentary Christians), Pomaks (Bulgarian speaking sedentary Muslims), Gagaus (Turkic speaking sedentary Christians) and Saracatsens (Greek speaking recently sedentarised former pastoral nomads). All groups, sedentary or former pastoral nomads, Muslims or Christians, Bulgarian or Turkish-speaking, invariably put Gypsies on the bottom of the scale.

One possible explanation is the traditional distrust of the agricultural population towards non-sedentary people. Most of the population in the Balkans until very recently were peasants. Pastoral nomads such as Muslim Yoroks or Orthodox Saracatsens are nowadays usually lower on the scale of prestige than sedentary Bulgarians, Greeks or Turks, but sometimes even higher than sedentary Pomaks (according to a minority of Pomaks themselves, as I shall discuss below) and always higher than Gypsies (Adanir 1989:135). Besides, Khorokhane Roma, Lingurari and other Gypsy groups have been sedentarised for centuries now (Marushiakova 1992:99), definitively earlier than Saracatsens. The natural question is: what commonalty is there in the image of nomadism held by sedentary people of these different nomadic or formerly nomadic groups?

Some groups feel the pressure of their low status and try to adopt a new ethnic identity. A large part of the Khorokhane Roma insist that they are Turks; Orthodox and Rumanian-speaking Lingurari claim to be ethnic Rumanians. Turkish identity, acquired via Islam and its associated politics may seem to offer the Khorakhane Roma (who are a considerable part of the Gypsy population in Bulgaria) a way from marginalisation to higher status (Marushiakova and Popov 1993:143). They are trying to imitate the customs and way of life respectively of Turks and Vlachs in Bulgaria. Neither ethnic Turks nor Vlachs accept that claim, so Khorokhane Roma and Lingurari remain Gypsy for their neighbours and solidly on the bottom of the ethnic scale.

The Muslim Bulgarians (Pomaks) from the Western part of Rodopi mountains are mainly farmers. The same families live for generations in the same villages, often in the same house and till the same lands. The mountain villages are poor and so there is a custom of sending young bachelors to the big cities or abroad to earn money. Before the Balkan wars of 1912-13 these young men were nomadic herders of large sheep flocks; they were in the mountains in summer and by the warm seaside in winter. There thus were and still are several possibilities for young men to leave their villages permanently, but they do not. The temptation of these possibilities is one of the reasons why Pomaks stress so heavily the moral values of their lasting links with their native lands, houses and villages which is one of their greatest sources of pride. The mechanisms which kept the people in their native places were effective and survived even the great rural exodus in Bulgaria between 1950 and 1960. The Pomak settlements are now among the most thickly populated mountain villages.

The Pomaks and sedentarism
One of the ways to stress the moral value of links with one's ancestral place is to comment on the nomads, traditional neighbours of the Pomaks, and emphasise the advantage of sedentarism. The archetypal nomadic stereotype now is, of course, the Gypsy. The Western Rodopi Pomaks often consider the typical Gypsy to be somebody 'black' and ugly, who roams all his life but also lives with dozens of his brethren in a ruined shack, who does not hesitate to steal but is a skilled blacksmith, lazy, hyper-sexual and without religion, even if he professes to be a devout Muslim. These images are deeply rooted and are not easily shifted by the facts. For example, there are no thefts in the vicinity of the Gypsy district in Dolno Drianovo village in Western Rodopi. The Pomak neighbors admit that, well, 'their' Gypsies are quite good, but the 'normal' Gypsies are ... and then the epithets above come pouring out.

Moreover, sometimes the image transforms the facts themselves. In the late 1940s a Gypsy family, Erlii (sedentary Muslim Roma) arrived in Dolno Drianovo village. They were former slum-dwellers from a neighboring town with no specialised trade. Like most Erlii Roma, the men, Djamal and Demir, had no particular skill, but the villagers *knew* that every Gypsy is a metalsmith by definition and so they had them repair their various tools. As old Demir explained to me, they had started out totally ignorant of smithing but over the years had acquired the necessary skills. So now in Dolno Drianovo there is a small Gypsy district of specialised blacksmiths who have clients from all the neighboring villages. Thus the image of Gypsies has moulded to a considerable extent the life of Dolno Drianovo Gypsies. Or, to put it another way, the facts adapted themselves to the image.

These stable images exercise an enormous influence on the Gypsies' life. A logical question to ask, therefore, is whether this cycle of reinforcement between stereotype and reality can be changed. This chapter takes the example of a similar image given by Pomaks to another nomadic group, the Yoroks (a pastoral-nomadic Turkic Muslim group) in Western Rodopi, to explain how and why it changed. My aim is to trace some details of the common stereotypes of Gypsies and Yoroks in Skrebatno, Valkosel, Dolno Drianovo, Laznitza, Godesevo and Garmen villages. I need hardly say these stereotypes do not portray their real characteristics.

As well as those who are their nomadic neighbors today, the Pomaks sometimes also speak about some nomadic 'shepherds' who could equally be Yoroks, Vlachs (Rumanian-speaking Christians) or Saracatsens (Greek-speaking Christians), who migrated (up to 1912) each spring and autumn, with their sheep, near Pomak villages. There were no serious conflicts during these migrations. The 'shepherds' paid in cash or in kind for the pastures, exchanged some small items with the peasants and departed. They had different languages and religions but for the Pomaks they were almost all the same. It is very difficult now to find any information about the social organisation, kinship-structure, folklore, etc. of these peoples. The villagers remember only the facts that they consider important. For example, in the early 1920s a group of these 'shepherds' was killed by some nationalist Bulgarian-Macedonian *comiti* near Valkosel. The peasants saw the sheep wandering about without shepherds and stole some of them. There was no retaliation and they decided to check what had happened. They found the corpses of the 'shepherds' with their dogs nearby, still running around the sheep. There is a "happy end" to this story as the villagers tell it. They took *all* the sheep and they still can tell whose family took more. They cannot tell whether those killed were Vlachs or Saracatsens. They disappeared as they always did, but this time they left their sheep.

The stories about the Yoroks blend with and are dissipated among the common memories about these typical and impersonal nomads. The details evoked in all the villages were almost the same. Everywhere the peasants remembered that the 'shepherds' had a specific kind of sheep, common to all the nomads but different from those of the Pomaks and adapted for long marches. Everywhere they recalled the kind of huts these peoples used, their clothes and how tongue-tied they were. Some of the memories have been washed away but some are clear. All the stories repeated in different ways that these people wandered all the time; they were not like Pomaks, they were different. The most detailed ones insist on this most important characteristic of shepherds – they were nomads. Their itinerary from the Rodopi mountains to the seaside (Nevrokop – Mousomiste – Leski – Koprivlen – Sadovo – Petralik – Linden – Vesme – Zarnevo – Eles – Guredsik – Kamarata – Prosetchen – Plevnja – Drama – Zdravik – Poreza – Kavala) is recalled with great precision.

The facts recalled in all the villages are almost the same but the comments varied greatly even in one village. Everywhere the Pomaks said that the Yorok women, like all the 'shepherds', had a specific traditional costume with hoods, oversleeves and leggings which covered their faces, hands and legs. The evaluation of this fact varied greatly, however. Some Pomaks said that the Yoroks, like all the wanderers, were so 'black' and ugly, that it was quite understandable they would hide their faces and skin from decent people. (Gypsies have the same reputation of being 'black' and ugly.) A minority of Pomaks, however, said that the Yoroks were the most pious Muslims, even more devoted than the Pomaks because their women had the examplary virtue to hide not only their faces but also all the 'flesh' of their bodies. Interestingly, the people who said this were either some of the most orthodox old men or younger people whose relatives had moved to Turkey or planned to move there. They had constructed their identity mainly around their religion and preferred the links with their brethren in religion from the other side of the border to those with their Bulgarian fellow-citizens with the same language and history.

As with women, so with sheep. Everywhere the Pomaks said that the Yoroks' sheep were quite different from theirs, leaner and more wiry, but the interpretations were again rather different. Some Pomaks said that these sheep were so lean because of their interminable wanderings, that in the end they looked more like homeless dogs than the normal, fat, calm and well-bred animals that would be a source for pride for any farmer. That is, the sheep are like their masters. But the minority Pomak group suggested a different explanation. The Yorok sheep were so well bred that they did not take even a blade of grass from another man's pasture and that was why they were thin. The pious man's sheep are as exemplary as his wife and do not steal.

Another example: as a rule, the nomadic group chose a representative to speak with the village authorities, to conduct the more important bargains, etc. The rest of the group did not communicate with the village people and all the shepherds had the reputation of being taciturn and rather reserved. The interpretations vary again. Some Pomaks say that the Yoroks were so 'savage' that they preferred not to communicate with civilised people. The minority, however, attributed their reserve to the Yoroks' highly developed sense of discipline and respect for the elders (unlike contemporary youth).

One final example: everybody agreed that several Yorok individuals would co-habit in one small hut. This often led to transparent allusions about their sexual behavior. The most outspoken bluntly said, "With the fall of night everybody in the hut took off their underpants." I heard the same allusions about big Gypsy families living in one hut. The minority of Pomaks, however, again offered a different interpretation. They explained that the Yoroks had not abandoned their old family values and so several generations of one family lived happily together, as the Pomaks themselves did in the old times.

This was the Pomaks' family ideal indeed, but it never was the Yoroks'. Moreover, nobody thought interpreting the big Gypsy families as closer to the ancient Pomak ideals.

Most of the Pomaks insisted that these shepherds were too savage to observe all the prescription of Islam, that they had no mosques and no learned imams thus they could not be considered true Muslims. These are practically the same grounds on which Gypsies are not accepted in the community of real believers. The pro-Yorok party claimed, however, that a hard life and continuous work made the shepherds better Muslims than the more spoiled peasants.

Thus, interpreting the same data, the Pomaks create two totally different images of the Yoroks. The first one is of a savage group without religion, of black and ugly people who cannot communicate with decent and civilised farmers and prefer to stay among their sheep, savage as their masters, except when they wanted to do something indecent. The second one is of a highly civilised people, an example for good Muslims, with sound families and flawless morals – so flawless, that they are transferred even onto their sheep. The first image has several traits in common with the image of Gypsies.

Perhaps the hypothesis put forward by Robbie McVeigh in this volume, that among sedentary peoples there are some common negative stereotypes about nomads, could explain the similarities in the images of Yoroks and Gypsies. The stable link with their native lands, homes and villages is one of the highest values of Rodopi Pomaks. This link is stressed in several domains. In folklore the ancestral house is the most sacred place. In economics this house and the family lands are never sold. It is the backbone of their identity. The Pomaks insist that they are the most ancient inhabitants of the Rodopi mountains, never migrated and were there before all the newcomers like Bulgarians or Turks. It is quite understandable that a group with such values may be that suspicious of people considered to be mobile by definition. So maybe the images of Yoroks and Gypsies are just variants of the same image of the uncivilised nomad. If that is so, however, it becomes interesting to examine how the important variations in the interpretation of the Yoroks' behaviour have occurred.

They probably have something to do with the big movements of population in the Rodopi mountains in recent decades. Their peak was the great exodus in 1989 but at the time of my research there remained a number of Pomak families who were still considering moving to Turkey as a viable possibility. Of course, this is just a hypothesis, which is difficult to prove in a totally satisfactory way because nobody recorded what the Pomaks were saying about the Yoroks ten or twenty years ago.

Migration, or the possibility of migration, provoked a serious tension in the traditional value system of the Pomaks. They had to choose between two principal values, their attachment to their ancestral homes and lands or that to the religion of their ancestors. Most of them did not favor the most radical solution, emigration to Turkey, but thought about it and had to find some moral sanction, some legitimation. Here they found the example of Yoroks, the almost forgotten people who moved but, nevertheless, were Muslim. Maybe this example was suggested from outside. Several Pomaks told me that Turkish radio stations in Bulgarian explained that the real ancestors of Pomaks were these same Yoroks, the oldest inhabitants of Rodopi mountains. I do not think that the principal aim of this propaganda was to solicit the Pomaks to migrate but to offer them a non-Bulgarian pedigree. The media helped anyway. Even if some help had to be given to evoke the fragmentary memories of this all-but-forgotten people, they were independently re-ordered and interpreted by some of the Pomaks in a new way to become the image of a positive example, as mythic as the negative old example of the savage shepherds. They offered a moral legitimation for people who hesitated to leave their homes and to become dangerously similar to wanderering nomads.

Of course, this is just a hypothesis. More important is the fact that an ethnic stereotype could be shattered in a relatively short period when there are the necessary conditions – tensions between values and maybe some help from the media. Now all Bulgarian society is undergoing a serious transformation which also needs its moral legitimations. The Gypsies are considered to be the most mobile and adaptable ethnic group in Bulgaria. We could learn a lot from those who can preserve their culture during different transformations and survive the changes without suffering shock beyond repair and loss of identity. Maybe such a positive example could change the present image of Gypsies.

References

ADANIR F 1989 "Tradition and Rural Change in south eastern Europe during Ottoman Rule" in D Chirot ed. *The Origins of Backwardness in Eastern Europe in the Early Twentieth century* University of California Press, Berkeley

HUPCHICK D 1993 "Orthdoxy and Bulgarian Ethnic Awareness Under Ottoman Rule 1396-1762": *Nationalities Papers*, vol. XXI, No. 2, Fall, pp. 89-90

MARUSHIAKOVA E 1992 "Ethnic Identity Among Gypsy Groups in Bulgaria" *Journal of the Gypsy Lore Society,* series 5, vol.2 (2)

MARUSHIAKOVA E and POPOV V 1993 *Tziganite v Bulgaria* Club 90, Sofia

Chapter 4 The Criminal Justice and Public Order Act and its implications for Travellers

Luke Clements, Solicitor, Thorpes, Hereford
Sue Campbell, Traveller Research Unit, Cardiff Law School

"While some travellers behave responsibly and live happily on authorised sites, far too many do not. The public expect the Government to take decisive action to bring this nuisance to an end. We will, therefore, review the present legislation". (Conservative Party Press Release 27 March 1992)

The government's review, prefigured by this press release, of the operation of the Caravan Sites Act 1968 led to a consultation exercise on its plans for the 1994 Criminal Justice and Public Order Act which received a massive response from local authorities, organisations and individuals both in this country and abroad. Many of these responses gave substantial details of caravan site operation and Traveller life which make them an unparalleled archive on Gypsy policy at the end of the twentieth century. A number of researchers are exploring this archive and will be doing so for some time. Ministers, however, claimed that no useful suggestions came from these responses. Since the opinion of everyone else is that a plethora of useful and sensible suggestions were made, the cavalier and dismissive attitude of ministers probably means only that the scale of response was just too great for their civil servants to brief them effectively. Independent scrutiny by a member of ACERT (Advisory Council for the Education of Romanies and other Travellers) showed that 93 per cent of county councils, 92 per cent of London boroughs and metropolitan authorities and 71 per cent of district councils responding believed the government's proposals will increase rather than "reduce the nuisance of illegal encampments". At the time we reported the dangers in an earlier version of this paper (Clements and Campbell 1994). Here we record for posterity the sections of the Act which are fulfilling those fears.

The twice yearly counts made by the Department of Environment of Gypsies in England and Wales showed that in January 1994 around a third (4,118 out of 13,794) still lacked anywhere lawful to camp. By January 1996 the total number of caravans counted by the Department of the Environment had fallen to 12,620 with under a quarter of these (2,819) reported as still on unauthorised encampments. These figures, however, may miss out many new Travellers and reflect decreased accuracy of reporting by local authorities to the Department of the Environment. The enactment of the Criminal Justice and Public Order Act in 1994 has visibly compounded the effects of previous legislation to criminalise unsited Travellers while, even on the government's figures, shrinking their numbers by under a third, leaving nearly 3,000 families in limbo.

The Legal position prior to the 1994 Act

The Caravan Sites Act 1968

This had proved to be the most important piece of Traveller legislation although it applied only to "gipsies" (sic) and was restricted to England and Wales. A "gipsy" is defined in this Act as a person of nomadic habit of life, whatever their race or origin. This definition under Section 16 of the Caravan Sites Act 1968 is retained under the new legislation. The Court of Appeal has attempted to exclude many new Travellers from this definition by a decision in which the judges imported into the word 'nomadic' the concept of purposeful travel, economic independence and (to a degree) a tradition of travelling (R. v. South Hams DC and others, CA 27 May 1994).

Part I of the Act provided very limited provisions for security of tenure on local authority 'gypsy' sites and is unaffected by the new Act (although they are excluded from the security of tenure provisions of the Mobile Homes Act 1983 by Section 5 (1) of that Act).

Part II of the 1968 Act dealt with the duty to provide sites and how council areas could be "designated" which gave authorities greater powers to evict Gypsies. The Act not only resulted in over 300 public Gypsy sites being built, it has also been used to restrict unnecessary evictions. In West Glamorgan County Council v. Rafferty (1 All ER 1005, 1987) the court prevented a council which had not provided enough sites from evicting Gypsies from its own land.

While the Act placed a duty on county, metropolitan and London borough councils to provide sufficient sites it also gave them the incentive of added powers to deal with Gypsies once they had provided these sites. These powers arose when the Secretary of State designated the council area, or stated that it had provided adequate accommodation for Gypsies. In certain instances, Section 12 of the Act enabled authorities to be designated where insufficient sites had been provided "where in all the circumstances it is not necessary or expedient to make any such provision". Section 10 made it a criminal offence (in a designated area) for a Gypsy to "station a caravan for the purpose of residing for any period", while Section 11 enabled magistrates' courts to make expedited eviction orders in respect of such Gypsies.

Over 180 councils were granted designation powers despite most of them having insufficient sites for Gypsies in their area. It was this combination of insufficient provision and criminalisation of Travellers which led to the European Commission of Human Rights declaring admissible a complaint (Buckley v. UK No.20348/92 decision 3 March 1994) by a Gypsy living in a designated area. The 1994 Act repeals the designation provisions but replaces them with even wider ranging powers. In the case of Buckley v. UK a decision was reached by the Commission in January 1995 (1995 19 EHRR CD 20). The Commission held, by seven votes to five, that there had been a breach of Article 8 by the UK. The case was referred to the European Court of Human Rights in February 1996 and a decision was given on 25th September. Unfortunately, technical complications led the Court to rule that June Buckley's human rights had not been infringed; but the case is to be appealed. Decisions on other, perhaps stronger, cases are also awaited.

The Town and Country Planning Act 1990 and other restrictive legislation
With limited exceptions the stationing of a caravan on land requires planning permission. (The exceptions come under Schedule 1 of the Caravan Sites and Control of Development Act 1960 and Schedule 2 (V) of the Town and Country Planning General Development Order 1988). Under Section 172 of the 1990 Town and Country Planning Act, a breach of such planning control enables the planning authority to issue an enforcement notice and now (since an amendment introduced by Planning and Compensation Act 1991 Section 9) a stop notice may also be issued which must be complied with (even if appealed). Failure to comply with a stop notice was made a criminal offence by Section 187 of the 1990 Act.

The Department of the Environment has sought (with no obvious success – see Mole Valley District Council v. Smith, 1992, 64 P and CR 491) to restrict these draconian powers by circulars urging toleration, for example, that "until enough sites have been provided gipsies (sic) should not be needlessly moved from place to place" (Department of the Environment 1977 para.36) and, more recently, that in deciding whether or not to commence enforcement proceedings "the existence or absence of policies for gipsy (sic) sites in development plans could constitute a material consideration" (Department of the Environment 1994a, para.26).

In addition to the legislation quoted so far, restrictions are also created by a large number of statutes and bye-laws including the Highways Act 1980, the Caravan Sites and Control of Development Act 1960, the Law of Property Act 1925 (camping on common land) and the Environmental Protection Act 1990.

The Children Act 1989 and the Housing Act 1985
Whilst the government has these extraordinarily wide powers to restrict Traveller activity, both the Childrens Act 1989 and the Housing Act 1985 provide some assistance to Travellers. Under Section 17 of the Childrens Act 1989 it is the duty of a social services authority to safeguard and promote the welfare of children in need within their area and, by virtue of Section 20, this includes the duty to accommodate, where a child's carers are prevented for whatever reason from providing the child "with suitable accommodation or care". This places the primary responsibility upon the social services authority to accommodate, but it nevertheless remains a powerful provision in assisting Traveller families, particularly where a county council (or other social services authority) is trying to evict as they

will have to show that the eviction does not frustrate their local authority duty to protect and accommodate children. (See R. v. Northavon DC ex parte Smith, House of Lords 14 July 1994.)

The duty to accommodate homeless people under Part III of the Housing Act 1985 includes those without anywhere to pitch their caravans. Paragraph 12.16 of the Code of Guidance (3rd edition) makes it clear that provision of accommodation under the Housing Act 1985 will (in relation to Travellers) often entail the provision of a caravan pitch.

The situation after the 1994 Act
The Criminal Justice and Public Order Act 1994 introduced a number of criminal offences relating to trespass which affect Gypsies. These are set out below. The sections of specific concern to Gypsies and Travellers are detailed later in the chapter.

Removal of trespassers
Section 61 of the Criminal Justice and Public Order Act repeals Section 39 of the Public Order Act 1986 and replaces it with wider ranging police powers. The new provision applies to two or more trespassers (regardless of whether their initial presence on the land was legal) where reasonable steps have been taken by or on behalf of the occupier to ask them to leave. In such cases the most senior police officer present can direct them to leave if any of the following three conditions are met:

> ■ if any of those persons has caused damage to the land or to property on the land
> ■ used threatening, abusive or insulting words or behaviour towards the occupier, a member of his family or an employee or agent of his
> ■ or those persons have between them six or more vehicles on the land."

Failure to comply with such a direction is a criminal offence.

"Land" is defined to exclude any building other than an agricultural building or scheduled monument. For the first time the powers are triggered by the trespassers doing "damage to the land". Section 61 (7) states that this includes "the deposit of any substance capable of polluting the land". In this respect the Minister of State, Mr Maclean stated that urinating on pasture land would constitute "polluting the land" but that dropping a sweet paper "would be a matter for the court to decide" (House of Commons Standing Committee Bulletin February 1994 col. 533).

The figure of "six or more vehicles on the land" has been reduced from the previous number of twelve under the Public Order Act 1986. The definition of "vehicle" has also been considerably extended and now includes "any chassis or body, with or without wheels, appearing to have formed part of such a vehicle, and any load carried by, and anything attached to, such a vehicle..."

Existing Chief Constable Guidance in relation to the appropriate use of these powers remained (Home Office 1991). The government indicated at the time that further detailed guidance would be issued on this and the other police powers introduced by the Act (House of Lords Hansard 11 July 1994 cols.15267 and 160). It was issued in the same year: Home Office Circular 45/94 now gives guidance to the police in the use of their powers under Section 61 and states that the police may wish to take account of the personal circumstances of the trespassers whose well-being may be jeopardised by a precipitate move. Although this circular is couched in less restrictive terms, it has been suggested in the January 1996 *Legal Action* that it may be unlawful for the police to make a Section 61 direction without taking into account the Travellers' circumstances. There are also court decisions in relation to the old powers contained in Section 39 of the Public Order Act 1986, notably Krumpa v. Anderson (1989 Criminal Law Reports. 295) which held that the question of what was a reasonably practicable period for a trespasser to leave the land was ultimately one for the court to determine, not the police officer.

Seizure of vehicles or other property
Section 62 gives the police power to seize and remove any vehicle on the land after the powers under Section 61 have been used. Section 67 allows for the retention of any seized vehicle (and prescribes regulations for the recovery of charges in respect of seized vehicles, disposal of vehicles, etc.). This means that the decision as to the seizure of what is, in effect, a home, may be left to a police constable. This provision represented a back-pedalling by the Department of the Environment on its promise (House of Commons Written Answers, 31 March 1993 col.292) not to permit the seizure of caravans.

Aggravated trespass
Sections 68 and 69 deal with the offence of aggravated trespass. Although these sections are not limited to Travellers (affecting most obviously hunt saboteurs) they are likely to have significant effect upon those Travellers involved in direct action against developments such as new roads. It has been alleged in the press that these sections were "kept as broad as possible to embrace anti-roads protests" (*The Observer*, 19 June 1994 p.3). The sections create an offence and provide police power to remove persons from land where a person trespasses on land in the open air with the intention of:

> "■ intimidating persons (engaged in a lawful activity on that or adjoining land) so as to deter them from engaging in that activity
> ■ obstructing that activity
> ■ disrupting that activity."

Trespassory assemblies
Section 70 inserts a new section (14A) into the Public Order Act 1986. It applies where a chief constable reasonably believes that a seriously disruptive/damaging and unlawful assembly is intended. In such circumstances s/he may apply to the local authority for an order prohibiting the holding of the trespassory assembly for a period of not more than four days. The section creates a variety of offences for those contravening such orders and Section 71 enables the police to stop persons believed to be going to such an assembly in contravention of an order under Section 70.

Squatters
Sections 72-76 provide new and amended powers in relation to displaced residential occupiers and protected intending occupiers, adverse occupation of residential premises and ex parte interim possession orders.

Unauthorised campers
Section 77 represents an amended form of the criminal designation provision which existed under Section 10 of the Caravan Sites Act 1968. It makes it an offence for a person residing in a vehicle on any land forming part of a highway, or on *any* other unoccupied land or on any occupied land without the consent of the occupier, to fail to leave the land as soon as practicable after receiving a direction from the local authority to move. Whereas Section 10 of the Caravan Sites Act 1968 applied only to "gipsies" (sic) the new section applies to any person; the new offence will, therefore, affect new Travellers. As the offence applies only to persons who are "residing" in a vehicle, it nevertheless remains restricted to Travellers. The new section essentially criminalises all Travellers without a secure pitch in England and Wales, whereas Section 10 of the 1968 Act applied only to areas where there had been adequate site provision (or where the Secretary of State deemed it otherwise expedient).

Although the heading to the section uses the phrase "unauthorised campers" this is not the case as the offence can be committed where a Traveller is on unoccupied land with the owner's consent (and causing no nuisance or other interference to neighbours, etc.)

During the House of Lords' debate on Section 77 Lord Ferrers gave assurances concerning its implementation stating: "We fully understand the problems which are experienced by genuine nomads without proper site accommodation; and we intend to reinforce our advice to local authorities that they should not evict gipsy (sic) families needlessly where they are camped on council or unoccupied land and are causing no nuisance. We will also advise authorities to continue to make emergency stopping places available to gypsies where they may stay for short periods... We intend to reinforce our advice to local authorities that they should not evict without good cause" (House of Lords Hansard 7 June 1994 cols.1121-2). The government also indicated at the time that formal guidance will be issued by both the Home Office and the Department of the Environment. This guidance (Department of the Environment 1994b) when issued was, however, a brief document urging only temporary toleration of Gypsy encampments, although in relation to all Travellers (Gypsy or New Traveller) it reminded local authorities of their duties under the Children, Housing and Education Acts.

Removal of persons and vehicles
Sections 78 and 79 effectively replaced the powers contained in Section 11 of the 1968 Act. A local authority can apply to a magistrates' court to obtain an order requiring the removal of a vehicle present on land in contravention of a direction to leave given under Section 77 above. On giving twenty-four hours' notice the authority is then empowered to remove the vehicle(s).

The power of authorities to move Travellers without the corresponding duty to provide accommodation (see below) has already begun to recreate the anarchy which gave rise to the 1968 Act. This power was described by Lord Avebury (House of Lords Hansard 7 June 1994 col.1118) as "thoroughly reactionary, taking us back to the bad old days prior to the 1968 Act when Gypsies were harried from pillar to post". In a twelve month period during 1966 - 1967, Wolverhampton, for instance, moved 1,456 caravans from its area in 251 separate operations (an average of five evictions a week), while absurdly, neighbouring Walsall was involved in the same activity (Adams et al 1975:200).

No duty to provide sites or pay grants
Section 80 is undoubtedly the most damaging section in Part V of the new Act and it attracted the most heated debate in the Houses of Parliament. It repeals Part II of the Caravan Sites Act 1968 as well as removing the Treasury's power to pay grants to local authorities to cover the capital cost of building and maintaining Gypsy sites.

Part II of the 1968 Act included the key sections which placed a duty on authorities to provide sites (Section 6), the power of the Secretary of State to direct councils to comply with this duty (Section 9) as well as the designation provisions (Sections 10-12). The repeal of this part of the Act has placed Travellers in an impossible situation. Those with sites find it very hard to undertake seasonal travel (because of new powers introduced by the new Act under Sections 77-79) and those without sites face prosecution under the same new powers but are unable to avail themselves of the limited defence provided by West Glamorgan County Council v. Rafferty (see above).

The abolition of the power to make 100 per cent capital grants towards Gypsy site capital costs is halting Gypsy site construction and will result in existing sites falling into disrepair and eventual closure, the Department of Environment capital programme having been used to refurbish vandalised and dilapidated sites as well as for new site construction.

Criticism of Section 80 came from such unexpected quarters as the National Farmers' Union and the Country Landowners' Association as well as the National Trust, the Town and Country Planning Association and the Association of County Councils (House of Commons Hansard 26 June 1993 col.972). The Association of Chief Police Officers, in a letter (15 January 1993) to the Labour Campaign for Travellers' Rights, opposed the repeal of the duty to provide sites, as well as the general effect of the legislation "to 'criminalise' the act of living in a caravan". The *Journal of the Police Federation* (anon. 1992) described the proposals as: "at best a knee-jerk reaction to the Government's wish to be seen to be doing something about this year's particular problem. At worst they can be construed as direct discrimination against a minority – a discrimination that would not be tolerated if Gypsies were Black, came from another country, or were homosexual."

The House of Lords did pass an amendment to delay the implementation of Section 80 until 1 July 1999 which would have left the 'West Glamorgan' defence intact until then and have represented a significant success for those involved in challenging the new Act. Unfortunately, the amendment was reversed in the House of the Commons.

Testing the new powers

Inevitably, it was only a matter of time before these new powers were to be tested by the courts. Recent developments in the case law have served to mitigate, to a limited extent, the harshness of these new powers.

The first case to reach the courts was R. v. Wealden District Council ex parte Wales (*The Times*, 22 September 1995). The case concerned a group of Travellers, some of whom were pregnant or had young children, who had been living on an unauthorised site in Crowborough for several months and upon whom a Section 77 Criminal Justice and Public Order Act 1994 direction had been served. The Travellers failed to comply and the Council applied for and was granted an order by the magistrates' court to remove the vehicles. Crucial to the case was that it was only after service of the Section 77 direction on the Council that the Council undertook enquiries into the personal circumstances of the Travellers as urged by Department of the Environment Circular 18/94, as a result of which the council gave undertakings not to evict some of the Travellers due to their medical condition. Other Travellers had obtained injunctions to prevent their eviction until their application for judicial review had been heard.

Two important issues were to be determined. Firstly, can a removal direction bind persons who arrive on the land after its service but who have or acquire knowledge of it? Secondly, what individual facts or circumstances should a local authority consider prior to issuing a removal direction? If no such circumstances are considered beforehand, whether and at what stage of an eviction process, can this failure be remedied?

On the first point, Mr Justice Sedley held that a removal direction applies only to those on whom notice of it is served and not to Travellers who subsequently arrive on site. On the second point, the court held that the considerations in Circular 18/94 paras. 9-13 had to be taken into account by a local authority before any removal direction was made and that failure to do so would result in the quashing of the direction and any subsequent removal order. These considerations are both statutory (based on the Children Act, the Housing Act and the Education Act) and what Mr Justice Sedley held to be "considerations of common humanity, none of which can properly be ignored when dealing with one of the most fundamental human needs, the need for shelter with at least a modicum of security" and these would have applied whether or not Circular 18/94 existed. Additionally, the court held that these matters have to be considered prior to giving a direction and must be reviewed at each stage in the eviction process.

Prior to Wealden, there had been suggestions that Circular 18/94 applied only to Criminal Justice and Public Order Act evictions but it now seems that the requirement to investigate personal circumstances prior to eviction applies equally to evictions under Order 24 (County Court) and Order 113 (High Court) (see *Legal Action* January 1996 p.11).

Many Travellers who live on their own land in contravention of the Town and Country Planning Act 1990 face eviction when a local planning authority takes enforcement action against them. In R. v. Kerrier District Council ex parte Uzzell (1995, 6 November, Queens Bench Division, unreported), Mr Justice Latham held that the same considerations of "common humanity ... must, it seems to me, be equally applicable to decisions in relation to enforcement actions".

Despite this judicial moderation, the plight of Travellers remains bleak and attention will almost certainly move to the European Court of Human Rights, as in the case of Buckley v. UK, noted above. In the House of Lords debate Lord Avebury (House of Lords Hansard 7 June 1994 col.1117) specifically referred to this eventuality stating:

> "The criminalisation of the Gypsy way of life under this clause would violate the recommendations made by the Committee of Ministers, which declared that: 'in their law and practice regarding the movement and residence of persons, States should refrain from any measures which would lead to discrimination against nomads for reasons of their lifestyle'.
>
> Will the government say whether they have considered the possibility of a flood of applications under Articles 8 and 14 being declared admissible by the Commission, and how they answer the charge that I now make, that what they are doing in this clause is a deliberate violation under the convention?"

References

ANON. 1992 Editorial *Police Gazette* September

ADAMS B, MORGAN D, OKELY J and SMITH D 1975 *Gypsies and Government Policy in England* Heinemann, London

CLEMENTS L and CAMPBELL S 1994 "Travellers Rights" *The Adviser* No.46, November/December, pp.8-11

DEPARTMENT OF THE ENVIRONMENT 1977 *Circular 28/77* DoE, London

DEPARTMENT OF THE ENVIRONMENT 1994a *Circular 1/94* DoE, London

DEPARTMENT OF THE ENVIRONMENT 1994b *Circular 18/94* DoE, London

HOME OFFICE 1991 *Circular 37/91* Home Office, London

HOME OFFICE 1994 *Circular 45/94* Home Office, London

Chapter 5 Sites of resistance: places on the margin – the Traveller 'homeplace'

Sally Kendall, Lecturer in Geography, University of Leeds

This chapter examines the concept of place in relation to notions of marginal space and how groups like Travellers come to occupy that space both physically and culturally. It goes on to analyse how the creation of a 'homespace' within such marginal areas can be seen as a method of cultural survival and resistance for the marginal group and as a space of direct cultural subversion by the dominant group. It examines the role Traveller women play in the creation of this 'space of resistance' in the context of gender roles and relations within the community. Although the processes, concepts and relationships consistent with the socio-spatial dialectic are pertinent to wider geographical settings, for the purpose of detailed analysis, examples in this paper will be drawn primarily from the experiences of the Travelling community in Leeds.

The concept of marginal space and place

Travellers are perceived as occupying 'marginal spaces', reflecting their physical and cultural marginality within the sedentary society. Marginal space may be seen as space occupied by marginal groups, either chosen by them or imposed on them by the dominant group. It may also be seen as any spatial arena where the dominant society is unable to define and/or control the physical and cultural use of space, at certain times and/or in certain places (Shields 1991). Thus 'marginal space' is not necessarily fixed in a particular location: it is subject to reinterpretation by groups, both from 'within' and 'outside' the margin and is likely to shift temporally and spatially. The following description of spaces frequently occupied by Travellers' unauthorised sites will highlight the continual renegotiation and redefinition of marginal space within society.

Travellers' unauthorised sites are often located on land which has been cleared for redevelopment such as the Cross Green industrial estate in south Leeds, just as homeless people may occupy derelict buildings which are earmarked for redevelopment. Within both these contexts the land or building is in the process of transition as it is moving from a strictly defined state, in which it is 'filled' with buildings and/or 'legitimate' people. At this stage the occupants and usage have legal, moral and ethical sanction within the frameworks of the dominant ideology. This definition becomes less clear and contested when the area becomes 'empty' awaiting future 'filling' via redevelopment by the dominant society. This middle state of transition and consequent vulnerability to 'outside' use provides marginal groups with the opportunity to usurp the power of the dominant society via their physical occupation of such sites. In turn the dominant group may attempt to reassert control by reoccupying or preventing unauthorised access to the building or land. Thus the marginal space created by the marginal group's occupation is usually transient; it is place and time specific. The degree to which Travellers successfully usurp control will be influenced by local conditions, including the attitudes of local authorities to illegal camping, characteristics of the landowner, the employment of 'gatekeepers' such as security guards, in addition to the status and nature of the land occupied.

Sites successfully usurped are usually located in 'marginal areas' such as those with poor or unsafe environmental conditions, next to sewage works, power stations or beside busy main roads. Due to the marginal nature of this land the sedentary society may turn a 'blind eye' to such sites, although Travellers are still occupying it 'illegitimately' as it has not been sanctioned for residential purposes. Consequently, eviction procedures can be instigated at any time; these may even be justified in terms of protecting the Travellers themselves, as in the case of an unauthorised site at the high voltage transformer station at Gelderd Road in Leeds. Although this is an extreme case it may reflect the paradoxical situation in which the Traveller lifestyle is associated with danger but this danger emanates from the lack of access to safe sites.

That space can be marginalised via direct association with a marginal group can clearly be seen when Travellers occupy land prized and valued by sections of the sedentary society. This is especially apparent and perhaps most contentious when that land is seen as a valuable amenity such as green spaces or recreational grounds within built-up, relatively deprived urban environments, such as Halton Moor in Leeds. Marginal status may thus be imposed by members of the local community on that site as a result of their inability to use the land for its 'legitimate', intended purposes inconsistent with the Traveller 'invasion'. Such examples highlight the inappropriateness of characterising marginal space as a static and rigid concept with fixed boundaries, instead they emphasise its fluidity and ability for renegotiation by groups and individuals, over time and between places. They also highlight the sedentary society's direct association of Travellers with marginality, including Travellers' perceived 'power' to turn the spatial environment into a marginal area.

During the latter half of the twentieth century 'marginal space' has become more clearly defined and restricted due to increasingly rigorous planning and environmental legislation, changes in land-use patterns and lifestyles (Home 1994). This reflects the continuation of an historical process since and before industrialisation whereby all land (even 'common' land) has to have an owner and hence 'controller'. During industrialisation the enclosure movement formalised the increasing exclusion of non-landowners, restricting their rights of access and usage of land (Mayall 1988).

> "There is no concept of land without proprietary interest. [Consequently when] Travellers stay on land which they have neither title nor consent to be on, they do so subject to the legal interests of others" (Swinhoe 1993).

The 'legal interests of others' will be those of the landowner who is generally, though not always, a member of the sedentary society or a state agency. Within the modern environment the degree to which land owners feel the need to 'protect' and 'barricade' their space appears to be increasing. Urban development is often denoted by bunker architecture, sophisticated surveillance equipment such as closed circuit television, security fences, electric gates and gatekeepers employed to ensure that 'undesirables' are not admitted (Thrift 1994). These developments reflect an increase in the dominant group's need to be seen to impose spatial constraints on some members of society. The creation of 'new enclosures' and the gentrification of the urban environment has led to the establishment of walled enclaves keeping other inner city dwellers, such as Travellers, out. Hence groups labelled as 'deviant' by the dominant society, occupying marginal spaces, e.g. Travellers, appear increasingly visible and conspicuous within this ordered and controlled environment (Home 1994:111).

It has been argued that these developments reflect a "space-time compression" (Massey 1993:59 and 1994:146). The world has become a 'faster' place via developments in communication and transport, increasing the mobility of people, information and capital. It is argued that this has resulted in the 'fragmentation of local cultures' supposedly for the first time. "We are living in 'placeless' times" (Massey 1994:162). This "globalisation of our local environment" has contributed to what appears to be an "increasing uncertainty about what we mean by 'places' and how we relate to them" (Massey 1994:146). Local identities and concepts of place have allegedly been transformed by 'invasions' of 'outsiders' and 'newcomers', by 'foreign' companies (both from within and outside national territories) and by the development of trans-global telecommunications. Places and communities have apparently lost their unique sense of identity as a direct result of these 'invasions'.

Massey (1994), however, also asserts that localities have always been open to extraneous influences and that the time-space compression currently experienced is neither a new phenomenon nor a universal one. The ethnocentricity and current acceleration of the time-space compression needs to be queried. The present 'invasion' of foreign goods and people is, she argues, perceived in the west and its literature from a white, western perspective only. If it was examined from the perspective of colonised countries, the time-space compression, i.e. the invasion of foreign goods and people, occurred a long time ago (Massey 1994:147). In addition, the phenomenon is not experienced universally, either regarding gender or social class, for example, women's mobility continues to be restricted by men. Social differentiation is also extremely important; modern developments and appliances such as washing machines may have increased the time-space compression for the relatively affluent members of society but not for those like roadside Travellers who still do not have access to running water. Those with power in relation to the space-time compression have also used it to control groups who are physically mobile, like Travellers. The 'tools' of space-time compression such as computers have been used to establish national and international intelligence agencies and computerised police records. Despite the above, a belief in the apparently universal experience of the time-space compression has been utilised by groups within society to perpetuate a defensive and reactionary sense of place. Current fragmentation is set against a past, idealised sense of place inhabited by coherent and homogenous communities. This in turn may lead to antagonisms towards 'outsiders' such as Travellers at a local, national and trans-national level.

At a national and trans-national level these concepts have also been utilised regarding discussions of notions of citizenship. People's sense of citizenship has traditionally been based on their sense of belonging to a spatial territory, one which will have particular identifying characteristics. If people believe or are led to believe that those characteristics are being threatened or eroded (by outsiders or institutions/companies representing them) they may feel vulnerable in the presence of these outside influences. This may in turn lead to an increase in nationalism because it is easier to externalise the threat by blaming outsiders rather than address internal problems. Within the European context Travellers are viewed with suspicion because they are seen to represent those outside influences. Travellers' ability (real or perceived) to cross spatial boundaries (including national boundaries) has been seen as a direct threat, particularly within Eastern European countries struggling to establish their 'national identities' after the break up of the Eastern Bloc. In addition, the creation of the European Union and the consequent relaxing of state boundaries has meant that travel between member states has become easier. Countries are finding it increasingly difficult to close down their borders to migrants as they did in the past when they felt threatened because the level of control is now moving towards the European Community. This has led to calls for the defence of 'our' national identity against erosion by immigrants. Roma, Sinte and Travellers are an easy target because they are perceived as a group without a national identity or an allegiance in another country. They represent symbolically, via their culture and physically, via their movement, a threat to national identity (Waever et al 1993). Their lack of state loyalty and aura of cosmopolitanism has made them a logical target for nationalist groups, particularly the New Right in Eastern Europe. They are portrayed as not possessing identifying characteristics from a particular place, their language and fashion is seen as 'something they have picked up along the way'. They do not 'belong', not 'here' anyway, providing justification for expulsions from one national European boundary to another.

As individuals and groups find it necessary to 'place' themselves in the world, the concept of 'home' can be used to provide stability, in the light of outside threats and invasions. It also aids the definition of individual and group identity, differentiating 'home' from other places in order to provide security in a fast changing world. This has led to calls to defend 'citizens' sense of home (and identity) against 'strangers' like Travellers and other ethnic minorities. Travellers can be held up as strangers because they do not belong. By establishing who does not belong, the dominant group assists in defining who does belong. Knowing what we are not helps define who we are. Thus the concept of place is important in defining notions of group identity and who does and does not belong to a particular spatial area. At the local level these concepts are utilised by the sedentary society to portray Travellers in Leeds as transient, ignoring the reality of a long association with the city, many having lived there all their lives (Save the Children 1991). It is also used to justify a denial of access to resources because 'they are not from here'.

It must be remembered, however, that 'places' are complex locations where numerous and frequently conflicting communities intersect (Massey 1994:164). The hegemonic culture influences non-hegemonic cultures and vice versa, they do not exist in a vacuum.

"Many cultural identities are hybrid forms; marginalised cultures are neither the same as the hegemonic group nor entirely different from them; cultures affect one another." (Rose 1994:49)

A static, isolated, idealised sense of 'place' stationed in the past with a seamless coherence of character and comforting bounded enclosure has been utilised historically to justify the exclusion of marginal groups like the Travelling and Asian communities in Britain. These images of place are also utilised to support romantic notions of the Traveller culture situated in a mythical past such as the rural Romany in a bow-top wagon. This facilitates the portrayal of the present culture as a shadow of its former self, eroded and tainted by modernism. This, in turn, aids the establishment of a dichotomy between a 'valued Romany culture' situated in the past and the 'vagabonds' and 'itinerants' of today, sited in a decaying urban environment, who need 'saving'. The dominant culture is represented as having destroyed the valued Romany culture, emphasising its fragility rather than its survival. The dominant society is attempting to make notions of place and culture static and rigid, in order to clearly define who is 'in' and who is 'out' – Travellers are 'out'.

There is, therefore, a need to reconceptualise the notion of place in order to break down this rigidity and prevent concepts of place being utilised by the dominant group to exclude marginal groups. The representation of 'place' is not solely one which is imposed on the marginal group by dominant society. It is formulated by interactions at different times and places and between different people and groups. Thus 'place' can be seen as a: "particular set of social relations, (some of those go beyond the spatial area of place being referred to), which interact at a particular location ... the singularity of any individual place is formed in part by the specificity of interactions which occur at that location ... and in part out of the fact of the meeting of these social relations at that location which will in turn produce new social effects" (Massey 1994:168).

'Sites' of resistance

Travellers' occupation of marginal spatial areas has already been discussed. Their marginalisation is both physical and cultural. Physically roadside and authorised sites are both usually spatially isolated in industrial parts of cities like the authorised site at Cottingley in Leeds or near sewage works or power stations. Cultural marginalisation emanates from a non-recognition or active suppression of the Traveller culture by the sedentary society. The creation of marginal space for Travellers was enshrined in British legislation with the 1968 Caravan Sites Act directing where 'gypsies' could and could not reside. The 1994 Criminal Justice Act goes further, criminalising the nomadic lifestyle and enforcing sedentarisation (Liberty 1994).

Marginal space can be perceived as 'space' (physical and/or cultural), created for designated groups, towards which they are channelled by the dominant society, in order to impose on them their marginal identity. This is done in order to control, homogenise and/or 'other' the marginal culture. The option, therefore, for the marginal group (from the dominant group's perspective) is either movement to the 'centre', i.e. cultural assimilation or, if they reject these advances, 'banishment' to the margins. Marginal groups like Travellers may reject the pressure to move to the centre, actively rejecting cultural assimilation/homogenisation and may consciously choose to remain on the margin in order to survive (hooks 1991). This action is seen as signifying still further their 'outsider' status by the dominant society. However Soja and Hooper (1993) argue that individuals can only *choose* to be on the margin if they are coming from a relatively central position. They assert that it is necessary for an individual or group to be in a relatively powerful position before they can attain the economic, social and political ability to consciously place themselves on the margin.

It is contended by hooks (1991) that the margin *can* be a position of power for marginal groups as long as it is chosen as such, that is to say they are not 'banished' to the margin by the dominant group. She goes on to say that any movement to the centre would entail the loss of the marginal group's position of power. Thus the margin may provide the opportunity for an arena where a positive ideology of resistance can be established. A marginal position gives individuals the capacity to resist, actively engendering and fostering resistance. Thus spaces of 'radical openness' can be created on the margin (hooks 1991). The margin can be viewed as a space (site) of oppression and resistance, e.g. Traveller sites. Outsiders are unlikely to enter these spaces without attracting the attention, suspicion or resentment of residents. Within visibly confined spatial areas like Traveller sites it is easy for residents to monitor invasions of outsiders. Thus the source of oppression can also become a source of protection, offering security for the marginalised group. Trailers will be arranged so that residents can monitor movement on and off the site and supervise children's play. Dogs also play a useful role in protecting/defending a family's spatial environment, actively deterring invasions of outsiders. Thus although this is a 'marginal area', it is one which Travellers adapt in order to increase their levels of control.

At certain times, within specific spatial areas the marginal group may take over the space of the dominant society, such as the Traveller horse fairs at Appleby in Cumbria and Lee Gap in Wakefield although the dominant group maintains ultimate control. The fairs play an important role in the maintenance of cultural identity including the opportunity to conduct business transactions, meet family and friends and even prospective marriage partners. The sedentary society may perceive the fairs as an exotic 'transgression' (both spatially and culturally) sanctioned for a brief period of time and within a confined spatial environment. The sedentary society is to a certain extent fascinated by such exotic cultures (and events such as fairs) as well as feeling fear and repulsion for the group. Comparisons can be made with the West Indian carnivals in Chapeltown in Leeds and Notting Hill in London and the 'carnivalesque' behaviour in Brighton explored by Shields (Shields 1991:89-93). The fairs and carnivals provide an example of how the dominant society is willing to take Travellers and other ethnic groups into their own space as long as they are able to commodify them and their culture. They are bringing the marginal group and their associated marginality into the centre. Shields analysis of 'places on the margin' can also be linked with 'cultures on the margin' (Shields 1991:5). Within the official discourse of the sedentary society the Traveller lifestyle can be seen to be reviled whilst at the same time it is a primary exoticised constituent of the sedentary society's own fantasy life, for example, the 'free Traveller', the 'roaming Romany' and the popularity of holidays in horse drawn bow-top caravans.

Throughout these exotic 'transgressions' (fairs) the controlling forces of the dominant society such as the police and RSPCA officers remain strongly in evidence. Despite this, Travellers at Appleby can be seen to be reasserting control of the spatial arena by taking over the main streets with their horses and motor vehicles although the actual racing of horses and accommodation is now situated outside the town. The parading of horses and cars along the streets of the town often leads to direct spatial conflict between the sedentary society defending 'their' space by blocking off roads and Travellers opposing these spatial constraints by running their horses through the barricades. Symbolically the fairs are fundamental in providing a time and a place where the marginal group can usurp the control of the dominant society. Even though it may only be for a brief moment in time it facilitates the maintenance of a positive and alternative cultural identity. Relationships are not necessarily conflictual; fairs provide opportunities for social, cultural and economic interaction between Travellers and the sedentary society in the pubs, cafés and stalls.

Although sites can be seen as spaces of 'radical openness' on the margin, occupants of these marginal areas may also seek to exclude other residents. The Travelling community is not an homogenous 'whole' and exclusion from the dominant society may lead to 'stronger' members excluding 'weaker' members, for example, English Travellers excluding Irish Travellers and men excluding women. This process of 'social closure' where an excluded group in turn excludes a weaker group in order to access resources, power and/or control for themselves, is termed 'dual closure' by Parkin (1979). Ultimately, the scapegoating of weaker groups, such as English Travellers blaming Irish Travellers for crime or mess, is used by the dominant society to discriminate against all Travellers (Acton 1974).

Creation of 'homeplace' on the margin

Travellers occupation of marginal space has already been discussed. It is now necessary to explore the concept of 'homeplace' on the margin. The term 'home*place*' rather than 'home*space*' is used in order to signify the home's position within a particular location. (This emphasis is particularly important for Travellers when the location of the home may be moving regularly). This in turn affects the meaning attached to the 'homeplace' for both the dominant and marginal group. For example, Travellers camped on a recreation ground are seen as far more threatening and intimidating by the sedentary society than if they were camped on a piece of 'waste' ground tucked away from public view. Thus the degree of visibility and the type of space occupied is important. The meanings assigned by each group will vary temporally and spatially. The creation of a 'homeplace' for 'marginal' groups like Travellers is necessary as a *site* (physically and culturally) of resistance (hooks 1991). Thus the 'homeplace' can be viewed as a space of sanctuary as well as one of control. In addition, symbolically the physical presence and difference in appearance of, for example, Traveller sites, offer a visual opposition to the norms and controls of the dominant society. The concept and existence of 'homeplace' for marginal groups also provides the opportunity for cultural development and/or resistance in a relatively safe environment. 'Homeplace' provides a structure on which to build resistance; it is a site of resistance on the margin.

The creation of 'home' as a community of resistance is particularly important for marginal groups as this may be the only spatial area where they have some form of control over their environment. In turn, its existence is likely to be viewed as directly threatening the dominant society's power over and control of, marginal groups. As a response to this threat the dominant group may attempt to destroy the marginal groups' means to create a 'homeplace' in order to achieve the goal of cultural assimilation and/or subjugation. The 'homeplace', seen as a site of resistance, must be destroyed, for example, via legislation such as the 1994 Criminal Justice Act. Travellers are the only group in Britain to have their freedom of movement directly controlled by legislation. This creates economic, social and legal structures making it far more difficult to establish a 'homeplace' which is not subject to violation and destruction. Therefore the creation of a 'homeplace' can be seen to have a radical political dimension, for both sides – for Travellers this will be their sites, whether unauthorised or authorised. Unauthorised sites are particularly 'strong' (powerful) places of resistance. Their existence directly contravenes/ opposes the norms and spatial controls of the dominant society. Establishing roadside sites transforms marginal pieces of ground, changing their usage via 'illegitimate' means and for 'illegitimate' purposes, thus becoming areas of contested space. The presence of the marginal group both physically and culturally is seen to represent a direct and exceptionally visible opposition to the norms and/or controls of the sedentary society. Those controls state "you can't live here" or "you can't live that lifestyle"; "not unless it is authorised by us" and "you abide by our rules".

Travellers' rejection of these rules by continuing to live their distinct lifestyle leads to a denial of their citizenship rights by the dominant society. They are seen as not 'deserving' a homeplace. They are the 'undeserving' poor because they are portrayed as members of an underclass and/or part of a dependency culture. Both underclass and dependency culture are useful concepts for a society wishing to exclude (spatially and culturally) marginal groups and deny them access to resources. Travellers are not perceived as making an economic, social or cultural contribution to society, they are not 'active citizens' (Kearns 1993) and may in fact be accused of consciously subverting the moral codes and norms of that society by, for example, claiming benefits whilst working. Therefore they do not deserve the 'benefits' (financial and social) attached to membership of society and their exclusion, particularly regarding their ability to establish a homeplace, is justified.

A brief discussion of why it is so important for the sedentary society to prevent or at least control the creation of a Traveller 'homeplace' follows. The creation of a Traveller 'homeplace' is viewed as particularly threatening by the sedentary society due to Travellers' real or perceived nomadism. Thus they are seen as difficult to control and/or monitor but especially threatening is their perceived freedom of movement. It is this perceived ability or potential to cross space more easily than the sedentary society which leads to fears that at any moment they have the ability to invade 'your area' because 'they' are not subject to the same spatial constraints as the rest of 'us'. Thus their perceived ability to cross space, seemingly unhindered and their resistance to sedentarisation, provides justification for the implementation of strict spatial controls in relation to the creation of a Traveller 'homeplace'. Travellers threaten the hegemonic spatial and social separation of society. Other 'undesirables' may successfully be segregated, for example, in 'dump' housing estates but Travellers, via their nomadism, oppose this attempted spatial exclusion, i.e. they oppose the locking of marginals into restricted spaces.

Travellers' nomadism contradicts the assumption that only people with power have the ability to move freely (*New Statesman* 1994:xii-xiii). Roads offer the opportunity to escape but only for the select few. Dominant interests within society restrict who can utilise these 'escape routes', thus nomadism is a form of spatial and cultural opposition. Travellers' trailers and vehicles give them the power to transport themselves around, to define their own living space and reassert control (Bird et al 1993). This, it can be argued, in turn, threatens the power base of dominant groups within the sedentary society. Nomadic Travellers in Britain are small in number, they have little political or economic power and it can, therefore, be argued that they have no real power and prove no realistic threat to the sedentary society. However, if this is the case why do Travellers incite such vociferous opposition? Why does their spatial proximity to residential areas lead to calls for immediate expulsion and accusations of criminal activity and dumping? Why has draconian legislation like the Criminal Justice Act been passed?

It is Travellers' ability to transport themselves around and cross spatial boundaries which is seen as a direct threat by the sedentary society. They oppose attempts at spatial and social exclusion and have the ability to cross into, for example, 'middle class space'. Their nomadism (real or perceived) locates them as 'strangers' within a spatial area. It is easier to blame 'strangers' for deviant behaviour (especially if they come and go) rather than blame your 'own' people and thus have to critically examine and possibly undermine or threaten the structure of your 'own' community. Hence when Travellers pull on to unauthorised sites in residential areas local residents transpose their fears onto them. As 'strangers' they provide the ideal scapegoat for undesirable behaviour such as criminal activity and the dumping of waste. This process also acts as an additional safety valve for the dominant group. By ascribing/transposing its negative character-istics onto a marginal group and by making those characteristics inherent within that group the dominant members serve to maintain their position of power and further weaken the position of the marginal group. It also means that those negative characteristics do not have to be dealt with by the dominant group within their own community because they 'belong' to/ are inherent in the 'deviant' group (Okely 1983).

Bauman (1990) would argue that Travellers are strangers rather than outsiders because of their physical presence within the community, albeit on the margins. Travellers are not unfamiliar to members of the sedentary society although contact is often limited and perceptions of non-Travellers are usually formed via media reporting and the appearance of roadside camps, i.e. invariably at times of conflict. However, they are familiar because in order to conceive of someone as a stranger you have to know something about them.

"Above all ... they (strangers) are bound to come time and again, uninvited, into my field of vision ... they sit firmly inside the world which I occupy ... and do not show signs of leaving" (Bauman 1990:54).

The last statement is particularly pertinent in relation to Travellers because the sedentary society is constantly trying to make them go elsewhere. Their spatial proximity ensures they appear more threatening because they can cross/redraw the boundaries between 'us' and 'them'.

Their ability to cross the boundary between the dominant and marginal groups exposes its weakness. In addition, it highlights the fluidity of the boundaries between the Travelling community and the settled population, interaction does occur regularly and it is not always conflictual. The dominant group perceives that boundaries (spatial and/or cultural) are drawn by them rather than by the marginal group. An acknowledgement that marginal groups also create boundaries is not considered as this would entail a recognition (by the dominant society) of the marginal group's power and ability to draw these boundaries or to even want to draw boundaries, as their perceived goal should be assimilation. Even the term 'Traveller' denotes people who were yesterday 'there' and today are 'here', i.e. they are not subject to the spatial controls imposed on the rest of 'us'. They challenge 'our' way of life because they have a different lifestyle which is 'alternative' to the established (and by inference) 'normal' way of life (Bauman 1990:59). Living a 'normal' lifestyle previously made the 'in' group feel comfortable now, with the appearance of 'strangers', they feel threatened and are likely to retaliate in order to defend that lifestyle, e.g. via legislation – the Criminal Justice Act, opposition to authorised sites, petitions against roadside sites, etc.

Gender differences and the concept of 'homeplace'

Gender differences in the meaning attached to the concept of 'homeplace' emerge via an examination of gender roles and gender relations within the Travelling community. For *all* Travellers 'homeplace' can be seen as a 'site' of control and resistance. However, this is particularly pertinent for Travelling women because they are subject to patriarchal control within the Travelling community in addition to discrimination from the dominant society due to their ethnicity and gender. This may be called a 'feminisation of racism', i.e. women suffer more acutely the discrimination experienced by the whole group. For example, poor living conditions mean that perinatal mortality within a sample of the Travelling community on council sites and the roadside was shown to be three times greater than within the general population (Pahl and Vaile 1986). Women play a central role in accessing resources within the Travelling community and are likely to experience external oppression and discrimination to a greater degree than men. The inability or difficulties experienced in the construction of a 'homeplace' adversely affect women because of their childcare and domestic responsibilities, for example, accessing healthcare and basic sanitation. Restrictions also come from within the community. In particular Traveller women are subject to strict moral codes regarding their sexuality. Crickley (1992:106) contends that when an ethnic group is under attack from external dominant groups, their oppressive control of female sexuality may be seen as a way of maintaining group boundaries as well as providing males in the group, already oppressed elsewhere, with ways of exercising some domination. This can be viewed as men constructing new sites of resistance, i.e. gendered sites. This can also be seen as a form of 'dual closure' (Parkin 1979). The reality of strict moral codes within the Travelling community is in distinct contrast to the sedentary society's traditional portrayal of 'Gypsy' women as sexual temptresses, freely available.

It is important to examine the position of women within the Travelling community because of their marginality *and* centrality. Women are marginalised because they are living in a patriarchal society/community but at the same time they occupy a central position because they are integral to the Travelling lifestyle. Their portrayal as 'victims' by the sedentary society merely serves to justify the cultural and spatial controls imposed on the whole community, a common stereotype is that 'they treat their women badly therefore they should be persuaded, (coerced/forced), into behaving more like 'us' ('civilised' people). What is implicit in this statement is that Travelling women are blamed for their own oppression brought upon themselves because they are Travellers, that is to say, their compliance leads to their oppression. This 'victim status' is a social construct utilised by the sedentary society to justify paternalistic assistance and enforced assimilation/sedentarisation. It also means that the dominant society does not have to address its own patriarchal system. Margaret Maughan, quoted by Anastasia Crickley, sums up the position very well when she says:

> "Settled women look down on Traveller women and give out about them for the oppression that they suffer. But what a lot of settled women don't see is that Travelling and settled women are in the

same boat when it comes to the way they are looked down on and treated in society by men" (Crickley 1992:101).

Within the Travelling community gender relations are unequal, as they are in the sedentary society, but they are formed from a different cultural base. However, all relations are developed in particular places and at particular times, that is to say, there are different forms of patriarchy shaped by the inter-relationships and inter-dependence between men and women, at different places and different times (Hanson and Monk 1992:572). Thus patriarchal relations within the Travelling community (as within the sedentary community) vary spatially and temporally. Gender roles are clearly defined and complementary. They are also inter-dependent, without the support networks provided by women's reproductive labour it would be impossible for productionist labour to continue.

Men ostensibly control female space, such as their freedom of movement and access to resources, but what the sedentary society ignores in its criticism is the reality that nomadism or the possibility of nomadism, is central to Traveller women's cultural identity, even if they are perceived as having little say about when and where they move (Crickley 1992:105). Thus sedentarisation in housing is not a solution to Traveller women's oppression, although it is often seen as such by resource providers within the sedentary society. This reflects the cultural bias of the resource providers and the belief that their own cultural perspective is the 'norm'.

Initial drafts of the 1994 Criminal Justice Act contained clauses stating that Travellers would be 'helped' and 'encouraged' to move into housing if they 'wished' to do so. Many Travellers in Leeds have moved into housing due to the intolerable living conditions on the roadside. According to Leeds Traveller Education Service (personal communication) there were at that time 200 families in houses in working class areas, predominantly in the south of the city, particularly in Holbeck, Beeston, Armley, Hunslet, Belle Isle and Cross Green. This is not, however, necessarily a permanent transition; the failure rate for housing Travellers in Leeds is 70 per cent (Leeds Citizens Advice worker) which reflects the cultural inappropriateness of a policy of sedentarisation. This mirrors a national trend; in 1987 Department of Environment research showed that "although 250 Traveller families took up a tenancy in a 12 month period about 100 were back on the road within a year" (Hawes 1995; Hawes and Perez, 1995). Traveller women find it particularly difficult to make the transition because they are more likely to be in the house all day, alone, without the support of relatives and friends to which they are accustomed. Rates of depression amongst housed Traveller women are particularly high due to the isolation they experience after moving from a supportive living environment where, for example, their sisters or mothers were always a few feet away (Daly 1990; Hyman 1989). Men generally find it easier because they are more likely to be out at work with other members of their family.

Women Travellers are thus marginalised due to their ethnicity and gender although gender relations vary spatially and temporally. However, an analysis of which 'marginalisation' they 'suffer' most acutely does not recognise the fluidity and social construction of relationships, it merely serves to establish fixed boundaries regarding ethnicity and gender. Even the terminology used in gender relations is highly emotive. Words like 'masculine' and 'feminine' are open to interpretation and geographical variation and can be viewed as social constructs (Rose 1992). Gender, spatial and even ethnic boundaries are fluid and open to adaptation and re-interpretation. There is, therefore, a need to look at the influence of space and place (including 'homeplace') on individuals and groups and to examine how they in turn influence the spatial environment and notions of place (Hanson 1992). An analysis of 'degrees of marginality' merely serves to perpetuate gendered static and rigid binaries of 'men/women' or oppositional forces of 'Traveller/non-Traveller'. The social construction of knowledge and discourse and the power relations embedded within them need to be recognised, as all interactions have a contextual location (McDowell 1992). Linking women (and by inference excluding men) intrinsically with, for example the home and private space can be seen as an ideological construct and constraint which serves to exclude women from particular areas rather than actually being based on the results of empirical research. The exploration of black oppression in the USA by hooks (1991:25) also has pertinence for Travellers. She contends that an analysis of spatial and temporal variations, contesting the gendered and ethnic stereotypes of 'us' and 'them' can be used to challenge the universal and static notions of ethnic identity. In relation to Travellers this approach could lead to opportunities to produce multiple Traveller identities challenging the representations of Travellers as one dimensional, reinforcing and sustaining the sedentary domination.

Space/time variations
The nature of gender relations vary spatially and temporally. They will also vary at different times in an individual's lifecycle. Gender relations within women-headed households are likely to be different from those within households headed by men. Women-headed households do give some Traveller women opportunities to control access to resources and relations within the family which they may have otherwise not had the opportunity to do so. They may still, however, be dependent on other, often male members of the household for their spatial movement; for example, if they are unable to drive, another family member will have to shift their trailers.

Another important variable is the differentiation between day and night. The geography of individual sites may change at night; this certainly occurs on the authorised site in Leeds. These changes have important implications for notions of 'male' and 'female' space and for gender use of space. Many of the women on the Leeds site are frightened to leave their trailers during darkness because of the actions of some men. Actions such as vandalism and joyriding serve to create 'spaces of intimidation'. Their behaviour, such as shooting out the street lights signifies to others that they 'own' that space; 'they are like cats – they only come out at night' (private conversation with Traveller man, site B, Cottingley Springs). These men, within this spatial context are controlling the temporal arena for other site residents, particularly for women. Their actions can be seen as a symbolic gesture showing others that they own that darkness and temporal space. They are playing on peoples' fears, particularly women's. This has resulted in women on the site saying that they are trapped in their trailers because they are frightened to go out but they are also frightened to remain inside. During the day, however, when many of the men vacate the site to go out to work, women may be seen to regain some form of control of the spatial arena (see the section on resistance below).

The temporal changes discussed previously also have a distinct spatial element. The authorised site in Leeds is divided into two parts 'A' and 'B'. There are distinct territorial divisions between the two and due to a number of factors including size of site, overcrowding and general appearance A is called 'Dallas', whilst B is called 'Hell'. There is friction between the two sites mainly because of their close proximity, highlighting how culturally inappropriate site design creates serious problems for residents. People from A are accused of coming onto B and 'causing trouble' such as dumping, vandalism, drug taking and joy riding, i.e. destroying B's space, which in turn leads to residents on B defending their space. In addition, people on B are accused of destroying their own spatial environment by burning the waste material that has been dumped. This has resulted in the hospitalisation of at least two residents because of the noxious fumes given off by the waste when it was burnt. Poor site design exacerbates and even creates many of these problems because there is not enough space to carry out work on the site. These poor environmental conditions manifest themselves in ill health, in particular, the occurrence of high rates of depression amongst women. Women on B have the potential for greater health problems because of the poorer environmental conditions in which they are living.

Homeplace as an area of resistance
Although 'homeplace' can be viewed as a site of control and/or oppression it can also be seen as a source of strength and power for women. This can be seen in relation to hooks' (1991) examination of the importance associated with creating a homeplace for black women in the USA. The homeplace is somewhere that Traveller women can restore their dignity, providing a 'safe' spatial area in which to learn to love and respect their culture outside the hostility of the sedentary society (c.f. fairs like Appleby and Lee Gap providing similar opportunities). Women control the inside of the trailer, especially when the men are away during the day, then it becomes primarily 'their' space. They have opportunities to have other women round and meet with family and friends, in *'their'* trailers, on *'their'* plots. 'Homeplace' provides the spatial environment where women can have control and instil in their families the concept of a 'Traveller identity'. Reference by other women is made to women's trailers rather than men's, acknowledging their influence within that spatial area. Thus they are not just providing a 'service' but are playing an important social role.

Within the spatial boundaries of the site, divisions can be seen between 'male' and 'female' space but these divisions are neither static nor rigid. Due to the integrated nature of the family and the interaction between 'homeplace' and 'workplace' men may physically leave the site to work but will return to sort scrap, tree loppings, etc. Because of the assignment of different gender roles, women (primarily responsible for childcare and domestic labour) are more likely to congregate in trailers, whilst men are more transient, moving between the trailer and outside whilst working (although they are more likely to actually congregate outside). Children move freely from one sphere to another. Thus, although childcare is ostensibly a female role, men will have children with them whilst they are working on the site or take them with them when they go calling. Both boys and girls may go out with their fathers, although when they become young adults (12/13 years) it is more likely to be boys as this is the time when they are learning their life skills (trade).

Children's concept of 'homeplace' appears to be the site rather than individual trailers. Toddlers will move independently from their trailers to those of relatives. The relative's trailer is seen as an extension of a child's own home. This also serves a practical purpose when families are living in trailers and space is extremely limited. The site also serves as a 'homeplace' for adults (although it is not always seen as a safe sanctuary as highlighted previously) but it remains an important spatial boundary, physically and culturally delineating where the 'Traveller world' begins and ends. People do not leave 'home' or the trailer, they go off and on the site.

There are additional temporal differences between male and female control of space. For example, when the weather is inclement and men are unable to go out to work (as the vast majority of work is conducted outside), women may lose the power to control their own spatial arena, i.e. the trailer. This may affect their ability to access resources or control their own spatial freedom, for example, attending outside groups and activities, such as the Women's Group in Leeds. This highlights how tenuous a woman's ability to control her spatial environment can be. Attending 'outside' groups may be perceived by some men as a direct threat to their patriarchal control. Thus the spatial and temporal context mediates in patriarchal control. In contrast many husbands and wives together attend outside organisations such as the church and one woman on the site said how she had been on holiday with her sister to Europe on a number of occasions but her husband had never been out of Yorkshire.

'Homeplace' as an area of socialisation

The 'homeplace' is the principal area of socialisation for men and women. It is here they learn their respective gender roles within the community. It is the spatial environment where women are socialised for domesticity and where, from childhood, girls learn to equate their femaleness with domesticity (Oakley 1974:113). This is an extremely important role within a community where the family is seen as the focus of individual identity and the women's role is primary responsibility for childcare and domestic labour. Consequently, a high birth rate may be a source of pride and status, not just a source of oppression for Travelling women. Non-Travellers tendency to focus solely on Traveller women's domestic 'drudgery' as a source of their oppression serves to ignore the positive aspects of their centrality within the community. The linking of gender oppression primarily to the Traveller culture and the nomadic lifestyle merely serves to discriminate against all Travellers, supporting arguments in favour of sedentarisation and assimilation. It also reflects the cultural bias of the sedentary society believing that their own cultural perspective is the 'norm' (Mohanty et al quoted in Mc Dowell 1993:164).

As within the sedentary society, from an early age the homeplace provides the arena for girl's and boy's 'apprenticeship' for future gender roles. For girls, this apprenticeship is part of the socialisation for the female gender role in a wider sense. The importance of domestic labour is intrinsically linked with a woman's own self-identity (Oakley 1974). Thus women judge themselves and their own 'worth' via their domestic proficiency. The appearance of their trailer is a source of pride and status for women within the community. Thus it is important to keep the inside and outside of their trailer in pristine condition as its physical appearance reflects directly on a woman's (and her family's) standing within the community. If the trailer is dirty and untidy they are perceived as having let themselves and their family down. This sense of responsibility is given at a relatively young age (12/13 years) and is a way of learning 'life skills' and also a source of cultural reproduction.

Gender roles will affect the ability of women to access certain resources, for example, employment, if they are primarily responsible for childcare. Cultural expectations also play an important role, particularly in relation to employment outside the home. Sibley (1986) has argued that the persistence of self-employment amongst Traveller men can be regarded as facilitating the maintenance of the marginal group's economic independence and cultural identity, i.e. social distance. Thus Traveller women taking formal employment outside the community and homeplace, working for non-Travellers, may be viewed as a direct threat to this independence and identity, as well as a threat to patriarchal control. The fact, however, that Traveller women have always been involved in labour outside the home, whether farmwork (where the whole family would be employed) or hawking, either with other female relatives or husbands, must be acknowledged.

The nature of women's employment is nevertheless changing. Whereas traditionally women would work for themselves or within family groups, today an increasing number are employed independently by non-Travellers. The vast majority of women in Leeds with permanent employment outside the home are relatively sedentary and unmarried (cultural norms dictate that most women give up waged work on marriage). Some young women have secured employment in local factories within walking distance from the authorised site, generally in couples or small groups in order to provide cultural and social support within the working environment. Despite what may be regarded as a radical departure from traditional roles within the Travelling community, changes in the nature of some women's employment does not necessarily signify the beginning of 'cultural assimilation' and may merely reflect the historical adaptability of the Traveller economy to changes within the economy of the sedentary society (Mayall 1988, Okely 1983). The spatial location of the Traveller homeplace also influences a woman's ability to access employment outside the home. If she is constantly shifting round the country or city it is virtually impossible to hold down a full time job. In addition, caring for a family on the roadside without basic necessities such as running water, sanitation and refuse collection is far more time consuming than living on an authorised site with facilities.

It can be argued that Traveller women cross spatial boundaries more freely than men since they are responsible for accessing many welfare resources and dealing with the gatekeepers of those resources in relation to claiming benefits, accessing healthcare and education. Traveller women in Leeds are entering different spatial arenas, for example, visiting the education service and schools, the Womens' Group and other community services. This is not to say that men are not doing this too but it does acknowledge that women are travelling between these spatial arenas and are, in many instances, crossing spatial boundaries to a greater degree than men. Although men have daily contact with non-Travellers particularly via their work, e.g. buying and selling scrap, dealing with customers, etc. the nature of their relationships with the non-Travelling community are far more detached than those the Traveller women are likely to develop. As stated previously increasing numbers of women who are relatively sedentary on authorised sites are taking paid employment outside the home. It is important to note that this is paid employment *within* the sedentary society, i.e. working for *gaujos* (non-Travellers). Traveller women are experiencing a greater intensity of interaction with the sedentary community than Traveller men who remain self-employed. This may lead to conflict, particularly gender and generational conflict. Many parents, however, are encouraging their unmarried daughters to go out to work (although attitudes often change on marriage) and some married women are also working outside the home.

The accessing of education is a particularly important spatial arena for Travellers traditionally denied access to their rights because of non-literacy. Women are at the forefront in accessing this resource both for themselves and their children. Education by the institutions of the sedentary society can be viewed as a vehicle by which the cultural norms of the dominant group are imposed on the marginal group; it may also influence the nature of gender roles within the family. Since school attendance removes children from the spatial arena of the 'homeplace' and its cultural influence, education can be perceived as a form of cultural assimilation. It may be viewed as a form of social control, fostering assimilation via a sedentary lifestyle and cultural hegemony (Sibley 1986). Education can also, however, be seen as a way that the community, via literacy, can gain skills in order to access resources denied them by the dominant society due to their non-literacy. The ability and desire to access education will be dependent on the nature of the homeplace and will vary temporally and spatially between families and individuals. Continuity of education is virtually impossible to achieve if a family is constantly being evicted, whereas families on authorised sites have greater opportunities to access education. Levels and rates of class attendance will be affected by parents' expectations, i.e. the extent that education is seen as worthwhile and relevant to their lifestyle and their own experiences of education. They will also be affected by the early adult status of young people within the Travelling community and parents' fears their children may learn different codes of behaviour, e.g. regarding sex and drugs. At the age of thirteen and over most boys will leave education to work with their fathers and girls are likely to leave to look after siblings and assist in domestic labour on a full time basis. Thus their spatial horizons change again; up to this point they could be viewed as fairly similar but at this time they diverge.

Children's attendance at school may prompt non-literate parents, particularly women, to learn to read in order to help their children's learning or because they feel embarrassed that they have to rely on their children to read, e.g. food labels in shops. A Traveller woman at Cottingley told me: "I felt so humiliated and stupid as a child not being able to read and write that I always swore that if I had children they would learn to read and write even if it meant us moving into a house". Note the emphasis on learning to read and write rather than attending school, i.e. the benefits of literacy are acknowledged but not necessarily the benefits of 'schooling'. Thus literacy can be viewed as a way of accessing resources without having to rely on members of the sedentary society to complete, e.g. benefit forms, tax or insurance documents, etc. It can also be viewed as an important tool to be utilised in the creation of a Traveller homeplace as a site of resistance; providing opportunities for Travellers to reassert control over their culture in the eyes of the sedentary society and providing Travellers with the opportunity to 'write' their own culture.

Conclusion

This chapter has explored the complex meanings attached to the concept of 'place' for both the hegemonic and non-hegemonic group and how these meanings are utilised by the dominant society in order to locate marginal groups in particular spatial areas. It contends, however, that Travellers' occupation of marginal space (both physical and cultural) within the sedentary society is neither given nor fixed and may be open to renegotiation by either side. Nevertheless, static, rigid and bounded concepts have been utilised by the dominant society to create reactionary and defensive notions of place which, in turn, have been used as a tool for the spatial and cultural exclusion of 'marginal' groups like Travellers (Massey 1994). Travellers are excluded from these bounded notions of place because of their nomadism (real or perceived) i.e. their ability to cross spatial boundaries. These concepts have also been utilised by the dominant society in the exploration of gender roles within the Travelling community. A static and rigid portrayal of gender roles has been used to support arguments that Traveller women's oppression is solely the result of their culture and lifestyle, rather than analysing the interdependence and reciprocal nature of gender relationships within the Travelling community (Crickley 1992).

The chapter's analysis of the different types of marginal space which Travellers' unauthorised sites occupy highlighted the transient nature of this space and the fact that it is a concept which is open to reinterpretaion spatially and temporally by both the dominant and marginal groups. It has also stressed the importance of locality for the development of inter-relationships between groups and how these inter-relationships, in turn, affect the nature of the locality. The environmental conditions experienced on sites such as the authorised site in Leeds clearly show the impact of locality on inter-relationships between individuals and groups and how this impact is experienced differentially in relation to gender. Thus the nature of the authorised site in Leeds clearly affects relations between residents on site A and those on B; these, in turn, affect the locality, e.g. the vandalism and joyriding experienced on B. The locality of unauthorised roadside sites in Leeds will also affect socio-spatial relations depending on the parties involved, past experiences of roadside sites in the area (i.e. temporal element) and inter-relationships with groups and individuals outside the immediate spatial environment, e.g. the local authority; these, in turn, influence the nature of the locality.

We need to reconceptualise notions of place in order that marginal groups like Travellers have the opportunity to *take* marginal space for themselves, actively locating themselves on the margin in order to reflect and signify their continued cultural, economic and social independence, both to themselves and to the sedentary society. Only then can marginal space be viewed as a *site of resistance'*(hooks 1991). Thus the creation of a homeplace on the margin can be viewed as a medium for reflecting Travellers' social and cultural independence. Traveller women play a central role within the community and are instrumental in creating and maintaining a homeplace on the margin. Despite economic, social and legal structures, aggravated by the Criminal Justice Act, making it very difficult for Travellers to create a homeplace which is not subject to violation and destruction, they continue to do so. This highlights their cultural survival and the strength/success of the mechanisms utilised to maintain their culture and their ability to adapt without assimilation.

References

ACTON T 1974 *Gypsy Politics and Social Change. The Development of Ethnic Ideology and Pressure Politics Among British Gypsies from Victorian Reformism to Romany Nationalism* Routledge and Kegan Paul, London

BAUMAN Z 1990 *Thinking Sociologically* Basil Blackwell, Oxford

BIRD J, CURTIS B, PUTNAM T, ROBERTSON G, and TICKNER L eds. 1993 *Mapping The Futures, Local Cultures, Global Change* Routledge, London

CRICKLEY A 1992 "Feminism and Ethnicity" in Dublin Traveller Education and Development Group *The DTEDG File: Irish Travellers: New Analysis and New Initiatives* Pavee Point Publications, Dublin pp.101-8

DALY M 1990 *Anywhere but here: Travellers in Camden* London Race and Housing Unit, London

HANSON S and MONK J 1982 "On Not Excluding Half of the Human in Human Geography" *Professional Geographer* 34 1 pp.11-23

HAWES D 1995 "Natural Born Travellers" *Housing* March 1995 pp.34-35

HAWES D and PEREZ B 1995 *The Gypsy and the State: The Ethnic Cleansing of British Society* SAUS Publications, Bristol

HOOKS B 1991 *Yearning: race gender and cultural politics* Turnaround, London

HOME R 1994 "The Planner and the Gypsy" in H Thomas and V Krishnarayan eds. *Race Equality and Planning Policies and Procedures* Avebury, Aldershot pp.111-27

HYMAN M 1989 *Sites for Travellers: A Study of Five London Boroughs* London Race and Housing Unit, London

KEARNS A 1993 "The Politics of 'Active Citizenship' and the Geography of 'Local Governance" Seminar presented to Institute of British Geographers' Conference, University of London, January

LIBERTY 1994 *Restrictions on Travellers and Squatters: Criminalising Diversity and Dissent* Liberty campaign briefing, London, February

MASSEY D "Power, Geometry and a Progressive Sense of Place" in Bird J, Curtis B, Putnam T, Robertson G and Tickner L eds. 1993 *Mapping The Futures, Local Cultures, Global Change* Routledge, London pp. 59-69

MASSEY D 1994 *Space Place and Gender* Polity Press, Cambridge

MAYALL D 1988 *Gypsy Travellers in Nineteenth Century Society* University of Cambridge Press, Cambridge

Mc DOWELL L 1992 "Doing Gender: Feminism Feminists and Research Methods in Human Geography" *Transactions* 17 pp. 339-416

Mc DOWELL L 1993 Space Place and Gender Relations Part I: Feminist Empiricism and the Geography of Social Relations *Progress in Human Geography* 17 (2) pp.157-79

NEW STATESMAN AND SOCIETY 1994 Criminal Justice and Public Order Bill Supplement 24 June 1994 iii-xv

OAKLEY A 1974 *The Sociology of Housework*, Basil Blackwell, Oxford

OKELY J 1983 *The Traveller Gypsies* Cambridge University Press, Cambridge

OKELY J 1994 "Thinking Through Fieldwork" in Bryman A and Burgess R G eds. *Analysing Qualitative Data* Routledge, London pp.18-34

PAHL J and VAILE M 1986 *Health and Healthcare Among Travellers* University of Kent, Canterbury

PARKIN F 1979 *Marxism and Class Theory: A Bourgeois Critique* Tavistock Press, London

ROSE G 1992 "Feminist Voices and Geographical Knowledge" *Antipode* 24 pp.230-3

ROSE G 1994 "The Cultural Politics of Place: Local Representation and Oppositional Discourse in Two Films" *Transactions* 19 (1) pp.46-60

SAVE THE CHILDREN 1991 *A Place of Our Own: A Survey of Leeds Travellers' Views on Sites and Their Future Provision* Save the Children Fund, Leeds

SHIELDS R 1991 *Places on the Margin: Alternative Geographies of Modernity* Routledge, London

SIBLEY D 1986 "Persistence or Change? Conflicting Interpretations of Peripheral Minorities" *Environment and Planning : Society and Space* 4 (1) pp.57-70

SOJA E and HOOPER B 1993 "The Spaces that Difference Makes: Some notes on the geographical margins of the new cultural politics" in M Keith and S Pile eds. *Place and the Politics of Identity* Routledge, London pp.183-206

SWINHOE L 1993 "Travellers and Land" Unpublished dissertation submitted as part of Masters Degree, London School of Economics

THRIFT N 1994 "Taking Aim at the Heart of the Region" in Gregory D Martin R and Smith G eds. *Society Space and Social Science* Macmillan, London pp. 200-231

WAEVER O, BUZAN B, KELSTRUP M, and LEMAITRE P 1993 *Identity Migration and the New Security Agenda in Europe* Pinter Publishers, London

Chapter 6 Razor blades amidst the velvet?
Changes and continuities in the Gypsy experience
of the Czech and Slovak lands
Chris Powell, Lecturer in Criminology, University of Wales

'Velvet' is the word widely used in order to describe the manifestly dramatic
events which have taken place in the Czechoslovak lands since 1989.
The argument is that given the collapse of a political and economic system
which had been in place for forty years, followed four years later by the
Czech/Slovak schism, potential catastrophes have been kept at arm's length
by a combination of good will and calm heads. Clearly there is some truth
in this version of events. This region has avoided the kind of militarised
conflict which has plagued the old Yugoslavia, Chechenia and Azerbaijan,
while the divide provided the opportunity for the newly formed states to
respond to changed circumstances at the pace each preferred. Hence the
Czech Republic could follow Prime Minister Klaus down the free market
route just as fast as the West would permit, whilst Slovakia under Prime
Minister Meciar was more reluctant to cast aside what many there
regarded as benefits deriving from the old 'socialised' means of production.
Velvet Revolution has, it appears, been followed by Velvet Divorce. It is
clear, however, that such a cosy view ignores substantial numbers of people
who have been adversely effected by the changes in economic terms. It is
even more clear that it ignores the plight of the Gypsies, or *Roma,* whose
situation has deteriorated in almost every way since 1989.

This was not, of course, the way it was meant to be. The activists in
the struggle against the Communists were well aware of the adverse
circumstances which most Roma endured under that regime. For example,
Vaclav Havel (1982), prior to the Velvet Revolution had described the public
attitude towards Gypsies in Czechoslovakia as somewhere between
indifference and racism. The communist state in his view had done little or
nothing to counter this attitude. "Czechoslovakia", Havel asserted,
"demands a more enlightened and more tolerant policy". Charter '77 (Havel

1982) proclaimed "Gypsies are the least protected citizens – a third world culture in the midst of a European Culture" and went on to assert: "Rights and freedoms should benefit all people regardless of their nationality or ethnic origins. Belonging to a certain nationality or race cannot be a reason for limiting a persons rights or depriving him of his rights". The implication was that Gypsies merited ethnic status, something the communist regimes of Poland and Hungary had acknowledged but Czechoslovakia had not. In the course of the Velvet Revolution Roma had close ties to the Civic Forum (an outgrowth of Charter '77) and both Czech and Slovak states have enshrined the above principles in their respective new constitutions.

One might have hoped, then, that such political liberation would lead to steady improvements in the broader social circumstances of Roma. However, if we consider some basic social stratificatory variables we find that such is by no means the case. In 1989 Kostelancik observed that 36 per cent of all Romani households lived in one room buildings. Such is still the case. The Romani population is overwhelmingly concentrated in what are officially recognised to be the worst housing conditions.

Roma have been and are heavily employed in seasonal occupations, by definition somewhat tenuous and insecure, and in reality poorly paid. Kalibova (1992) has demonstrated that Romani people born in 1980 can expect to live approximately thirteen years less than can non-Gypsies. In terms of education it is still the case that only 29 per cent of them advance to vocational schools (Kostalancik 1989). The number of Roma entering higher education establishments is minimal and those teaching in such places virtually non-existent. Truancy rates are over eight times higher than those for non-Gypsies. Over a quarter of all Romani children are officially in special schools. As 20 per cent of all Romani children are officially designated as mentally retarded, this is perhaps predictable. Officially the Romani proportion of the overall population (4 per cent) is responsible for half the robberies, 60 per cent of the thefts and 20 per cent of overall crimes (Ulch 91). Such data parallel the Communist period during which Gypsies accounted for three quarters of all charges laid for endangering the morals of youth and a quarter of those for parasitism. Arguably then 'over-criminalised' by regimes old and new, Roma have remained massively over-represented amongst the imprisoned population for whom conditions have remained quite appalling.

Perhaps it is unrealistic to expect that in a period of rapid change such inequalities could be reduced in a short space of time. The status of Roma as an 'underclass' was by no means the product of the Communist Regime and hence should not be expected to alter as an automatic spin-off from its demise. Rather, the history of the Roma in the Czech and Slovak lands is one of continuous oppression since the mid sixteenth century when legislation was passed to expel them on the alleged grounds that they were spying on behalf of the Turks. The later part of the following century found the regime ravaged by the aftermath of the Thirty Years War. Guy (1975) refers to the country as "depopulated, plague-ridden, starving and continually troubled by serf uprisings and robber bands recruited from discharged soldiers. Meanwhile the Turks (and French) mounted new and more menacing attacks. It was a terrible time for Roma." Many Gypsies were expelled but many others, less 'fortunate' were slaughtered and their corpses left hanging from trees on the borders to deter future immigration.

Guy tells that this kind of persecution collapsed throughout the Hapsburg Empire in the eighteenth Century. The Age of Enlightenment was defined by attempts being made to transform lands into national and 'rational' centralised states. The intention as far as Roma were concerned was to transform them into productive peasants ultimately controlled by the state. Such attempts at assimilation were proceeded by the provision of new houses and compulsory employment. To 'rational' ends then, Roma were to be prohibited from travelling and from owning wagons and horses. Furthermore they were forbidden to wear 'outlandish' clothes.

People were officially forbidden to speak the Romani language and Gypsies became abolished linguistically, to be reconstituted as 'New Farmers'. Happily all these assimilatory measures collapsed only (less happily) to be superseded by routine harassment of Roma throughout the nineteenth century. For example, they were required to register with the local police who very often tried to 'escort' them off their patch. In the 1920s Roma shared with convicted thieves the doubtful distinction of being required to carry identity cards. This was part of an attempt to restrict nomadism – a practice which became illegal unless formally sanctioned by the local police and local authority. The Nazi period brought about another, albeit a more 'successful' attempt at exterminating the Roma. Whilst those in the Slovak lands avoided this fate, the Czech-based Roma were virtually eradicated.

The post-war Communist government promised that anti-Gypsy discrimination would not be tolerated. The preferred form of social control became assimilation again. With this objective in mind, in the 1950s laws were passed aimed at the remaining minority of nomads, denying them the right to travel. Wheels were forcibly removed from carts and wagons and horses were shot. Even the Czech Circus was affected. This law on restricting movement could be applied to Roma who just happened to be travelling somewhere or visiting friends or relatives. Those officially categorised as nomads could be imprisoned for terms ranging from six months to three years. Essentially whilst such measures succeeded to some extent in limiting Romani patterns of movement, they failed to achieve assimilation. Indeed, rendering the population static resulted in the institutionalisation of the special segregation of Roma in terms of amenities and low quality settlements or ghettos.

The negatively differentiated treatment of the Romani populations of the Czech and Slovak lands thus needs to be understood in terms of important continuities. Whether by elimination or assimilation the intent has been to inhibit Romani autonomy and the outcome to consign Roma to the bottom of the social stratificatory heap. The aftermath of the Velvet Revolution and Divorce has further worsened the situation of the Roma.

It is abundantly clear that both the Czech Republic and Slovakia are currently rife with expressions of anti-Gypsy racism. This racism manifests itself in a wide variety of areas. For example, on the streets, people point to Roma, pull faces at them and obviously avoid them. One woman I was with visibly shuddered when she saw them. Everyone had a ready off-the-peg anecdote to tell about Gypsy criminality. Gypsy visibility on street corners, in city centres and on public transport (perhaps especially public transport) is a matter for public concern. Graffiti proclaiming 'Gypsy free area' are common. In public places such as pubs, clubs, discos and restaurants Roma have been effectively blacklisted by many businesses. Signs contrary to the constitution declaring "Gypsies not welcome" have been ignored by local authorities. More blatantly Roma have had dogs set on them when they have attempted to go into bars. Owners typically deny their own prejudices. One restauranteur, for instance, was reported in the *Prague Post* in 1992 as excusing himself by saying: "Germans come to the restaurant, see them [the Gypsies] and leave".

Racism also occurs at sporting events. For example, soccer clubs from places like Trnava and Kosice (where there are relatively high proportions of Roma) are subjected to the kinds of racist chants most British soccer fans are used to hearing directed at black players.

There has also been a dramatic intensification in anti-Gypsy feelings amongst young people. Most obviously and violently skinheads have taken and continue to take their anti-Gypsy sentiments onto especially (but by no means exclusively) the Prague streets, calling for gas chambers to be introduced for the 'impure' race. A Ku Klux Klan group has been established. Possibly more worryingly, Nougayrede (1992) reported an upwardly mobile, rather "Americanised group of sixteen and seventeen year olds in Prague". They consider the slogan 'Foreigners out!' to be intolerable. "Tolerance and friendship between people ... especially the Europeans" they chant in unison but they make major exceptions to the rule, especially in the case of Gypsies, although not liking "Gypsies doesn't make you a racist, they assert serenely!" This kind of casual racism is allowed to seem normal. In the course of a televised beauty contest, one young woman quite matter of factly observed that her ambition was to become a lawyer so that she could help her community get rid of all the 'dirty' Gypsies. Her interviewer gave no indication that this was in any way controversial. The media indeed plays its part in expressing and reproducing anti-Gypsy prejudices. It has, for instance, run campaigns linking Roma with diseases such as typhoid. Furthermore, the crime-reporting policy has been to identify the ethnic origins of people involved only on the occasions when Roma have been the offenders, ignoring such an ethnic dimension when the victims have been Roma.

The police have proved to be reluctant to act where violence has been targeted against Roma. Indeed, such is their anti-Gypsy reputation that Romani victims often decline to report incidents for fear of becoming doubly victimised. Those events which are reported are by no means automatically recorded and those which are recorded are left bereft of their ethnic dimension. Helsinki Watch (1992) has provided evidence to the effect that the police routinely interact aggressively with Roma and regularly conduct unauthorised searches of their houses. Express efforts have been made to 'cleanse' the streets of Roma, especially in tourist areas and in those areas where businesses wish to locate themselves. The police might also use the low credibility of Roma as a good opportunity to steal from them. It seems that many police officers use coercive measures against Roma as a means of re-establishing their credibility amongst the population at large. In recent years a number of businesses have been established offering private 'security services'. The so-called 'black' sheriffs are developing a real reputation for their vigorous anti-Gypsy actions. Public opinion polls indicate that 85 per cent of Czechoslovaks wanted Roma to be excluded from their neighbourhoods and 92 per cent believe that all Gypsies are criminals. Hardly anyone could countenance having a Gypsy as a friend and 83 per cent believed that Gypsies should be denied all welfare benefits.

Such rampant racism is both rooted in and reproduces the social stratificatory characteristics identified above. Since the two 'velvets', for example, Romani housing conditions have actually declined. Helsinki Watch (1992) found that throughout the region landlords had felt at liberty to remove windows and turn off electricity and water supplies so that Roma would be forced out of their apartments. In terms of the labour market those state employment agencies, whose responsibility it is to enforce equal rights legislation, largely fail to do so. They 'justify' advertising jobs with private companies which expressly exclude Gypsies in terms of avoiding mutually embarrassing encounters. However, positions in the public sector are also openly declared as not for Gypsies. Whilst legislation prohibits firms from requiring job applicants to identify their ethnic origins, in practice Roma are required to declare themselves as Gypsies. Finally, Roma are experiencing new forms of discrimination in formal educational terms. In 'mixed' schools their children are often segregated 'for hygiene reasons'. Increasingly 'dirty' children are sent home. This results in the state withdrawing welfare payments from their parents for refusing to send their children to school! One has to draw the conclusion that since the Velvet Revolution and Divorce, the structural position of the Roma has deteriorated. There is a tendency, perhaps understandably, for concern over the treatment of the Czech and Slovak Gypsies to be focused on manifest expressions of violence and symbols of such violence. It is relatively easy for liberals in the West to be horrified by the racist graffiti which is now commonplace and by the knowledge that skinhead razor gangs frequently rampage through towns and cities looking for Gypsies. Consciences are almost as easily pricked by an awareness of the discriminatory practices identified earlier. The reality is, however, that the latter are potentially dialectically linked with the structural location of the Gypsies.

'Potentially' is the key word here. Throughout the Communist period the Gypsies in structural terms constituted an 'underclass'. The Romani activist Scuchka (1993) refers to a situation of "State Racism". During that time, the official policy of assimilation required, however, that discrimination against Roma should remain relatively invisible. Whilst anti-Gypsy prejudices were held and expressed by a large proportion of the public, discriminatory powers were substantially within the control of the state. The state-controlled media restricted overt anti-Gypsy output and the authorities stamped down hard on public acts of violence against Roma. In an important sense the collapse of the communist state has 'liberated' people; they are now free (and are more likely to have the power) to discriminate and indeed to engage in physical violence. Scuchka observes that state racism has been replaced by citizen racism. It is now in the open.

However understandable, Scuchka's conclusion is, it is somewhat limited. 'Citizen racism' is not a product of 'natural' impulses which any given state can inhibit as it chooses. Citizen racism cannot be analysed in isolation. It has to be understood in terms of a complex interplay between state, economy and global politics. A given state may attempt to inhibit, release or wash its hands of citizen racism but it makes its attempt within a far broader context which determines the parameters seeming to limit the 'choice' of the Czech and Slovak states appear to an alternation between 'handwashing' and 'releasing'. Many changes which have adversely effected Roma have been (on the surface at least) brought about by the state. Although skinhead razor violence has been publicly denounced, no measures have been forthcoming to deal with it. Indeed Leicht (1992) alleges that in at least one Bohemian town officials have gone so far as to engage skinheads to help in guaranteeing security and order. Police have been all too willing to victimise Roma in promoting the interests of more powerful social groups. Both the Czech and Slovak states have been quite prepared to break and bend their own rules when the issue concerns Gypsies. The case of employment rights has already been commented on. It is also the case that contrary to law 'Gypsy registers' have been compiled in some areas. Peoples' houses have been illegally entered and some Roma have been forcibly removed from the Czech Republic. In Slovakia a local authority imposed a curfew on Roma who were not allowed on the streets between the hours of 11pm and 4.30 am. The local police chief observed that this was illegal but effective. Apologists for the regimes argue that they are trying to contain 'citizen racism' by being seen to be actively engaged in controlling what they describe as anti-social behaviour perpetrated by Gypsies. The reality is, of course, that such state action actually legitimates rather than inhibits citizen racism. A 'kind' reading is that a strong state has been superseded by a relatively weak one, not adequately equipped and indeed somewhat reluctant to oppose public expression of opinion, even when racist. A harsher reading would be that the lack of response to citizen racism and the enacting of state-implemented racist measures is less an outcome of loss of power and more a policy designed to enhance state power. Such an account is supported by the increasing tendency for officials and researchers to make public pronouncements which are liable to promote anti-Gypsy feelings and actions. Academics for instance, now feel free (or are tacitly encouraged?) to refer to Gypsies as 'alien' and to repeat a catalogue of very familiar sounding anecdotes and prejudices.

For example Gypsies are alleged to:
- commit crimes to get a bed on a cold night
- coerce doctors into giving them false medical certificates saying they are unable to work
- breed more prodigiously than 'normal' people and thereby threaten to swamp the country
- have a large number of extended kin in limited accommodation
- not know how to live in a normal house and use the floorboards for firewood
- work with mechanical things, spoiling the neighbourhoods both visibly and audibly
- make and sell illicit alcohol
- urinate in bushes!
- dispatch the women to the tourist areas for the express purpose of prostitution.

During the communist period Charter 77 termed as 'genocide' state attempts to pressurise women into having abortions and sterilisations. There is no evidence of recent changes. Officials are still rewarded for meeting assigned sterilisation quotas and Gypsy women are given bonuses five to ten times those given to other women (Ulch 91).

Gypsies are seen as doubly deviant. They may be workshy scroungers but the state indulges them by providing undeserved welfare. For some reason provision of free buses to take Gypsy children to school (a clear social control measure, surely) seems particularly galling for those 'normal' citizens who do not get this service.

Alternatively Gypsies are seen as 'Gypsy Kings' driving around in Mercedes and mocking their less fortunate and more honest non-Gypsy neighbors. Of course, the academics are balanced. They talk of the positive aspects of Gypsy culture as well – how musical they are – perhaps they have 'natural rhythm'? (!) Such willingness to accentuate the victimisation of a social group which has been traditionally victimised bears a marked resemblance to the so called New Realism which has infected British political life throughout the past decade.

Official and quasi-official casting of the Gypsy as alien in the metaphorical sense is currently being reflected in the legal sense in the Czech Republic by their new citizenship regulations. After the Second World War many Roma were forced to leave 'shanty' homes in Slovakia to go to the Czech part of the Republic where they were employed as part of the industrial labour force. Given the virtual extermination of Czech-born Roma by the Nazis the overwhelming majority of Czech-based Roma since that time have had Slovak roots. In 1968 the Czechoslovakian Republic was fused into a federal state and every citizen assigned Czech or Slovak status according to birth. At the time that Rooker (1995) observes this did not seem very important. Regardless of where one lived, Czechoslovakian citizenship seemed to be all that really mattered.

Come the Velvet Divorce, however, this changed dramatically. Slovak-born Roma and their descendants (who may never have been to Slovakia) became obliged to apply for Czech citizenship should they wish to continue living there. The Czech state has made it clear that citizenship should be regarded as a 'gift' rather than a 'right' and has laid down criteria for the granting of citizenship which have proved very difficult for Roma to fulfill. One of these requires that applicants must have held permanent residence in the Czech Republic for five years. Zoon (1994) reports that many Roma discover that their apartments are classified as temporary rather than permanent. The 'temporariness' derives not from the length of time a property has been inhabited but from an official recognition that it is, in sanitation terms, uninhabitable. Citizenship is also refused to people with criminal convictions. The law does not distinguish between serious crimes and the petty offences of which many Roma have been convicted. Given the historical trend has been for an 'over-criminalisation' of Roma, their disadvantage is compounded. Another potential difficulty is a clause which requires that applicants have mastery of the Czech language. Whilst to date according to Rooker (1995) this does not seem to have been significant, it is clear that mastery is open to variable definition. Does the Czech language have to be the person's first language? Is the mastery required of oral or written language? What about the illiterate? What about primary Slovak speakers?

In 1994 the Tolerance Foundation interviewed ninety-nine Slovak Romani applicants for Czech citizenship. Forty-eight of them had been born in the Czech lands, the rest had lived there for up to thirty-five years. None had been able to acquire Czech Citizenship. As stateless people (applicants have to renounce Slovak citizenship in order to apply for Czech) they became ineligible for welfare benefits from June 1994.

How can we explain the continuities in the Romani experience of discrimination and how can we explain the changes? Traditional theories of racism clearly have some value. At a sociological and a social-psychological level, for example, we must take account of the symbolic meanings the Roma have for the non-Gypsy population. Gypsies are stereotyped as unrestrained, rootless – indeed *free*. Romantic and romanticised tales of the roving life (sometimes, of course, recounted by Roma themselves) fuel these sorts of belief.

For the majority of the population this assumed freedom is the antithesis of their own life circumstances and is at one level an object of desire. The assumed holders of the freedom become objects of resentment. Jock Young (1971) put it in a different context: this hedonism is unlicensed and unmerited.

There is also perhaps an hypocritical element of resentful dependence and projection of guilt. Historically, Jewish traders and financiers faced prejudice from the very Christian population who used their services but simultaneously held them in contempt for doing so. Today, Roma provide services (alcohol provision, cheap motor repairs, unregistered labour) of which the majority population, slightly shamefacedly, take advantage while putting all the blame for illegality on the Roma.

Without defining sin, we cannot say who the saints are. If 'now' in the post-Communist era the Czech Republic is really a cultured and civilised nation ready to take its place in the bright new Europe, perhaps it is rather functional to have what Nils Christie (1984) has termed a 'good enemy' around enabling people to feel reassured as to their own virtue. 'Good enemies', of course, do not just remain so – they require combatting. In terms of the Czech Republic this is clearly happening with respect to the Roma.

Economic factors assist us with our understanding of both continuities and changes in anti-Gypsy racism. Kenedi (1986) shows how, in the communist period the poor officially had no excuse for their poverty and mainstream public consciousness saw the Gypsies as in some way degenerate. Now in the harsh new market-driven world Roma are even more likely to be scapegoated in doubly deviant terms. The few who make it are 'flash', getting above themselves, objects of envy and resentment. The majority who do not make it are to be condemned for their shiftlessness, their idleness and their stupidity.

For a society unaccustomed to it, the fear of unemployment is almost certain to generate dissatisfaction – dissatisfaction which requires an easy victim or scapegoat. For people whose wage level fails to enable them to afford the new consumer items available in the shops, seemingly unemployed and highly visible Roma constitute a predictable target for blame. It might also be argued that the nature and the sheer speed of economic change has led to a form of moral vacuum in which traditional solidarities wane and traditional hostilities wax. More contentiously this might be formulated as a suggestion that the adoption of a capitalist ideology by the state in a period of rapid change leaves it particularly susceptible to moral vacuum. Whilst officially abhorred, discrimination is both intrinsic to the logic of the system and renders considerable benefits for those in positions of dominance within that system. Hence it may be argued that the intensification of anti-Gypsy racism in the Czech Republic is to a large extent the product of a choice made by that state to pursue the path that it did. That 'choice' was, however by no means an entirely free one, but rather a context-bound one.

An important and consistent policy objective of successive political regimes in the Czech lands has been to restrict Gypsy mobility. To the extent that the vast majority of Czech-based Roma can now reasonably be described as sedentary these policies might be said to have been successful. Nonetheless, much of the image of Gypsy culture remains that of unregulated mobility. Certainly some Roma have been mobile within Czechoslovakia and others have regularly crossed international borders. Communist policies fluctuated, proclaiming assimilation and but often achieving only ghettoisation but still repressing nomadism and discouraging mobility except when expedient for fulfilling specific localised labour needs. In the communist period, borders with the west were rigorously policed but within the old Eastern bloc some Roma did move around relatively unhindered. They followed harvests and went to warmer climates in Romania and Hungary, for example, in winter time.

In the light of contemporary developments in western Europe concerning open borders, eastern European states are increasingly coming under political and perhaps economic pressure to police their own national borders. Utrat-Milecki (1992) makes the point for Poland. "If we do not 'improve' our policy towards foreigners then the western countries will not open their frontiers for us." The 'open' borders sought during the Cold War have increasingly been restricted to those defined by the powerful as economically productive or tourists or the very rich. Governments do not intend to allow uninhibited free movement for all. The ideologically useful proclamation of open borders runs alongside attempts quietly, and sometimes not so quietly, to inhibit the movement of a variety of social and ethnic groups categorised as undesirable. In Czech public consciousness Gypsies are the archetypal mobile and disreputable section of the population – a prime target for surveillance and control. This is reinforced by surrounding states. Austrian police have already operated in an assistance role on Slovakian soil. Agreements are also in place with Germany. An expansion of this rather one sided co-operation is likely, together with legislation which although ostensibly focused on the Romani population (which would of course virtually guarantee it almost 96 per cent support) in practice would afford the state the power to monitor general population movements both within and across borders. One Czechoslovak precedent for this kind of move was that in 1958 when the 'Nomad' legislation was passed. At that time 'everyone knew' it was meant for the Gypsies, but it did not specifically say so. In practice, the 'Nomad' legislation facilitated the control of movement of any undisciplined group the state or its functionaries felt merited control.

The collapse of the Iron Curtain has been succeeded by the construction of Fortress Europe. The borders of the old West have been rendered exceedingly tight by the implementation of rigorous anti-migration measures. One of the most important of these has been to engage the authorities of the old Eastern bloc to assist in this endeavour in exchange for various kinds of economic rewards. This assistance takes the form of guaranteeing close monitoring of the movement of 'problematic' populations. The promise of controlling Gypsy movements provides part of the legitimisation for states such as the Czech Republic in terms of 'selling' such policies to its own citizens.

The New (Fortress) Europe promotes itself on the basis of maximising security and freedom for its citizens but can only do so by increasing levels of insecurity and control for those deemed ineligible or unwilling to accept the nationalistic and statist assumptions underpinning citizenship. Within the Fortress, Gypsies would seem to fit these categories. In the Czech Republic they are victims of internal razor gangs, racist local officials, scapegoating state politicians, local and international entrepreneurs and Fortress Europe. So much for Velvet!

References

CHRISTIE N 1984 "Suitable Enemies" Paper given to the Howard League conference, Oxford

GUY W 1975 "Ways of looking at Roms" in F Rehfisch ed. *Gypsies, Tinkers and Other Travellers* Academic Press, London

HAVEL V 1982 *Human rights in Czechoslovakia* Conference for Security and Co-operation in Europe, New York

HELSINKI WATCH 1992 *Struggling for Ethnic Identity* Human Rights Watch, New York

KALIBOVA K 1992 *Romany children in Czechoslovakia* Charles University, Prague

KENEDI J 1986 "Why is the Gypsy the scapegoat and not the Jew?" *East European Reporter*

KOSTELANCIK D 1989 "The Gypsies of Czechoslovakia" *Studies in Comparative Communism* Vol XXII, No.4

LEICHT L 1992 "Gypsies, a vulnerable minority in Europe", Paper submitted to Unicef

NOUGAYREDE N 1992 "All eyes on the New World" *The Guardian*, June 28

ROOKER M 1995 "Stateless and Marginal" paper given to conference *The Criminalisation and Victimisation of Gypsies in Europe*, Onati

SCUCHKA E 1993, quoted in *Het Parool*, (Dutch newspaper), January 13

ULCHO 1991 "Integration of the Gypsies in Czechoslovakia" *Ethnic Groups* 9 (2)

UTRAT-MILECKI J 1992 "Poland, the bridge or the wall of Europe", paper given to European Group for the Study of Deviance and Social Control Conference, Padua

YOUNG J 1991 *The Drugtakers* Penguin, London

ZOON I 1995 *Notes on the Czech Citizenship laws* Tolerance Foundation, Prague

Chapter 7 Foreign Gypsies and British immigration law after 1945

Donald Kenrick, Researcher and Consultant, London

How useful it would be if we could find a list, however incomplete, of speakers of Indian languages passing through, for example, Baghdad in the ninth century. I hope that future historians will find this list useful, although there is no way of knowing which of the groups mentioned will become important in the history of Gypsies. I have concentrated on showing how the Gypsies were able to enter Britain and what work they did. For the purposes of this list, I will define 'foreign' as 'not born in Britain (or left Britain as a child and spent most of the time in a foreign country)'. 'Gypsy' I will use here as a synonym for 'Romany' which will refer to the descendants of a group of people who emigrated from India between the fourth and tenth centuries and moved west into Europe and who identify their language as Romany. I will not discuss groups such as Irish Travellers who can move freely between the two countries. I will disguise the identity of some of the individuals mentioned to protect their privacy. Much of the information summarised in this chapter is based upon their private and confidential information and so cannot be referenced in the normal way.

When the Second World War ended in 1945 the Gypsy population of Britain consisted of Romanichals and the Welsh Kaale, together with a small number of Kalderash and Rudari who had spent the war in the UK. At least one of the latter served in the army. A certain number of earlier Rudari immigrants had intermarried with the Romanichals.

The Kalderash
Kalderash or Coppersmith Gypsies have been coming to Britain since 1860 as serfdom in Romania came to an end. There was a small influx in 1911-13 and a large immigration in the period 1929-40 which was described in several articles in the *Journal of the Gypsy Lore Society* (Winstedt 1913;

Anon. 1934; Myers 1943, 1945; Holmes 1978, 1988:64). In the 1930s there were two large families – the Stirios and the Yevanovics. These two are the progenitors of the majority of Kalderash in England since 1945.

First, there was Tom Stirio with his four wives, only two of whom produced offspring. To their children and grandchildren we must add the descendants of two of his wives in other marriages. Their descendants number some 200.

The other important family are the children of Zyorzyi and Maria Yevanovic wrongly listed in the *Journal of the Gypsy Lore Society* (Yates 1942, 1943) as the children of Tanas and Tereza Yevanovic. Again we theoretically have 200 children and grandchildren but there have been marriages between the Stirio and Yevanovic families and recently cousin marriages within each extended family. All in all, there are about 300 living descendants of the 1930s Kalderash. The surnames have been anglicised. The men work mostly with metal and the women tell fortunes except for the strict Pentecostals (cf. Kovalcsik 1985).They tell neighbours they are Greeks or Italians and thus hide their Romany identity. At least one man, married to a Romanichal, still lives in a caravan.

They occasionally come to the notice of the press. In 1973, D. came to the attention of the *South London Press* (2 March 1973) when neighbours complained of the noise. The headline was "Decibel diary of a Gypsy family". K. was in the national press when thieves burnt her hand on a stove to make her reveal where she kept her savings. "Raider burns palms off a palm reader" said the tasteless headline in *The Sun* on 12 April, 1989.

Only rarely do the London Kalderash make the news with fortune telling as they arrange to give the money back if clients complain. One occasion where the police did intervene was when, as the *Daily Mirror* (3 September 1983) wrote: "Gypsy Rose runs out of luck" when she took £500 from a nurse so that it could be washed in holy water to make evil spirits vanish. Rose received a prison sentence. Rose was in fact the Gaji wife of a Rom.

Groome wrote in 1899: "Fifty years hence very likely ... the ancient corporation of the Calderari will have undergone dissolution". He was wrong.

British Citizens

While some Kalderash were in Southend in 1914 Igrava Maria gave birth to a son, George. He acquired British nationality which may have helped to save the lives of his children and grandchildren who were held in an internment camp in Italy during the Second World War. His children, the three brothers Philipov, now regularly come to England to work as coppersmiths.

Kalderash children who were born in England in the 1930s did not, on the whole, automatically become British citizens at birth. Most of them became Canadian or Australian citizens as they were living in those countries when they reached the age of sixteen. But if they did come back to England after 1945 then they were often given British passports on request or a permanent residence permit.

British citizens were at one time able to bring their husbands, wives or fiancées to the country with little trouble and the spouse obtained British citizenship often on the same day as the marriage. A.E. had obtained a

British passport at the age of about thirty. He married a French Gypsy and she was issued with a British passport at the British Consulate in Paris after which the couple came to reside in England. The only difficulty is that there has to be a legal marriage which means that if the marriage breaks down there has to be a legal divorce.

P. married a Serbian Gypsy woman at a registry office who could not adapt to the strict Kalderash customs. He then tried to get an annulment on the grounds of non-consummation of the marriage but his wife's description to a lawyer of the wedding night put a stop to this plan. Thus he had to wait two years to get a divorce on the grounds of desertion. Meanwhile, his plans to marry a Canadian citizen were held up as she needed a legal marriage to enter Britain. How much easier was life in the time of Bahram Gur!

The most well-known foreign spouse is perhaps the Slovene Sinti, Zilka Heldt, who married a Romanichal. The story of how she survived the Second World War in Yugoslavia and Italy is told by Kenrick and Puxon (1972:109-11, 1995:86).

For a woman to bring in a husband might be more difficult but not so necessary, as the custom among the Kalderash in particular is for the bride to join the husband's family. So L. who married a Greek Gypsy went to live in Athens.

Commonwealth citizens

In the early years after 1945 the British government showed its gratitude to the Commonwealth countries that had aided the war effort by a liberal attitude towards immigration. Many Kalderash came from Canada and Australia and retained their citizenship but were given permanent residence permits. The majority of these were children of the 1930s Kalderash.

With the expansion of the Commonwealth regulations tightened up. The new rules put Canadian and Australian citizens largely in the same position as other aliens – they could come as tourists for six months but after the expiry of this six months could not return for a further six months. In practice, the women were allowed to tell fortunes although they were on tourist visas while the men engaged in traditional tinning and moved into the second-hand car trade. A few families, Rays and Johns, who came from South Africa, were more distantly related to the core 1930s Kalderash families. A London policeman kept a benevolent eye on the comunity and, if they did not overcharge clients, they were left alone.

In the last few years immigration controls have been tightened up and several couples with different nationalities who are not legally married have to spend six months in Canada and six months in the UK each year if they want to stay together with their children.

Two brothers with Canadian nationality who wish to stay in London with their widowed mother, a British citizen by marriage who was seriously wounded in a robbery, have been refused leave to remain. The Home Office argues that the woman should be looked after by her daughters although it has been put to them that the Romany custom is for daughters to move into their husbands' homes and look after their parents-in-law, not their own parents. One brother has been deported while the other waits for a change of heart from the Home Secretary.

Frank S., a Canadian citizen, was refused entry on 3 February 1995 on the grounds that he was 'not likely to leave at the end of his six month's stay' although he had entered and left three times in the previous three years. Frank's elderly father and three siblings are in the UK with leave to remain. His mother and two brothers are British citizens.

On one occasion being checked on arrival at immigration proved lucky: C.F. was arrested in 1985 and charged with a fortune telling fraud. Then it was discovered from her passport that she had arrived in England after the date of the fraud.

A small community of Gypsies from Cyprus with British passports lives in London and works in the catering trade. Later arrivals from Turkish Cyprus have not been so fortunate. A group of asylum seekers was returned to Cyprus.

The Australian Kalderash who came to the UK in 1975 were part of the Stirio or Yevanovic families. They came with Australian passports as tourists and stayed on. The women (mother and daughter) told fortunes throughout England under various names: Mrs Shiner in Leeds, Madame Shasha in Bedford, Madame Treena in London and Birmingham, Madame Anna in London and Bristol, Madame Clarissa, Madame Superior, Sister Kelly, Sister Mary and Madame Freda in London and finally Madame Cariba in Gloucester where they came to grief when dissatisfied clients complained. The press had a field day, with headlines like:

"Women faked powers of supernatural" (*The Times* 20 July 1978)
"Prison for the phoney fortune tellers" (*The Express*
18 August 1978)
"Fortune tellers' dim future" (*The Guardian* 18 August 1978)
"Madam Carib (sic) jailed for Demon plot" (*The Daily Telegraph*
18 August 1978)
"Gypsy Queen accused" (*The Sun* 20 July 1978)
"Fortune tellers' reign of terror" (*The Daily Mail* 20 July 1978)

A spin-off from this affair was that the Home Office gave permission for relatives who visited 'Madame Cariba' in Pucklechurch Prison to speak in Romany. Previously policy had been that theoretically there had to be a member of the prison staff available who could understand the language, otherwise the conversation at a visit had to be carried out in English. I expect that the increasing number of foreign languages spoken by prisoners has led to an end to this policy but at the time it was seen as an advance.

The Canadian Kalderash again were descendants of the 1930s families or their wives.

American tourists

The American (US and South American) Kalderash who have come here are not related to the Stirios and Yevanovics except, rarely, by marriage. They have no chance, and probably no desire, to switch their nationality to British as the Canadians and Australians have sometimes been able to do. They always come as tourists for a short stay. The women rent offices in London on the whole, while advertising leaflets are usually distributed by young men recruited from their non-Gypsy neighbours. A fortune-teller calling herself Mrs Green was working here in 1972 and there have been others each summer. Because these US fortune tellers do not want or need to build up a regular clientele (as they can only stay for six months) they tend to charge larger fees than the native Kalderash who want their clients to return regularly. The men rarely work (except giving out leaflets occasionally and protecting the women against unruly customers). One exception was a male fortune teller whose methods were somewhat dubious.

In 1985 *The Sun* (20 May 1985) ran an exclusive on "a Gypsy gang of phoney spiritualists who have conned gullible victims out of more than £1 million" and this story was picked up by the South London Guardian Group in August that year, much to the annoyance of the London-based Kalderash who feared for their clientele.

"Police estimate that a hard core of 30 North American Gypsy psychics are currently plying their ploys in South England" wrote *The Streatham Guardian* (29 August 1985).

On one occasion the men from this group also went round hospitals buying used X-ray plates for recycling. Exceptionally, a single man came over to buy hydraulic jacks (and to try to find his wife who had disappeared). Romanies holding Puerto-Rican passports have also lived in Kensington while telling fortunes on at least two occasions.

More recent European Kalderash and Lovari

Three 'Polish ' Lovari were reported in the newspapers in 1978; Lovari arrived from Ireland in the following year. Lovari from western Europe have been coming at intervals, the most well-known of whom was Koka Petalo who used to sail from Holland and stay in southern England most summers. He was well known for the marquee-like tent he slept in and the fact that he was probably the first to have a citizens' band radio (the precursor of mobile phones) and would phone his wife from afar to tell her to start cooking the supper.

The European Kalderash and Lovari travel around to the markets in caravans or dormobile-type vehicles. Usually they have had Italian or Dutch passports.

If large numbers turn up at the port of entry at the same time they get sent back on the grounds they are not genuine tourists. Fifteen families were stopped at Southampton in 1966 and another group in 1970. Once here although they do pass for tourists (as they don't have lorries) and stay in tourist camp sites or pay a farmer for a week's stay. Crystal Palace and Hackney have all seen regular visits by western European Gypsies in large cars with tents or Volkswagen caravanettes. In some cases when the camp authorities realise they are dealing with Gypsies they ask them leave on the ground, perhaps, that they had forgotten there was a large group of English children coming to camp the next day. In 1989 a North London caravan site refused a group of European Gypsies and they spent the night parked outside the gates.

It seems unlikely that many Gypsies came to the UK merely as tourists to see the House of Commons and the Changing of the Guard. Because of the immigration laws most European Romanies who came do so with the status of tourists and for six months. When they are here they travel to markets in small towns selling mats and carpets or sell flowers in London streets and restaurants and, more recently, have attended evangelical conventions. In 1986 there were twenty French Gypsies in six caravans parked near Brentwood in Essex.

German Sinti also come regularly to trade in antiques but since they attract little notice and have no problems to be solved, they have not appeared in the newspapers or the records of Gypsy organisations.

A Lovari group who were trading in the markets did come to public attention after accusations of shoplifting. Because the different members of the family had been born in different countries the police decided they were dealing with an international gang who had come to England to embark on a vast criminal enterprise. In fact, the older man had come with his new wife to escape from the attentions of his first wife's brothers in Sweden who were not pleased at his changing affections. But neither the police nor the press could be convinced of this. The Home Office wanted to deport them to Bulgaria where the father had been born. The Bulgarian authorities refused to accept him as he had 'emigrated illegally' at the age of five. Help came in the shape of a Danish passport with which he was able to return to Sweden to face the possible wrath of his ex-in-laws. It took several more months before he received compensation for a large amount of jewellery which had disappeared in transit between two police stations in East Anglia where he was being held but for which, fortunately (perhaps to the surprise of the police), the family had kept receipts.

An earlier group of Lovari who had been calling on houses to sell craftwork was arrested on suspicion of burglary. Unusually they were given plots on a Gypsy site in east London while awaiting trial and had the chance to meet Yul Brynner when he visited the education project on the site. An emerging friendship between a young Romanichal lady and a Lovari man was nipped in the bud when the charges against him were dropped and he was deported for overstaying his visa time.

Another Lovari visitor was Tanya Kuzhikov who was earlier recorded in Italy as a folk story teller.

Muslim Romany visitors
Most Muslim Romany visitors to the UK were born in Yugoslavia but emigrated from the 1950s onwards and perhaps obtained Italian, French or Dutch right of residence. The first press references in the United Kingdom are from 1980 ('women in vans'). Entering as a tourist means that the authorities can deport anyone who worked and, therefore, broke the conditions of their entry to Britain. This did happen in the case of one group of Yugoslav flower sellers (with Dutch passports) who were caught during a drive against dark-skinned flower sellers and beggars in central London in 1985. They were hauled in to Paddington Green police station and an official from the Home Office was called in to inform them offically that they had broken the terms of their entry permit and they would have to leave within twenty-four hours. These families were Jehovah's Witnesses, having been converted in Holland and had been hoping to visit the movement's centre in London to which they had an invitation.

A second group of Yugoslav flower sellers was unluckier. They were arrested at the Chelsea Flower Show on suspicion of pickpocketing. They were found to be carrying a "large" sum of cash – £200 (!) but, of course, no other form of finance such as credit cards or travellers cheques. On this basis they were held in custody and brought to court. One of the juveniles was taken to a children's home. The magistrate realised that there was no evidence to convict the women of pickpocketing so he said he would free them if they agreed to be bound over to keep the peace and left the country that night. The alternative was to stay in custody for several weeks for a trial. They chose to leave. "Flower Show Romany Gang freed", as the *Kensington and Chelsea Times* (17 June 1988) put it. Meanwhile their car had been impounded outside the courthouse which in fact stopped them leaving that day.

Some Cherhari (or Chergashi from Bosnia) were regular visitors from 1984, sometimes in caravans and sometimes renting flats (Kenrick and Bakewell 1988 pp.11-12). The men went early to the then Covent Garden Market to buy flowers wholesale which the women then made up with silver paper during the day. At night the men sold the flowers in the West End. They were doing so well that they toyed with the idea of buying a Rolls Royce until a relative by marriage was found to be claiming social security as an EC citizen on a false Italian passport. Worried about their status, if stopped and questioned, they all left London in a hurry. This particular extended family has travelled in Italy, Germany and Holland before and after coming to England.

Not all brushes with authority were as serious. The Gypsy Council office was once called for someone to go and explain the significance of wiggly lines to a Yugoslav family who had parked their caravan for the night too near a zebra crossing in Shepherds Bush. In 1989 a Yugoslav girl was fined £700 for trying to smuggle in a puppy.

One Nawwar (or Middle Eastern Gypsy) family came here in 1978 with Iranian passports. They returned two years later with Somali passports. This time they were unfortunate as two of the women wearing veils were arrested on the suspicion of being a couple of veiled women who had been shoplifting. They were released but not before the police had discovered their passports were false. The Home Office had a problem in deciding which country to deport them to and this became more difficult after the arrest of the father on an unrelated charge. In the end they were put on a boat for Holland where a brother lived.

Missionaries and politicians
The first missionary to England was Oscar Lyck, a Belgian Traveller, who was based in Kent for several years in the early 1970s. The various missionaries and political leaders who have come to England for short visits usually come as tourists, to avoid bureaucracy.

Political leaders have included Vanko Rouda in 1966, Rudolf Karway in 1970, Stevica Nikolic in 1980, Mitko Markov of Eurom and Rajko Djuric of the World Romany Congress. Amongst the missionaries was Mateo Maximoff who has paid several visits to this country. The first Pentecostal missionaries to the London Kalderash were Nono and Nene in 1970. They were followed by others and the work was extended to the Romanichals and Irish Travellers.

Some politicians have combined this with business, such as a group of Spanish Gypsies from one of the Madrid-based organisations and a Danish Kalderash who visited several Romany organisations and, as a sideline, was trying to get sponsorship for a boat trip round the world and a publisher for a book of Hans Andersen style fairy tales.

Students

The first students to come to the notice of the Gypsy Council were the Finnish Blomerus sisters who came with a school party from Sweden but wished to meet English Gypsies while here. Luckily they had a broader view than Katerina Taikon who, after visiting London from Sweden said on radio words to the effect that there were only two genuine Gypsy families in England and only about 200 in Europe. One of the sisters returned with her family to buy saree material to make the traditional Finnish Gypsy dresses – purchases which they had previously made in Paris.

A small number of Romanies from eastern Europe have also come as students. One Polish Gypsy has carried out advanced studies at Oxford. A Romany teaching assistant from Norway was coming to a conference on multi-cultural education but was stopped at the frontier – because of her dark appearance, we must assume – and removed from the party for a lengthy examination before being allowed to continue her journey. Some Romanies from Scandinavia have been studying English and the bible at colleges in Surrey. One missionary student from Finland found the climate in London too damp and asked to be transferred to Canada.

Medical treatment

Occasionally Gypsies have visited England specifically for medical treatment. They include S. from Yugoslavia who came in 1979 for eye treatment and stayed to arrange a marriage for a young woman acquaintance and a Finnish Romany from Stockholm who was sent by the Swedish health authorities to a private hospital in west London for a heart operation. More recently the growth of private hospitals (especially near the east coast) offering minor operations more cheaply than in Europe has led to a certain amount of Romany participation in the growing 'medical tourism'. Relatives of the patients have occasionally sought Gypsy Council help if they run up against immigration problems while trying to visit during convalescence.

Musicians

To discuss all the Romany Spanish flamenco artists who have come to Britain would take too much space. The Maya company should, however, be mentioned as they brought a politically orientated flamenco show to Sadlers Wells which looked at the history and suffering of the Gypsy people over the ages. An explicitly political message was also given by the presence of the emigré Russian Romany singer, Raya, who played at the Hampstead Festival after the World Romany Congress in 1971. Manitas de Plata paid several visits and was to be followed by his relatives from a younger generation, the Gypsy Kings. Jazz artists in the Django Reinhardt tradition such as Birelle Lagrene also make regular visits as do Loyko, a partly Gypsy group originally from Russia but now based in Ireland. Hungarian Romungri musicians are also recruited on short-term contracts for restaurant work from time to time.

In 1988 a Gypsy Festival at the Institute of Contemporary Arts in London was notable for the lack of Gypsy artists but if few in number the quality was high, including both the Gypsy Kings and Kalyi Yag before they had reached fame. Kalbelia dancers from India were included in the Rajasthan folk group which appeared at the Albert Hall.

European Community citizens

With the establishment of the European Community EC citizens could come to Britain freely. For a short period they could also draw Income Support for up to six months while establishing themselves as self-employed or finding a job. Two families and a number of young people with French citizenship related by marriage to the Yevanovic clan did this. The family of 'D', mentioned before, managed to build up a trade in repairing copper utensils, came off income support and remained in the UK for some months. The younger people stayed for six months after which their Income Support was withdrawn and, as they had not found England particularly welcoming, they returned to France.

In 1994 the Government changed the rules and EC citizens found it more difficult to get Income Support (which was not a problem) but also Housing Benefit – which was, as they found it impossible to pay the high prices for rented property on the proceeds of repairing kitchen utensils. Unlike the Americans they did not have the wives' second income from fortune telling. There were, however, some ten Kalderash families with French nationality in London around Christmas 1995.

Refugees

The largest influx of Romanies to Britain between 1945 and 1989 came after the Hungarian counter-revolution of 1958. Many took the opportunity of easy admission in the Cold War atmosphere when anyone who came here from a communist country was offered political asylum if they asked for it. The greater proportion of those who stayed were men and they have taken non-Romany wives while others have disappeared into the general population and so a new community has not been created.

For much of the post-war period Hungarians have not needed visas (as so many came to watch international football matches) so some relatives have come to visit the refugees. In one case in Bristol in 1981 the visitors quarrelled with their hosts but could not go back to Germany where they had been resident as their leave to remain there had expired. Nor could they get any money from social security as they were here 'illegally' – they had outstayed their six months. They relied on the charity of a Gaji Hungarian refugee until the German authorities could be persuaded to take them back.

At the time the conflict started in Bosnia in 1992 there were a number of Bosnian Gypsies in England staying at tourist caravan sites in London and Essex. They included Kalderash, with some Muslim Rom linked to them by marriage (Acton 1995:89-97). They were born in Yugoslavia, mostly Serbia or Bosnia. As well as Yugoslav passports, some held Italian or French passports or had achieved the right of residence in those countries and were intending to travel back to Bosnia through Europe. With the outbreak of the conflict they applied to stay in the UK. They were given the status of asylum seekers but were rarely properly considered for asylum and most were simply allowed to remain. Many returned to their caravans after a short stay in housing and travelled around the country selling carpets at markets.

Many of their relatives then joined them. They usually told of how they had been driven from Sarajevo to the border with Croatia and then smuggled in closed lorries to England. Some had bullet wounds to show. As they did not know which route they had come through they could not be sent back to France or Belgium to apply for asylum there. These Gypsies stayed in houses mainly in east London. The authorities split up the families in accordance with strict rules. In one case the grandmother was given a flat in Stratford on her own, a daughter and baby was placed in Hackney while the son was put in a flat in Dagenham some five miles away. It was explained that they were three family units and had to be given three flats. They cheered up slightly when they discovered they could get three crisis loans for furniture and that they could all live in one flat and leave the other two empty.

Some of the Bosnian refugees who had been used to begging outside mosques – and on traditional Rom Yugoslav begging trips to Italy – tried begging in the underground but, after being arrested a few times, gave up.

Life in London was not easy. Neighbours complained about the Bosnians' chickens and perhaps with more justification when they slaughtered a sheep in the back garden for a feast. A group was arrested in front of their house for what seemed to be a new crime 'speaking loudly in public in a foreign language'. They were bound over to keep the peace. Another was stopped for parking on a zebra crossing and then eventually arrested for not producing a driving licence. He did, in fact, have one but until he heard the magic words 'Fuhrerschein' ('driving licence', in German) from the court interpreter had not the slightest idea why he was being charged. Many have now moved to Birmingham and Scotland.

In 1991 a pogrom at Mlawa marked the renewal of anti Gypsy racism in Poland, scapegoating Rom for economic problems after the political changes in 1989. There has been a substantial flight to Britain of Polish Gypsies, both from the Polish Kalderash and the older established Polska Roma group. The emigration of the latter is significant because they had not joined refugee movements after earlier periods of persecution in the 1980s which led to the flight of much of the Polish Lovari and Kalderash communities. Most of these went to Germany or the United States, although two young people, Grofo and Lalla, did reach London in 1970 (after an earlier failed attempt to land at Dover) and claimed political asylum. They later went to Sweden.

As passports were then issued freely and visas were not required for entry to the United Kingdom a large number of Rom came to Britain seeking asylum on the grounds that they were being persecuted because of their race. At a peak in 1995 there were over 1,000 Polish Gypsies in England. As asylum seekers they are not allowed to work for six months but receive income support at a reduced level and are given at least hostel accommodation. Those arriving by boat are sent back to the continent to apply for asylum there under the so-called 'first-country rule'.

The British government has begun to get worried about the numbers. According to one report, the Polish government was asked to stop Gypsies getting on planes for London but the Poles refused saying they could not make a distinction between one ethnic group and another.

The British government then started the tactic of imprisoning the men while they were waiting for a decision on their application. The women and children were, in general, released on temporary admission to remain in freedom while their husbands' cases were being considered. At least two men could not cope with the conditions in the detention centres, abandoned their claims and voluntarily returned to Poland.

In September 1995 the British government announced that from February 1996 there would be no income support payments to asylum seekers after a first refusal. As asylum seekers are not allowed to work until they have been here six months. This means they would have no source of funds if their first application is refused and will have either to rely on begging or give up their claims and return to the country from which they came.

It is likely that by the time this paper is printed the Polish Gypsy refugee community will have shrunk considerably.

Conclusion

Time will tell if any of these more recent immigrant groups become part of British Gypsy communities as have the Stirios and Yevanovics. If not, their visits have served to raise the consciousness of the English Romanichals and the Gypsy organisations to the existence of these *wavver-themengre* Gypsies with their traditional clothes and fluent Romany.

References

ACTON T 1995 "Les refugiés Roms de Bosnie et de Serbie au Royaume Uni" *Chimères* No.26, Autumn

ANON. 1934 "Supplement: Greek Gypsies:An opportunity for Research" *Journal of the Gypsy Lore Society* 3rd Series Vol.13(2).

GROOME F H 1899 *Gypsy Folktales* Hurst and Blackett, London

HOLMES C 1978 "The German Gypsy Question in Britain" *Journal of the Gypsy Lore Society* 4th Series Vol.1(4)

HOLMES C 1988 *JohnBull's Island: Immigration and British Society 1871-1971* Macmillan, London

KENRICK D and BAKEWELL S eds.1988 "They call me Shaikh" *Traveller Education* No.23

KENRICK D and PUXON G 1972 *The Destiny of Europe's Gypsies* Chatto Heinemann, London

KENRICK D and PUXON G 1995 *Gypsies Under the Swastika* Hertfordshire University Press, Hatfield

KOVALCSIK K 1985 "Oláh Cigányok Londonban" *Zenetudomány dolgozatok* Budapest

MYERS J 1943 "The Greek nomad Gypsies in South Wales during August 1942" *Journal of the Gypsy Lore Society* 3rd Series Vol.XXII pp.84-100

MYERS J 1945 "Supplementary jottings on the customs of some Greek nomad Gypsies" *Journal of the Gypsy Lore Society* 3rd Series Vol.XXIV (3) pp.88-94

WINSTEDT O 1913 (?) "The Gypsy Coppersmiths' Invasion of 1911-13" *Journal of the Gypsy Lore Society* 2nd Series Vol.6 (4), dated 1912-13 but actually published in 1913 or 1914

YATES D 1942,1943 "The 'Greek' nomad Gypsies in Britain, 1929-40" Parts 1 and 2 *Journal of the Gypsy Lore Society* 3rd Series Vol.XXI (3) 87-110, Vol. XXII (1) pp.9-33

Chapter 8 Burakumin in contemporary Japan

Ian Neary, Professor of Japanese Studies, University of Essex

Some Japanese, especially those who live in the area around or to the north of Tokyo, may genuinely be unaffected by prejudice and unaware of the extent of discrimination against Burakumin. A recent national survey of the attitudes of more than 24,000 people found that only 41.4 per cent of those living in Hokkaido and Tohoku and 73.1 per cent of those living in the Kanto area were aware of the problem. This compares with 95.3 per cent of those in the Kinki region (*Sômuchô*, March 1995:29).

There is also some disagreement about the significance of the prejudice and discrimination that remains. Even the most radical Burakumin activists would accept that over the last thirty years their situation has improved. Discrimination is no longer as blatant; living conditions in the Buraku communities are no longer as obviously impoverished as hitherto. There continues to be a problem though, as the following anecdotes suggest.

Mrs Kato, born and brought up in the north of Japan, had to move with her family to the Tokyo area after her husband was transferred by his company to work for a time in the head office. They decided to live about an hour's commuting distance from central Tokyo. When they were looking for somewhere to live they came across some apartments which were significantly cheaper than the others. She and her husband started to make arrangements to rent one of them but the estate agent suggested they should think again. Without saying anything directly, he hinted that the reason they were so cheap was that they were in a Buraku area. At first the family decided to go ahead anyway. They had no strong prejudices, were unconcerned about living in such a community and anyway they would only be there for a couple of years. But then they realised that people might start to regard them as Burakumin and more importantly that their children might be treated as such in local society. In the longer term this might even damage their children's marriage and employment prospects. Reluctantly, they decided to live in more expensive accommodation rather than take the risk of becoming the victims of discrimination. Later, when they moved from Tokyo to Fukuoka they enquired discreetly in advance so as to avoid repeating the same mistake.

One man who married a Burakumin woman about twelve years ago describes his experience as follows:

> "My parents said I could not have any relationship with them. I have two sons aged eleven and nine. My father met the first one once when he was a baby and the second time a few months ago by accident at the hospital where when we were visiting my grandmother." (*Daily Telegraph,* May 24, 1994)

The two families have lived eight miles apart from each other for more than a decade with virtually no contact. His father refuses to relent even though his Burakumin daughter-in-law died of cancer two years ago. The shame of untouchable grandchildren appears too much for him.

Happily this kind of attitude is becoming less common. Surveys suggest that only around 5 per cent of the population would still take such an uncompromising stance.

Burakumin are racially and ethnically identical to other Japanese and so how can people tell them apart? The traditional test of whether someone belongs to such a Buraku community or not, was the test of common knowledge. In any village people knew who the Burakumin were and where their community was located. However, one might have expected that the rapid urbanisation of the last fifty years would have destroyed both the old communities and the patterns of thinking that marginalised them, except perhaps in remote rural areas. However, when the first modern family records (*koseki*) were produced in the mid nineteenth century, many local officials made sure that former outcasts would continue to be identifiable by marking the new registration form in some way. In some areas they even insisted that all the 'new commoners' adopt the same surname so that it would be easy to distinguish between them and the rest of the population. The family registers were open to public inspection making it easy for a potential employer or parent-in-law to check out an individual's family background. In the late 1960s there was a campaign to close these records. Local governments were the first to restrict access and in 1976 the Koseki Law was revised to close them to the public. However, at the end of 1975 investigation agencies began to offer to sell *Chimei sôkan* (comprehensive guide to place names) to major companies. The one and only use that can be made of these is to ascertain from an individual's family address whether or not he or she might be from a Buraku community. Using these lists the family, company or private detective agency can investigate an individual's status background. There is plenty of evidence that people still use them. (Tomonaga 1995, Upham 1980:65)

If the 'how' of discrimination can be explained fairly simply, the 'why' is more difficult. This chapter will discuss the evolving situation of Burakumin in Japan looking at the three themes of origins, protest and policy, concluding with a brief assessment of their prospects.

Origins

To begin with what they are not: early this century there was a common belief that Burakumin were racially distinct from mainstream Japanese; that they were the descendants of slaves from the ancient period, descendants of Koreans or even, descendants of the lost tribe of Israel that somehow ended up in Japan. There is no historical foundation for these ideas and they were publicly repudiated in the 1965 Deliberative Council Report (see below), although some 10 per cent of the Japanese population still believe Burakumin are racially different from the mainstream (*Sômuchô* 1995:29).

Research produced during the 1970s showed how policies adopted in the Tokugawa era (1600-1868) had created Buraku communities where none or few had existed before. This stress on their relatively recent formation served a number of purposes. First, it reinforced the idea that Burakumin were unequivocally Japanese. Secondly, it suggested that, as a relatively recent social creation, the possibility of eliminating prejudice and discrimination and, indeed the communities themselves, in the near future was not a Utopian ideal. Thirdly, it provided a clear target for Burakumin protest. Ultimate responsibility for discrimination could be ascribed to the Tokugawa regime and the inability or unwillingness of its successors in government to deal with the problem.

Japanese society during the Tokugawa period was divided into four main classes; a ruling elite of samurai comprising about 6 per cent of the population, the peasantry who made up around 80 per cent of the population and the residents of the castle towns, artisans and merchants in descending order of status. Strict rules regulated the behaviour of those who made up these social classes and relations between the classes. Only samurai, for example, were permitted to own or wear swords. No intermarriage was permitted between members of these four main groups.

Outside mainstream Japanese society, however, there existed a number of communities which were subject to informal or organised discrimination. There was great variation in the functions performed by these outcast groups, the regulations to which they were subject and even the names they were called, although *eta* and *hinin* were most common. Local authorities were given a significant degree of discretion in these matters. From the 1720s increasingly detailed sets of regulations were imposed on most aspects of their lives. Their content varied from place to place but usually they were permitted only certain types of clothing to ensure they were clearly visible, they were often not allowed to enter towns at night and banned from entering religious sites. Efforts by members of these communities to ignore or evade regulation were rewarded by ever more detailed sets of rules. The result was that segregation and discrimination was at its peak shortly before the start of the Meiji era (1868-1911).

As outcasts were not considered a fully human, they were not included in the periodic censuses that took place from 1720 onwards. These demonstrate that, overall, the population of Japan increased hardly at all in the period 1720-1850. Meanwhile, it is estimated that the outcast population may have increased by as much as three times and there are examples of communities which grew more than six fold. In part this was because bad luck or bad behaviour would force people to leave their homes and they would end up living in the outcast areas. Even those who moved to work the land in the seventeenth century, becoming in many ways indistinguishable from peasants, often maintained their connection with leather-making or some handicraft trade which made them less vulnerable to periodic crop failures. Their access to meat also made them better able to sustain themselves following poor harvests. Finally, they were less likely than the majority to restrict the size of their families by selective neo-natal infanticide. The outcast population which had been scattered, fairly small and did not loom large in the public mind had, by the mid nineteenth century, become large, visible communities, tightly regulated to segregate them from the majority and regarded with contempt by most of them.

The process of dismantling the Tokugawa state included the elimination of all the regulations that had restricted the outcast groups. However, whereas in Japanese society at large, consciousness of one's former feudal status quickly became irrelevant, prejudice and discrimination against the former outcasts continued. They remained on the margins of society and were largely excluded from the development of the capitalist economy. Their attempts to take advantage of the new possibilities, for example, by establishing modern shoe factories usually failed. Where they did become involved in the process of industrialisation, as in the development of the coal industry in northern Kyushu, they were to be found doing the dirtiest jobs usually in small mines with poor capital investment.

Until recently Buraku histories emphasised the continuity between the Edo and Meiji periods and criticised the lack of positive effort by the Meiji regime to help Burakumin to slough off the disadvantage accumulated over the previous centuries. Now it is argued that the Liberation Edict of August 1871 should be regarded as the start of a new phase in Buraku history, much as the start of the Tokugawa era had been. The Buraku communities which grew in the second half of the nineteenth century were in urban areas such as Osaka or Tokyo or newly developing regions such as the north of Kyushu, not the Buraku which had grown in the Edo era. This suggests different social processes were now at work.

There is also a clear change from the institutionalised discrimination of the Tokugawa period to social discrimination of the Meiji era. Discrimination in marriage, education and employment which the young Burakumin encountered in the later nineteenth century simply had not been possible in the highly regulated feudal period. They should be regarded as new phenomena. In this connection we should note a document of 1918 which describes Buraku discrimination as being based not on custom but because they are unhygenic, unschooled and poor. In other words, they were unable to fulfil the duties of the citizen of the Japanese empire: to serve in the army, to be educated and to pay taxes. This indicated a new rationalisation for discrimination had developed within the discourse of modernisation and the creation of the Imperial state structure (Watanabe 1993:10-12).

Protest
Burakumin were not passive participants in this process and, freed from the feudal regulation, they took part in the resistance to the creation of the emperor-centred Meiji state. Thus, for example, we find that as the liberal

ideas of the *Jiyuminken Undô* (Popular Rights Movement) percolated down to the educated peasantry in the 1870s, there were discussion groups formed in Buraku communities to study these ideas. After a brief blossoming in the 1870s these groups fade away only to revive as an active force in the 1890s when they begin to consider ways in which discrimination could be overcome. One imagines that this was, in part, a response to a realisation of the discrepancy between the notions of the equality of the citizen's obligation to the emperor as expressed in the Meiji Constitution and the reality of the inequality faced even by younger, educated Burakumin. Groups were formed in areas across the west of Japan and there developed a realisation that there was a set of problems that were being faced by similar groups all over the country. This was the necessary precursor to a desire to create a national movement. Indeed, in 1903 the first national conference of Burakumin, the *Dai Nippon Dôhô Yûwakai* (Greater Japan Fraternal Conciliation Society) was held in Osaka. It was attended by 300 Burakumin from all over Japan but it failed to develop into a sustained organisation. One characteristic weakness of these early groups was that they accepted the dominant idea that there was something wrong with them that had to be put right before they would be accepted by society at large.

The *Suiheisha,* perhaps the most interesting organisation for comparative analysis by students of Romani politics, was formed in 1922 in the social context of the rapid increase in activity of tenants groups and labour unions and the related ideological context of the rapid spread of socialist ideas which followed the revolution in Russia. It had a much more radical agenda. In their initial declaration they announced, "The time has come when we can be proud of being *eta*" and declared that they sought "to organise a new collective movement through which we shall emancipate ourselves by our own effort and self-respect" (Neary 1989). Several hundred Burakumin attended the founding conference, soon Suiheisha groups were formed in nearly every major Buraku community and at its peak it could claim over 50,000 members. At annual conferences held over the next twenty years, activists discussed and devised new strategies for the movement.

As is the case with most mass movements, after the first few years of enthusiastic activity there was a lull and debates erupted about the most appropriate theory and tactics to guide the movement forward. And, like most social movements of the time, there were three main factions – the anarchists, the Bolsheviks and the social democrats – each of which had a different diagnosis of the movement's ills and a different solution for its problems. Moreover, the government attempted to regain its control over the Buraku communities by creating a rival, the *Yûwa* movement, which offered an alternative national leadership structure and a solution to the Buraku problem which lay within the perfection of the emperor centred state system.

Despite the often fierce internal debate and external pressure, the Suiheisha outlived all its contemporary social movement organisations. It remained active until 1937-8 and only finally capitulated to demands that it dissolve in 1942. Two factors enabled it to stand out so long against the pressure to conform. Firstly, Buraku leaders were determined to "emancipate ourselves by our own efforts and self-respect". Experience showed that they could not rely on the efforts of others whether they be communists or government officials. They had rejected the idea that the problem was something to do with their inadequacy and instead argued that it was social attitudes that needed changing not Burakumin. Secondly, the development of the *kyûdan tôsô* – denunciation struggle – became for the Suiheisha what the strike was to the labour union and the rent-strike was for the tenants' union – their weapon in the class struggle or at least in the battle against discrimination. At one level the aim was simply to encourage Burakumin to protest about discrimination when they encountered it rather than accepting it as an inevitable part of their lives. In the first few years of the movement's existence the tactic was adopted enthusiastically, if indiscriminately, and activists attacked in word and deed all who were regarded as discriminators. Fights broke out which sometimes developed into more extensive violence. However, as the movement matured, the leadership was able to be more selective about which campaigns it chose to pursue and they tried to use the denunciation process and so it had an educative impact both on the discriminator and the wider society.

In 1945, only days after the surrender was announced, former Suiheisha leaders met to consider how the Suiheisha might be reformed (Asada 1969:171). In 1946 the National Committee for Buraku Liberation (NCBL) was launched as a successor to the Suiheisha with the support of most of the left-of-centre parties. Both the communist and socialist parties (JCP and JSP) included support for Buraku liberation in their first post-war manifestos and nine Burakumin were elected to the Diet in 1947, seven of them as members of the JSP. However, it proved difficult during the occupation to arouse much enthusiasm for the project of Buraku liberation. Most people needed to spend so much time and effort in maintaining a bare existence that they had little time for political activity. Moreover, the reform of Japan instigated by occupation forces included guarantees of human rights in the constitution, land reform and education reform suggesting that the democratisation of Japan was underway and that this would include the elimination of Buraku discrimination. Indeed, the JCP endorsed this view. Even before the war they had argued that the Buraku communities were a remnant of the feudal era that had remained because of the incomplete nature of the bourgeois revolution of the nineteenth century. It seemed to them that the US occupation with its dismantling of the aristocracy, dispossession of the large landowners and similar reforms was completing that process so that Buraku discrimination would naturally disappear.

In 1951, just before the occupation ended, an incident occurred which demonstrated that segregation and discrimination were being recreated in post-war Japan and that there was an important role for the new Buraku movement. In October of that year a pulp magazine, *All Romance*, published a story entitled *Tokushû Buraku* set in a Buraku community in Kyoto. It portrayed a "hell on earth full of black marketeers, illegal sake brewing, crime, violence and sex" (Wagatsuma 1976:352-8). It turned out that the author of the story was employed in the Kyoto city offices and, as the word spread, a campaign was mounted which criticised not only the publisher of the story but also the Kyoto authorities. The incident became a hook on which the NCBL could hang a *kyûdan tôsô* campaign about the continuing poverty and deprivation of Buraku. They demanded that:

> "...officials in charge of various administrative districts mark on a
> map all sections of the city lacking public water supplies, sewage
> disposal, fire hydrants and all areas with inadequate housing,
> high rates of TB, trachoma and other public health problems,
> high absenteeism in the schools and high concentrations of
> families on relief. The result was a vivid demonstration of
> Burakumin problems since the marked areas fell entirely within
> the eighteen Buraku areas of Kyoto and its environs." (Devos and
> Wagatsuma 1973:76)

Embarrassed by these findings the Kyoto city government began a
programme of improvements to the environment ensuring an adequate
water supply and sewage system and starting rehousing schemes and
building nursery schools. During the 1950s NCBL groups, particularly in
the larger cities, launched similar 'administrative struggles' against local
government in which instances of discrimination were used as the basis for
campaigns which came to include demands for the provision of improved
local facilities. Possibly because the movement was seen to be able to
deliver real improvements, it attracted more support and in 1955 it was re-
launched as the *Buraku Kaihô Dômei* (Buraku Liberation League – BLL) a
name which was thought to have more mass appeal than the 'vanguardist'
national committee (Asada 1969:269).

The movement's growing significance prompted the political parties to
take the issue more seriously. In 1957 a JSP committee produced a report
which argued that, although complete Buraku liberation was only possible
through the creation of a socialist society, even within the capitalist
structure it was possible and necessary to improve the Burakumin living
environment and their life chances. They called for the creation of a special
commission within the Prime Minister's office with a remit to devise a
comprehensive policy (Neary 1986; 560-1; Morooka 1981:383-7,446-50).
Shortly after this the JCP produced its own Buraku policy which linked the
issue more closely to the reactionary rule of US imperialism and Japanese
monopoly capitalism. They rejected the view that there was anything
special about the problems faced by Burakumin workers. Their poverty was
just one product of the contradictions within capitalist society and therefore
the main target of the Buraku struggle should be the overthrow of the class
system rather than making special demands on that system which would
weaken their solidarity with the rest of the working class movement
(Morooka 1981:392-5).

Policy

The creation of discussion groups by the radical young men in Buraku
communities was a source of concern to local government leaders in the late
nineteenth and early twentieth centuries. In an attempt to control their
activities many prefectures began to encourage the formation of *Yûwa*
(conciliation) discussion groups which were placed under the watchful eye
of a trusted member of the community such as a schoolteacher.

There were even some places where local government bodies provided
small amounts of money to relieve Buraku poverty. A national structure

was imposed on the Yûwa organisations in the mid 1920s to create a rival to the Suiheisha and a special budget was created to fund the new body and also to provide some additional unemployment benefits and housing improvements for impoverished Burakumin. A Ten Year Yûwa Plan to solve the Buraku problem was launched in 1935 but it did not survive the changes in government priorities at the end of the 1930s. The policy was not revived immediately after the war but, as we have seen, in the late 1950s the JSP was suggesting the creation of a new comprehensive policy.

This was a time of unusually wide interest in the problem. Over the winter of 1957-8 the topic was discussed in newspapers and magazines, on radio and television. The BLL argued that the fragmented improvements funded by local government would never be sufficient to have a significant impact on attitudes or living conditions, a national strategy was required to co-ordinate policies and to provide new resources. Even the then Prime Minister, Kishi Nobusuke, expressed his view that the continued existence of discrimination against Burakumin was 'regrettable' and he undertook to introduce appropriate policies (Morooka 1982:297-8; speech made on 11 March 1958). Nothing came directly from this promise but in October of that year the LDP set up a committee – the Dôwa Policy Committee – to consider the problem. In March 1960 the LDP Dôwa Policy Committee proposed to the cabinet the creation of a special commission of enquiry and the bill was passed in August 1960.

The report that the Commission of Enquiry on Dôwa Policy published in August 1965 came very close to what the BLL was requesting. It divides into two parts. The first section gives a brief history of the problem in which it made three very important points. Firstly, that there is no substance to the widely held view that Burakumin are in some way racially or ethnically different from mainstream Japanese. This is something that was particularly important given the tidal wave of literature emphasising Japan's uniqueness that was to sweep across the country over the next thirty years. Secondly, it did not accept that the problem was a remnant of feudalism that would disappear with the development of advanced capitalism. And, thirdly, it also rejected the view that the best solution is to ignore the Buraku issue since discussion or special action only serve to perpetuate a problem which, if ignored, would disappear. A solution to the problem, it argued, must be based on knowledge not ignorance.

The second section is a survey of the state of Buraku communities. The report portrays ghetto-like communities located on land liable to flooding where the quality of the housing stock was poor and often totally lacking in such public services as sewers, tap water, street lights and fire protection. Standards of educational achievement were well below the national average, few Burakumin were employed in major firms or had 'lifetime' employment and there was a very high degree of dependence on unemployment benefit. The report concluded that it was the duty of the state to take steps to eliminate some of these problems beginning with the introduction of legislation which would enable government to address the social deprivation described in the report (Harada and Uesugi 1981:252-9; Neary 1986:563-4; Upham 1987:84-6).

In 1969 the main recommendations of the report were written into the *Dôwa Taisaku Tokubetsu Sochihô* (Law on Special Measures for Dôwa Projects – SML) which established a Ten Year Plan. Broadly speaking there were three main types of programmes implemented. Firstly, there were the projects which targeted the physical environment – improving streets, schools, clinics and community centres and constructing high rise housing to replace the old housing stock. Secondly, there was a system of grants that were paid directly to Buraku families. Upham describes the situation in the 1970s where a family in Osaka with two children could receive over Y400,000 annually from a combination of grants rewarding school attendance, twice yearly grants given to all, not to mention the one-off payments on marriage or the birth of a child (Upham 1980:49). The third type of programme related to education: both programmes within the school classroom and enlightenment programmes which aimed to change public attitudes.

However, the act was vague about who was to receive these benefits. It talks of the residents of 'target areas', "where the security and improvement of living environment has been obstructed for historical and social reasons" (Upham 1980:46). By the late 1960s, however, many Buraku communities also had residents who were poor Japanese whose ancestors had not been outcasts or, especially in the Osaka area, who were Koreans. Should these non-Burakumin benefit from the programmes? The JCP view was that they should but the BLL argued successfully that they should not. Moreover, the BLL was anxious that the various programmes might be used by central or local government to pacify Buraku radicalism and put them under some kind of administrative control. There was also a fear that if the Dôwa administration adopted a method to identify 'genuine' Burakumin this would create a set of records that at a later stage could be used for the purpose of discrimination. So, in many areas applicants for benefits from the programmes were screened by a committee which was composed of members of the BLL and local officials. Rather than being co-option of the BLL into the state structure, it was regarded as the only way of guaranteeing that Burakumin were not co-opted. In 1978 the programmes were extended for three years and since then, mainly due to successful lobbying by the BLL, they have been renewed several times with the current programme set to expire in 1997. Between 1969 and 1993 the total amount spent on SML projects was Y13,880 billion. Most projects were carried out at the level of the municipal authorities (city, town, village) where the cost was split 20:10:70 between the state, prefecture and local authority. Each time the programmes have been extended their scope has been redefined and narrowed. First to go were the generous grants and later the scale of the construction programmes has also been curtailed (Sômuchô 1995:7).

The JCP and its supporters within the BLL had long held a different view of the fundamental causes of Buraku discrimination from the movement's mainstream. Not surprisingly then, in contrast to the cautious welcome the JSP and BLL gave the report of the Commission of Enquiry, the JCP was highly critical both of the report and the subsequent Ten Year Plan. They argued that it would separate Burakumin from the wider working class movement thus weakening opposition to the LDP domination of politics and the capitalist structure (Morooka 1982:352-3). The tension between the two rival wings of the BLL was formalised with the creation in 1970 of a separate group within it which aimed to change the movement's policy to make it closer to the JCP line. Over the next few years JCP policy continue to argue that Buraku communities are no longer a necessary part of the Japanese social system. There is therefore no structural foundation for discrimination and no reason why it should continue to exist through into the twenty-first century. Parallel to the development of this new policy there was violent disagreement between the two groups within the BLL that precipitated the creation of a completely separate, JCP-oriented, organisation in 1979, the *Zenkoku Buraku Kaiho Rengokai – Zenkairen*.

Prospects

After forty years of BLL activity and over twenty-five years of special improvement programmes the question arises of what remains to be done and who should be doing it?

What more could be done to improve conditions in Buraku areas? One can begin by pointing to the existence of non-designated areas. For the purposes of SML administration, local governments had to formally designate certain areas as target areas but, for a variety of reasons, some local authorities declined to do so or missed some out. Some 4,603 target areas were designated but it is estimated there are between 800-1,000 which were not and which therefore have not benefited from the SML policies. What is to be done about them?

There is copious evidence about the current state of the 'designated' Buraku communities following the publication of a 2,000-page report which is based on surveys carried out in 1993 of all 4,603 designated Buraku, nearly 60,000 Buraku households and of the attitudes of 60,000 Burakumin and over 24,000 non-Burakumin (Sômuchô1995). This is the most extensive and most sophisticated survey of conditions and attitudes ever undertaken and its very extent defies summarisation. All one can do in the space available is to mention some of the features relevant to the argument presented here.

First, there is some evidence of improved income levels: only 52 per cent of Buraku households received livelihood security support in 1993 compared to 76 per cent in 1975. However, this is almost twice as high as the non-Buraku households in the same areas (28.2 per cent) and well above the national average of 7.1 per cent (Sômuchô 1995:4). At the same time while a substantial proportion of the Buraku population own their own homes (62.7 per cent compared with a national average of 59.8 per cent) around a third live in publicly owned apartments. As such they pay very low rents, on average Y8,138 compared with a national average of Y33,762 (Sômuchô 1995:21-2).

The evidence about educational performance shows a similar pattern, suggesting both improvement and unresolved problems. Overall, the entry of Burakumin children into senior high school is close to that of the mainstream, 91.8per cent compared with over 96 per cent for the non-Buraku samples. However, the rate of persistent, long-term absenteeism of Burakumin children from primary and junior high schools is almost twice the mainstream averages; 1.6per cent and 4.5 per cent compared to 0.8 per cent and 2.4 per cent respectively. Less than 2 per cent of Burakumin over the age of fifty-five had any experience of higher education whereas over 20 per cent of today's Buraku teenagers can expect to continue their education past high school (Sômuchô 1995:10-11, 15). This is a considerable improvement but still lags behind the figure of nearly 40 per cent for the population as a whole. Probably linked to this difference in educational achievement is the fact that only 10.6 per cent of Burakumin were reported to be employed in enterprises of over 300 employees, well below the national average of 23.3 per cent (Sômuchô 1995:20). Since it is only the larger enterprises that can provide stable employment, higher salaries and fringe benefits, these figures might suggest that Burakumin remain marginal to Japanese society.

Such differences in employment might also be explained as the result of continuing discrimination in the employment practices of the larger companies. The discovery in 1975 that lists of Buraku communities had been sold to many Japanese companies showed that many firms did seek to avoid employing Burakumin. It is hard to be certain that this no longer exists. When asked about their experience of discrimination, only one third of the Buraku respondents reported feeling their rights had been violated at some time. Most frequently this was in incidents which took place at work, at school or involving marriage (Sômuchô 1995:25). Few of them did anything about it; the largest single group, 46 per cent of the sample, kept quiet and put up with the treatment. If marriage outside the Buraku community can be regarded as showing the decreasing power of discrimination there is some encouraging evidence. Around 80 per cent of those over eighty married fellow Burakumin but this had dropped to less than 25 per cent of those under twenty-five.

It may be though, that the survey underestimates the degree of improvement to educational achievement and employment opportunities. There is a trend for younger, more successful Buraku-origin families to move out of their community to live in better housing elsewhere. This group was not covered in this survey and they are likely to be that part of the Buraku community that has the better record of academic and employment achievement.

In the 1950s it was a key BLL aim to persuade central government to fund an improvement programme and, having succeeded in this, to have the various programmes extended. However, in September 1992 Uesugi Saichiro, chairman of the BLL, announced that the movement would not demand any further extension to the SML when it expires in 1997. This came as something of a shock to many of the movement's activists and it marks the start of an ongoing debate on how the movement should prepare for its 'third era'. The first era was that of the Suiheisha which came to an end in the late 1940s. The 'second era' really began with the formation of the BLL in 1955 but for most of its latter half it has been characterised by its involvement in and the support it has got from the various improvement programmes. Preparing for the 'third era' the BLL must devise new tactics.

Three key questions were posed:

■ What would amount to a 'solution' to the Buraku problem?
■ What is the link between Buraku discrimination and poverty?
■ What international dimensions to the problem exist? For example, to what extent do Japanese companies practice discrimination abroad?

Proposals were presented to the BLL conference in May 1995 to allow for wide debate within the movement over the following twelve months so that the new policy can be adopted by the movement at its next conference in March 1996, well before the expiration of the SML. The proposed set of aims and principles has set aside a 'class history' perspective in favour of one founded on democracy and human rights. It outlines what a society without Buraku discrimination would amount to and links this to a vision of a 'Suiheisha for the whole world' (*Kaihô Shimbun* 8 May 1995:9-10).

The debate about the movement's next steps has been a lively and wide-ranging one. One commentator has pointed out that over half of those attending the BLL conferences and study sessions have their expenses paid in some form by the Dôwa programme. Will the movement get such enthusiastic support when people have to pay all their own expenses? (Ohga 1993:34-5). For others, the start of a new era suggests the need to redefine the movement's aims; it is not enough just to seek an end to discrimination. Just as peace is more than the absence of war, so the aim of the BLL should not simply be the abolition of prejudice but the creation of a society in which there is a positive respect for human rights. As a part of this, the movement should move beyond demands for 'reparations' in recompense for the damage cumulatively inflicted by discrimination in the past and begin to formulate demands for the creation of a rights based society – from fighting the results of discrimination, to combating its causes. In this way the BLL's demands could act as a catalyst for rapid social change in Japan in the window of opportunity provided by the breakdown of the 1955 system (Okuda 1994:95-107).

The decision not to press for an extension of the SML beyond 1997 was tactically shrewd given the fairly common perception that Burakumin these days are privileged compared to other Japanese. The low rents paid by many Burakumin seem to be a sore point with many people. But the end of the SML is a threat to the movement. If all subsidies cease then both its publications and series of meetings and conferences may have to be curtailed as it may not be possible to fund them from the BLL's own resources or those of its members. Secondly, it will have no influence over the flow of tangible benefits and therefore there will be no material benefit to be gained from BLL membership.

Since the mid-1980s the BLL has campaigned for a Basic Law on the Buraku Issue. Such a law would institutionalise national commitment to the goals of the 1965 report, establish a legal framework for a comprehensive approach to the Buraku problem and prohibit a wide range of discriminatory acts providing the statutory basis for direct legal attacks on discrimination by individuals and groups. Government would be expected to submit an annual report to the Diet and conduct a survey on Buraku conditions every five years. Moreover, it is proposed that a Buraku Deliberative Council be created to investigate long-term problems related Buraku discrimination (BLRI 1994:27).

The campaign for the Basic Law has been opposed by the JCP, much of the LDP and has not had wholehearted support from within the BLL. The justification for the denunciation tactic has been that it is appropriate and constitutional because private and public legal redress are not available when individuals find their rights are infringed. If a law were introduced to create just that kind of legal machinery, there would be no legal or theoretical justification for the denunciation tactics; the decision of whether and how to deal with a specific instance of discrimination would pass out of the hands of the BLL and into those of the state. If the Basic Law campaign were to be successful it would lose its role as the instigator and co-ordinator of denunciation campaigns and the Buraku Deliberation Council would take over some of the functions of the BLL leadership. Not only would the movement lose one of its central functions but it also risks giving the state the kind of influence that it has sought since the time of the Yûwa movement.

Improvements funded by the state have made significant differences to living conditions in the Buraku communities and improved the life chances of their inhabitants. It is clear that discrimination remains and continues to be reproduced. The Japanese state has studiously avoided introducing measures which would make discrimination itself a punishable offence arguing that it is not appropriate to legislate about matters which are 'affairs of the heart'. Yet this is precisely what is being demanded at a time when demands for material improvements have been dropped. There are risks to the strategy but the BLL clearly feels that remaining stigmatisation can be eliminated if it is impeded by anti-discrimination legislation. At the time of writing the chances of the legislation being passed are good. While it is unlikely to have much affect on the very extreme feelings of, for example, the father described at the start of this chapter, it would probably discourage the estate agent from making discriminatory remarks which recreate prejudice and would amount to the state taking a moral lead.

References

ASADA Z 1969 *Sabetsu to Tatakai Tsuzukete* (The Struggle Against Discrimination Continues) Asahi Shimbunsha, Tokyo

BLRI 1994 *Suggestions for Human Rights Policies in Japan* Osaka, Buraku Liberation Research Institute

BURAKU LIBERATION NEWS 1985 Osaka, January

BURAKU KAIHÔ UNDÔ SUISHI IINKAI 1971 *Madoguchi Ipponka* (The Single Window Policy) Osaka

HARADA T and UESUGI S 1981 *Long Suffering Brothers and Sisters Unite!* Buraku Liberation Research Institute, Osaka

ISHIMOTO K 1994 "Buraku no Henka to Gendai Kenkyû no Kadai", (Changes in the Buraku and Topics of Recent Research) *Buraku Kaihô Kenkyû* Vol. 97, pp.77-94

KAIHÔ SHIMBUN 8 May 1995 No. 1718 Osaka, Kaihô Shimbunsha

MOROOKA S 1981-2 *Sengo Buraku Kaihô Ronsôshi* (A History of the Post-war Buraku Liberation Theory Debate) , three vols, Tsuge Shobo, Tokyo

NEARY I 1986 "Socialist and Communist Party Attitudes towards Discrimination against Japan's Burakumin" *Political Studies* Vol. 34 , pp.556-574

NEARY I 1989 *Political Protest and Social Control in Pre-war Japan: the origins of Buraku liberation* Manchester University Press, Manchester

OHGA M 1993 "Daisanki no Buraku Kaihô Undô ni tsuite" (On the third era of the Buraku Liberation Movement) *Buraku Kaihô Kenkyû*, Vol. 94, pp.31-40

OKUDA H 1994 "Daisanki no Buraku Kaiho Undo e no Mondai Teiki" *Buraku Kaihô Kenkyû* Vol. 95, pp.95-107

SÔMUCHÔ 1995 *Heisei Gonendo Dôwachiku Jittai Haakutô Chôsakekka no Gaiyô* (Outline of the Results of the 1993 Surveys to Assess Conditions in the Dôwa Areas) Sômuchôkan Kanbô Chiiki Kaizen Taisakushitsu, Tokyo

TOMONAGA K et al.1995 "Buraku Chimei Sôkan Jiken Niju nen" (Twenty Years After the First Publication of the Chimei Sôkan) *Human Rights* Vol 84, March pp.2-21

UESUGI S 1995 "'Dotaishin' Tôshin Sanjûnen to Buraku Kaihô" (Thirty Years After the Deliberative Council Report and Buraku Liberation) *Human Rights* Vol. 85, April 1995, pp.2-7

UPHAM F 1980 "Ten Years of Affirmative Action for Japanese Burakumin: A Preliminary Report on the Law on Special Measures for Dôwa Projects" *Law in Japan: An Annual* Vol. 20, pp.39-87

UPHAM F 1987 *Law and Social Change in Post-war Japan*: Harvard University Press, Cambridge, Masachusetts

UPHAM F 1993 "Unplaced Persons" in A Gordon ed. *Post-war Japan as History* California University Press, Berkeley

WAGATSUMA H and DeVOS G 1973 2nd.ed. *Japan's Invisible Race* California University Press, Berkeley

WAGATSUMA H 1976 "Political Problems of a Minority Group in Japan: Recent Conflicts in Buraku Liberation Movement" in W A Veenhoven and W Crum-Ewing eds. *Case Studies on Human Rights and Fundamental Freedoms* Martinus Nijhoff, The Hague

WATANABE T 1993 "Ima 'Buraku Rekishi' o toinaosu" (Time to review 'Buraku History') *Buraku Kaihô Kenkyû* Vol. 94, pp.1-28

Chapter 9 "New Age" Travellers: identity, sedentarism and social security

Colin Clark, Lecturer in Social Policy, University of Newcastle upon Tyne

"The heavens themselves run continually round, the sun riseth and sets, the moon increaseth, stars and planets keep their constant motion, the air is still tossed by the wind, the waters ebb and flow, to their conservation no doubt, to teach us that we should ever be in motion." (Burton, quoted in Chatwin, 1987:189)

This article seeks to address one of the questions raised by Sinéad Ní Shuinéar in this volume. Ní Shuinéar reflects that one issue which requires further examination is:

"Why do New Age Travellers inspire such fanatical hatred? Why single them out, instead of simply lumping them in together with other travelling groups?"

In this chapter I want to argue that such 'fanatical hatred' is at least partly founded on misrepresentations of New Traveller identity. Connected to this important issue of identity is also the perennial 'moral crisis' over Travellers, work and social security payments – just one example of such a 'moral panic' in operation. This latest example of the 'politics of prejudice' has taken some interesting forms (which will be discussed later in the chapter) and has been primarily actuated by explicit anti-nomadic policy and practice rather than traditional anti-fraud considerations. New Travellers, for social security purposes, really do constitute a 'class of their own'.

Robbie McVeigh's chapter in this volume makes clear the contemporary psycho-social sources of sedentary aversion to nomadic people and illustrates the importance of the historical context of the 'wandering traditions' that earlier scholars such as Burton (1577-1640) refers to in the above passage and throughout his writings on nomadism. This context aids our understanding of the dominant sedentary ideology and complex theoretical structures which lie behind the prejudice displayed with such conviction by settled people and, unfortunately, some 'Traditional' nomads towards New Travellers in the 1990s. One such example was the 'exclusive' two-page *Daily Express* (2 December 1993) article entitled "Pitchfork Rebellion" which told of the villagers' protests, in alliance with local Gypsies, in Middlezoy, Somerset, against a planned transit site for New Travellers. One resident of the Gypsy site who was interviewed spoke of the protest taking place:

> "We take turns with the villagers on the picket line. We just don't want these people there – it will make it bad and awkward for us. We will get the blame for any trouble they cause. These hippy folk claim to be like us Gypsies but they're not. They don't live like us and they don't think like us. They have taken to the road because they like their drugs and their festivals."

Though we must be aware of press misrepresentations, generalisations and other such simplifications, it does seem that this is not an uncommon sentiment – although such feelings are usually kept private and not aired in such a public manner.

There are many assumptions which underpin the social security system in Britain: the implicit economic demands for sedentarism that lie within the structures of the labour market are particularly important when considering anti-nomadism. The development of the welfare system placed great emphasis on the organisation of the labour force, hoping to eliminate all forms of casual labour. Indeed, there was an obsession to regulate labour and an assumption of full-time wage labour work as the norm (Harris 1972; Whiteside 1991). However, with the recent development of part-time work (mainly amongst women) and current preoccupations with more flexible labour markets, the rigidity of the system has been brought into question. In many ways, New Travellers – being prepared to travel to find work, accepting self-employment – could be seen as a paradigm for greater flexibility. If old stereotypical assumptions did not linger quite as long as they tend to do, then this might be the case. But, it is not just the problems of any one 'client group' that are of concern but also the nature of the system itself and its inflexibility. The social security system explicitly penalises an itinerant way of life as do other government policies. It will be shown in this chapter that many social security regulations contain inherent assumptions which mean that the welfare system, in conjunction with other departments' policies (for example, the Department of the Environment), are acting as instruments of social control which demand the settlement of Travellers if they are to have their legal access to public social services.

The social security system, accounting for one-third of all public expenditure – approximately £83 billion in 1994/5 – is a good example of the sedentarist-materialist basis of a society which assumes all of its citizens lead a 'settled way of life' and bases both policies and laws on this sedentarist premise. A question to be addressed is how this society copes with increasing numbers of people who 'opt-out' of what is regarded as the 'conventional', i.e., sedentary, way of life and choose (either freely or through necessity) what the Government regards as an 'unsettled way of life'. The DSS (via the Benefits Agency which operates DSS policy) differentiates 'unsettled' itinerants and the homeless from their 'settled' claimants and the production-line system of benefit delivery by using such terminology as this.

Indeed, the 'production-line system of benefit delivery' is an expression used by staff I came across in my office fieldwork. Although the new ethos of the BA insists that claimants are now called customers, for many staff the former still applies. When I was engaged in office fieldwork, 'punters' was often how staff referred to customers when talking amongst themselves in the office environment away from the counter area and this term was usually used when referring to claimants as a homogeneous group. Claimants who fall out with the production-line, including those who are classed as being no fixed abode, are generally taken 'off-line' and are dealt with clerically as the DSS computer system cannot keep up with those individuals who are highly mobile or unsettled. However, 'transitory clients' is the phrase used in a recent Department of Employment circular to describe New Travellers (Employment Services, 1992). It states that:

> "Considerable media coverage has recently been given to 'new age travellers' and the way they continue to receive benefit when they do not *appear* to meet the benefit conditions... It is also important that the *additional problems* caused by the attendance of these people are addressed, particularly the *safety and security aspects*" (my italics).

Within this document, and others like it (see Income Support Bulletin issue 24/93) we can see certain assumptions that lie behind the legislation implying that the norm is single-occupation fixed wage labour which is in direct contrast to 'deviant' itinerant and Traveller multi/flexi-occupations and self-employment. This is a key theme and fits in with the demands for sedentarism and a fixed address.

Who are the 'New Age' Travellers?
Despite their increasing visibility both on and off the roads of Britain, New Travellers ave not received a great amount of in-depth academic study of their lifestyle. This lack of informed knowledge has led, I would argue, to a widespread belief and common acceptance of many media-inspired myths and stereotypes about them as a group, as individuals and as citizens. Even though "history has always dismissed the nomads" (Deleuze & Guttari 1987:394) it does appear to have dealt the so-called New Age variety a particularly difficult hand.

However, it is worth noting that despite the large amount of informed academic work on Gypsies and other traditional Travellers, such as Acton (1974), Okely (1983), Fraser (1992), it is the negative and derogatory media stereotypes that are still being employed in their popular representation. Academic discourse is either ignored or rebutted and when Travellers attempt to speak for themselves, they are commonly shouted down or harassed. Such frequently misinformed views seem likely to have affected their relationship with, and treatment by, the wider society and its public institutions.

The practice – as opposed to theory – of defining groups of people in society often appears to be based more on ostentation rather than considered and selective categorisation. This practice can lead to numerous problems, not least those of omission, exclusion and over-simplification. I do not wish to reinforce simplistic stereotypes which are held by those who do not particularly care about Travellers as people. It is not my intention to define who New Travellers 'really' are, for that would be impossible. During my own research, one Traveller commented to me on a site in Scotland:

"There are as many different types of Travellers as there are people in society. Just face it, you can't put us in a box – we're all different. We don't all think the same way and we don't all behave the same way. If you ask me, you are wasting your time trying to define us ... let us define ourselves ... (pause) ... as individuals."

However, bearing this in mind, some kind of clarity must be brought to the identity of New Travellers to simplify the task of those working with and writing about them. For whilst we may have problems identifying this particular 'group', it is clear that oppressive and prejudicial action is being taken against a particular group known as Travellers (however vaguely defined) rather than seeking to accommodate (constructively or otherwise) specific types of behaviour and lifestyle. It should be remembered that any definition will need to remain flexible and broad if it is to have any meaning at all. Generalising greatly, it could be said that New Travellers are persons of "nomadic habit of life regardless of their race or origin", (as the 1968 Caravan Sites Act phrases it, even though New Travellers are not usually provided for under this now repealed legislation) but differentiate from other cultural/ethnic groups who occupy the British Isles known as Romanichals (English Gypsies), Kale (Welsh Gypsies), Nawkens (Scottish Travellers) and Minceir (Irish Travellers).

Although unclear and bound up by much mythology, it is generally regarded that the first-generation New Travellers came into being largely through choice. The beginnings of 'convoy culture' are said to date back to the early 1970s after Jimi Hendrix and others played the Isle of Wight Festival. Those without tickets watched Hawkwind play for free and the beginnings of a 'free festival' nomadic lifestyle was born as people began to live in the vehicles they used to travel to the festivals. Wally Hope, coming from the London squatting scene of the late 1970s to early 1980s, was later to be one of the figureheads and main organisers who helped to establish the network of free festivals that exist today for New Travellers and other young people coming from the nearby towns. (See Earle et al. 1993:1-20 for a fuller discussion of this).

Many second and third generation New Travellers now exist with young families who were born on the road: a point to bear in mind when considering them as a social/cultural phenomenon. Does this self-reproducing factor give New Travellers a form of 'ethnic' status and thus a need for legislative protection as a 'racial' group with clearly defined rights? Gypsies are protected under the 1976 Race Relations Act – why not other Travellers? By using 'ethnicity' in this sense, I agree with Griffin's use of the concept, meaning no more than:

> "...the social identity any individual derives – or has ascribed to him or her – by contrast to others from an apparent sharing with still others of enduring cultural signifiers." (Griffin 1987:11)

The so-called New Age Travellers are just one part of the New Travelling community. This sub-group are generally regarded as being from middle-class backgrounds, degree-educated, 'alternative', anti-materialist and ideologically/philosophically rooted in the eco-spiritual enlightenment of the late 1960s which emanated from Europe and the USA. Or, as one New Traveller suggested to me during my own fieldwork, they are: Travellers with bank-accounts.

The 1980s saw many clashes between New Travellers and the police, probably through escalating numbers joining the convoys and a Government wanting to preserve its strong law and order reputation. In 1984 at a festival at Nostell Priory in West Yorkshire, police and Travellers clashed and there were some 250 arrests. A year later, Operation Daybreak resulted in the 'Battle of the Beanfield': "a watershed in the history of confrontation between police and Travellers" (Lowe and Shaw 1993:68). The Beanfield saw over 400 arrests and much police violence. Subsequent court proceedings by twenty-four plaintiffs against the police did lead to the awarding of compensation in early 1991 though they did not see any of the money as it was absorbed by legal costs. In 1986 at Stoney Cross, it is said that the police, in conjunction with other bodies, attempted to 'decommission the lifestyle' by employing different tactics and not just plain assault and battery, as witnessed at the Beanfield. Two different tacks were adopted: the police impounded vehicles on small technicalities and, with the aid of local social services, they planned a dawn-raid to take the children into care. A sympathetic social-worker forewarned the parents however and as a result all forty-seven children who were named on the care-orders were off-site by 4am when the raid commenced, (as told by 'Spider', an eyewitness, interviewed by Lowe and Shaw 1993:91-2).

Moving into the 1990s, police figures have suggested that there are just 2,000 live-in vehicles and 8,000 people involved in the all-year New Traveller scene in England and Wales (*The Guardian*, 22/4/94). An intelligence drive was also launched against New Travellers and rave organisers by the Police and one of the aims of this operation was to build-up a database of information about them which will help police prevent gatherings such as Castlemorton in 1992. This latest drive is a follow-up to Operation Snapshot in 1993 which detailed Travellers' movements, locations and vehicle registration numbers. It must be said, however, that the above figures are widely criticised as undercounting the true numbers of New Travellers in Britain. So-called DIY organisations such as Travellers Itinerant Truss and Friends and Families of Travellers estimate a figure at least double this, if not more. Indeed, during the early 1990s Save the Children Fund estimated that anything up to 50,000 New Travellers were living on the road.

During the mid 1980s, with the onset of the social effects of Thatcherism starting to take effect, I would suggest that many of the urban dispossessed and young homeless saw a new life for themselves in the countryside and joined the Travellers' ranks. Life in a shared bus or van seemed more promising (and fun) than cardboard city. Indeed, with many sixteen and seventeen year olds denied benefits as a result of the 1988 social security changes there was little other option for some.

Those people were, in a sense, 'economic refugees', taking the forced choice offered to them, seeking refuge from unemployment, hostile government policies and bleak inner-city environments. By escaping to rural sites which appeared to offer new hope, a real sense of community and all the things that were missing in life when stuck in the high-rises of city centres, these 'refugees' sought to find a new identity and meaning to their lives, looking for a fresh start. To illustrate, witness Claudia's story:

> "I was sick of living on the twenty-seventh floor in a squat, basically with a kid. I grew up in London and I didn't see much future for myself there. I left, I sort of escaped my destiny, if you like, and I didn't want my two children to have the same future. It's not an unnatural instinct to be nomadic. A lot of people have got a nomadic instinct in them – they don't want to see the same thing outside their window every day – and I'm one of those people. It's a community where you're not isolated. If I was living in a city, on my own, I'd be isolated, with two children. I would never have the degree of freedom that I've got. I know that here I'm safe to leave my children. They are not going to get snatched – everyone keeps an eye out for each other. I look after other people's kids." (BBC TV 20/5/93)

For Claudia then, and many like her, travelling is a year-round way of life. The reasons for that choice have been well thought out and are deliberate and continuing. Her way of life is not just a summer outing as it is for the other 'weekenders' who come out into the country from the cities to make up the Travellers' ranks at the festivals and gatherings. Claudia is just one New Traveller whose nomadism constitutes a 'settled way of life'. It may not be settled according to the DSS or the government but it is to her and her children.

Indeed, this adoption of a nomadic existence (rather than being born into it) is an interesting and recurring theme. Accounts of how and why they took to the road is often the first discussion point for many first-generation Travellers when asked about their lifestyle (Lowe and Shaw 1993). One Traveller I met, Scrumpy, told me that he had been on the road since around 1976/77. He had been in the medical corps of the British Army and posted over in Northern Ireland for a time. A serious incident involving an explosive device resulted in his losing his left arm. Upon being medically discharged from the Army, he found it difficult to adjust to both civilian life and his disability and drifted (his word) into the early squatting and then Traveller scene. Scrumpy now annually participates in and follows closely the free-festival calendar of events, knowing where he will be in the country at a certain time in order to go to the festivals and meet friends. For Scrumpy, as with the thousands of others like him, his form of nomadism offers him a very settled way of life. This lifestyle has specific arrangements to it with established routes and venues and seems very similar to how commercial nomads operate. The free-festival circuit is his economic niche and opportunity to earn a living. Gypsies, who are engaged in various forms of economic activity, such as tarmacking or scrapping, often travel around traditional routes selling specialised goods and services to settled people. For New Travellers the free-festival season, running from about May through to September, offers the year-round Travellers a focus for this economy to work and a common meeting point to exchange news. Again, in many ways, these New Traveller festivals reflect and echo the purposes of the traditional Gypsy horse fairs (such as Stow-on-the-Wold) which revolve around economic trade and the transference of news.

The Department of Social Security and 'New Age' Travellers:
The Department of Social Security has recognised the pattern of movement associated with the free-festival calendar and many of its nomadic 'customers'. In conjunction with local authorities, the police, the Department of Employment (and now Education), the Post Office, landowners and other interested parties, the DSS has adjusted its operational procedures in order to handle 'surges' of claims at small district offices near to festival sites. A DSS National Task Force now monitors the movements of Travellers, informs offices of their approach and numbers, provides assistance in the processing of additional claims and investigates cases of suspected fraud. Income Support Bulletin issue 24/93 entitled *New Age Travellers* sets out the remit of the Task Force. This widely leaked document introduced new operational guidelines and strategies for handling claims from New Travellers. The task force was essentially set up to 'police' New Travellers' benefits. Foucauldian notions of sophisticated 'monitoring and surveillance' strategies could not be more applicable in this situation, the BA being part of the Government's 'information and observation machine'. As mentioned previously, Operation Snapshot carried out by the police in 1993 aided and abetted the DSS in their objective to control and monitor Traveller movements by documenting Traveller vehicle registration numbers and occupants of the vehicles. Databases now exist to hold this information and it is shared among those involved in the Task Force, (see *The Independent*, 16/5/93 and *Police Review* 4/6/93).

The DSS was swift to react to the wave of adverse media attracted by an incident on a festival camp at Kerry in Wales during the summer of 1992 where social security staff were recorded handing out claim forms to a few travellers on-site, helping them to fill them in and paying out benefits. This was allegedly carried out at the request of local police who wanted the Travellers moved out of their area as soon as possible. The giros were required quickly to allow the Travellers to get diesel to facilitate this move. Others have regarded this incident in a conspiratorial way, suggesting that the whole event was staged for the media by the government to justify a clamp-down on benefits to Travellers and other 'undeserving' customers in the light of the resulting media and public protests. As the spokesperson for the Stonehenge Campaign Group wrote to me (27/3/93):

> "Travellers became the media and political scapegoat last summer. This was clearly shown at the DSS propaganda exercise where a handful of people received giros on site at a Welsh free festival – all in a blaze of publicity" (see also Earle et al., 1994:132-3).

Although this is debatable, it is certainly true that the criticism of the DSS by the media led to a tightening-up of existing regulations and new administrative measures under consideration being implemented; namely, tightening-up the 'actively seeking work' (ASW) regulations and also cutting hardship payments to single persons where they were found to be not ASW. These changes, of course, affected not just New Age Travellers who "descend like locusts" to "demand benefits with menaces" as Peter Lilley put it at the Conservative Party Conference in 1992 but all unemployed single people found to be not ASW. Despite the Social Security Advisory Committee warning against such action at the time, the government pushed the reforms through saying: "We are not in the business of subsidising scroungers". Although Travellers were the public target, the net had been widened to catch other 'workshy' individuals.

The efforts of the Nomadic Claimants Working Party (DHSS 1986) in the mid 1980s to address the issue on nomadism and social security has not helped Travellers access the benefit system and many still do not receive the full range of social security benefits to which they may be eligible. This is due to a host of different factors ranging from a lack of basic information to outright institutionalised and individualised discrimination because of their nomadic way of life. Under current DSS regulations, Travellers who occupy unauthorised sites without a postal address are registered as people of No Fixed Abode (NFA), not householders. Being NFA means they can receive only a basic personal allowance benefit and are not entitled to premiums (unlike those who are on fixed sites or those who can provide a 'Care of' address).

Constant evictions from one DSS area to another often results in the loss of Child Benefit, Family Credit and Incapacity Benefit payments. Unforeseen moves can also cause delays in payment of Unemployment Benefit (renamed Jobseekers Allowance in October 1996) and Income Support. In order to be eligible for Income Support and Unemployment Benefit you must prove you are available for and actively seeking work. Claimants who are transferring to a new office must now answer a set of additional Employment Service 'jobsearch' questions which ask: where they last claimed benefit, when they decided to move and when they arrived, how the move will affect their chances of getting a job, what steps they had previously agreed to take in looking for work and what steps they have actually taken. Thus, moving into an area with high unemployment may be interpreted as failure to seek work and a reason for suspending benefit. In the same legislation, entitlement to hardship payments was curtailed and the requirement of issuing a warning letter before suspending benefit for not actively seeking work was withdrawn.

The nature of the Traveller lifestyle and the actions of other bodies such as local authorities and the police, when located within the broader context of sedentarist policies in contemporary Britain, affect the access, take-up and delivery of social security benefits to nomadic people. It is notable just how negative this kind of social control is. With the passing of the Criminal Justice and Public Order Act in November 1994 and the resulting increase in evictions, more Travellers are being penalised by DSS policies as a direct result of having to move more often from one area to the next. Each move to a different area requires a new claim to be lodged and this can take days to come through leaving a problem of immediate need to be met by a crisis loan – if one is awarded.

Method of payment procedures are not standardised and some Travellers have to sign-on daily in order to meet the Employment Service 24-hour contact rule; this is connected with the availability and actively seeking work rules. Other Travellers are permitted to sign on either weekly or fortnightly in the usual procedure, picking up their giro via counter-payment personal-issue forty-eight hours after signing. There are many variations in Travellers receiving benefit payments, in keeping with local offices' new freedom to manage their own affairs.

It is apparent that many Travellers have great difficulty claiming any benefits at all, especially those that choose or are forced to move on with great frequency. Claiming Child Benefit is particularly difficult for some. Child Benefit is normally paid at a designated Post Office and for Travellers who choose or are forced to move on frequently, claiming can be a problematic experience. Families who are on Income Support may actually be underpaid as it is often assumed that they are already in receipt of Child Benefit (and One Parent Benefit if the claimant is a lone parent). 'Sue', a Traveller on a site just outside Bristol, told me about her local DSS office. They had a policy of issuing order books for Income Support/Sickness Benefit with all the change of Post Office spaces stamped out so they could only be cashed at the main Post Office in the centre of town, some way from the site. The main reason for this policy would appear to be to contain Traveller claims to one Post Office. This is not an isolated policy specific to that part of the country and is clearly to do with social control.

One of the main problems for Travellers in claiming social security is that of proving address and identity. The regulations do not detail exactly what evidence will be accepted. Decisions about what is required are left to the discretion of a DSS officer acting on behalf of the Secretary of State. Such decisions cannot be appealed to a Social Security Appeals Tribunal (SSAT) and a claimant who is not satisfied about an unreasonable demand for evidence would have to appeal to the courts, using the judicial review process. This would then examine whether the DSS had acted outwith their powers, or had behaved 'unreasonably'. This all takes time, and for highly mobile Travellers such an option is an unrealistic course of action to follow through.

Staff guidelines in the Adjudication Officers Guide suggest (they are not legally binding, being only a working interpretation of the complex social security laws) that claimants can be required to produce evidence of their identity, address, income, the existence of a partner or dependants, their housing costs and their age. Clearly then, Travelling people who have no permanent address and who are self-employed may encounter difficulty providing the sort of evidence that is required by the DSS. Some BA offices sometimes insist on having a National Insurance number with which to work when processing a claim. Many Travellers simply do not have one for one reason or another and finding acceptable evidence of identity can lead to delays (Action Group for Irish Youth 1993.) New identity guidelines were drawn up by the BA in late 1994 and it was hoped that these would ease most of the difficulties. Early reports seem to suggest that there are still problems and delays.

Collecting Family Credit is also problematic for many nomadic and working Traveller families. This benefit is paid in twenty-six week periods on evidence of earnings over the previous five to six weeks. Earnings from seasonal/temporary work tend to fluctuate wildly and evidence is not always available due to the nature of the work and the frequent movement of Travellers – which is often in order to find work. Again, the demands for sedentarism and a fixed wage labour occupation are much in evidence via the workings of Family Credit.

Likewise, the Social Fund is a cash limited and discretionary benefit which comes in the form of loans (Budget and Crisis) and grants (Community Care). The guidance on social fund requests states that a Community Care Grant payment could be made to those who are seeking a 'settled way of life' as this can fit into the 'priority cases' criteria. Some BA staff seem reluctant to award Social Fund loans or grants to Travellers as they assume that people who move on will be harder to trace for repayment. However, the recent computerisation of the Social Fund, which makes tracing debtors easier will, it is hoped, allay this fear and more payments will be made to Travellers after being solely judged on their ability to repay the loan.

It should be noted that some New Travellers refuse to claim benefit at all due to past negative experiences with the DSS or through strong ideological beliefs which seem to be rooted in ideas of self-preservation and independence. A Traveller of eleven years I spoke with, 'Weasel', pointed out to me the high incidences of police arrests of New Travellers and other peripatetic 'customers' for outstanding warrants in BA offices – the police apparently being informed in advance when a certain claimant was going to be in a particular office at a particular time. 'Weasel' suggested to me that this is not just coincidence (or a conspiracy theory). As he said:

"I mean, fair enough if it's for fraud or that, they've got a job to do, but when it's for something totally unrelated to the Social, that's when it's just not on ..."

Indeed, the legality of this is questionable. Having spoken to a senior DSS official about this issue, in the hope of substantiating 'Weasel's' theory, it was confirmed to me that a 'certain level' of BA/police collusion goes on in 'pinning people down' for outstanding criminal offences, especially if they are without an address. Although this same officer assured me that such information would only be passed on to the police if the offence was of a serious nature, such as armed robbery or attempted murder, I have heard reports from some New Travellers who have been arrested in BA offices for driving offences and other minor charges. Many Travellers are understandably very concerned but not terribly surprised, about such practices.

New Traveller representation:
what is the difference between myth and reality?
The intrinsic link made in the media between New Travellers and their claiming of social security benefits is almost always represented in a negative, if not outright hostile, manner. Headlines in the popular press such as "Sponging scum" (Daily Star, 29 July 1992) and "Hippy scroungers must get jobs or starve" (The Sun, 1 August 1992) do little to warm the general public to the situation of their Traveller neighbours. The

Government appears unconcerned with such malicious reporting, perhaps due to a desire to reduce the huge social security budget. The myth is that all New Travellers (or "*Giro-Gypsies*" as another infamous *Daily Star* headline put it) are drunken, drug-taking, bone-idle scroungers who are living it up at the expense of the hardworking tax-payers. It would be untrue to say that no Travellers conform to this tabloid stereotype; indeed some do but no more so than some settled people on so-called 'sink' estates. The point must be that there are many people suffering from the effects of poverty, disadvantage, marginalisation and social exclusion who head towards a self-destructive pattern.

As Claudia puts it:

> "There are hundreds of other dole scroungers, we're just the ones that everyone really hates. I don't understand. If we were in cities, in houses, we'd probably still be on the dole, you know. It doesn't mean to say our job prospects would go up if we were living in houses." (BBC TV, *Roaming Free* 1993:11)

Negative headlines and inaccurate representations of nomads by the media and other vehicles of popular culture is not, of course, a new thing. In the Irish Republic *The Report of the Commission on Itinerancy* (1963:1) recommended that "the solution of the itinerant problem" could be tackled by implementing basic 'liberal' reforms. These would include making state benefits to caravan dwelling 'itinerants' payable in voucher form rather than cash, "so as to overcome abuse by dissipation on intoxicating liquor". Indeed, this is a measure that Peter Lilley, the current Secretary of State for Social Security, may well be considering reviving in the 1990s in order to deal with the so-called brew-crews within the New Traveller community. This is not so unrealistic when you consider that there has been reports from some parts of the country of social fund crisis loans being paid to some New Travellers in the form of food-only vouchers. However, when I recently spoke to a Higher Executive Officer (HEO) within the DSS in London about this policy, he informed me that this discretionary practice is not specific to Travellers and can be applied to any case where there is a reasonable degree of suspicion about the nature of the request for a crisis loan and what the money is being used to finance. This level of discretion in decision-making is one aspect which concerned Lipsky (1980) when he wrote of "street-level bureaucrats" and the power they had in making policy as well as implementing it. Similarly, Cooper (1985) reported on the prejudicial decision-making that went on under the Supplementary Benefits Scheme. One of his case studies involved a pregnant Gypsy woman who did not receive her full legal entitlement and was treated harshly – a victim of the "they all look after their own" syndrome.

A contemporary classic example of a myth taken too far was the the *Daily Mail* story about why New Travellers had so many dogs. The reason offered by the *Mail*, which claimed it was a quote from a Traveller, was the fact that for every dog a Traveller had the owner received an extra £8 a week in social security benefit to feed it. Although complete fabrication, it is amazing how many times this suggestion still appears in media reports – and in DSS offices. The real facts are, of course, a little different. Travellers have dogs for much the same reasons as anyone else – they make nice pets.

In addition, because Travellers sites are vulnerable targets for the disgruntled locals and vigilante groups, dogs are a good advance warning system. As well as being guards, some dogs are used for hunting (e.g. lurchers) and others for breeding – a good source of income.

It is true to some extent that many Travellers cannot find suitable work, are unemployed and signing on to claim state benefits. This is due to many reasons, such as the increasing mechanisation of agriculture swallowing-up traditional seasonal work – a process which has hit Gypsies equally hard. Many New Travellers do manage to make a living through various occupations, such as labouring, scrapping (rescuing all sorts of scrap from tips to sell on for recycling) and activities which are based around the festival circuit – making clothes, jewellery and food to sell. The festival economy will be discussed shortly.

A common criticism often levelled at New Travellers is that whilst they claim to be following a lifestyle which can be described as 'outside' society they still depend on society's benefits. This is a rather simplistic argument and in itself a highly questionable value judgement. Is anyone really 'outside' society? Do all New Travellers even claim to be? It also neglects the simple fact that we are living in an era of mass unemployment. Pursuing a life on the road can be a far more attractive alternative to a life on Income Support whilst living in a squat or tower block, as was reflected in Claudia's story. In many cases, just like nomadic Gypsies, New Travellers actually travel the country in order to try and find work, not to avoid it. The idea that every Traveller could get a job that would enable them to lead what society regards as a 'normal' (sedentary) life is highly unlikely (as Claudia mentioned earlier). It is very difficult to get work when you live on the road. Although many Travellers have a variety of skills (e.g. welding, mechanics, crafts) tales of them being turned down for jobs when potential employers learn of their nomadic way of life – living in a bus on a lay-by – are all too common. In reaction to press criticism of their way of life, many Travellers have pointed out that by living on the road they are saving the Government money by not claiming the Housing Benefit to which they would be entitled if living in a house and unemployed. This fact seems to have been conveniently overlooked by those in Whitehall and Fleet Street.

Another problem which is the cause of much discrimination from settled people towards New Travellers is the belief that they all live in filthy squalor and 'smell'. Obviously, in some circumstances, this is quite true. By living in rather basic conditions in muddy fields, bits of wasteland and lay-bys, pursuing the same hygiene practices as house-dwellers is difficult, if not impossible. Travellers develop hygiene practices which are suitable to their circumstances and environment. Some Travellers with larger vehicles install showers and keep themselves clean and tidy. Most tend to rely on friends who live in houses, public baths, showers in local sports centres and other such facilities. Travellers being denied access to public transport, pubs, libraries, health centres and other public services is not uncommon on the grounds of personal grooming.

There is a myth that all New Travellers traipse around the country invading privately owned land, leaving a trail of destruction in their wake. The Criminal Justice and Public Order Act, which received Royal Assent in November 1994, aims to deal with the 'problems' associated with New

Travellers and other 'folk devils' (including squatters, hunt saboteurs and ravers), amongst many other varied concerns. Section's 61, 62, 70, 71, 77-90 directly effect the Travelling way of life and section 61, which covers 'aggravated trespass', triggers police and criminal (no longer just civil) law into action where:

> "aggravating factors exist ... The measure is not aimed at cars and caravans but at mass invasions of land by new-age convoys...It is not aimed at the *genuine* Romany or other Gypsies because they do not indulge in mass invasion of people's land." (David Maclean, Minister of State, Home Office. Hansard, 26/7/93; my italics).

Despite this new legislation and the tabloid headlines, it is true to say that most Travellers do not look for trouble. Most would much rather occupy sites in out-of-the-way places where they are not going to upset the locals. They would much rather park-up on common land or council land than private property but this is much easier said than done. Small numbers of New Travellers have even attempted to get onto official sites only to be told that their types of vehicles cannot be accommodated. It is this access to land and the freedom to travel, stop and stay that have always been major issues for Travellers in Britain. Travellers are the first to re-cycle and their environmental credentials are second to none. A great respect for their immediate environment is shown when on the road and when parked-up. New Travellers have been made easy and convenient scapegoats for those landowners who wish to deny them their rightful heritage to roam the land and make their living.

The primary reason that New Travellers have been singled out for particular derision by the authorities is, perhaps, the fact that their lifestyle is at such odds with that of sedentary society. Although many Travellers would reject the 'Age' part of their New Age label as being 'hippy rubbish', some groups have opted to live an 'eco-friendly' existence in loose communal frameworks (Griffin, 1987). This is where the New Age aspect of the community is evident. Although many Travellers share similar social, political and ethical values with young people who live in the settled community, it is still true that they are 'different'. The difference comes from the way the New Traveller lifestyle in a world of crisis has shown a way out of the darkness for those that are part of it. It is certainly no Utopia or Nirvana in itself but the problems of urban and rural youth poverty have brought the remainder of a materialist, consumer-oriented society into confrontation with its own internal failures, contradictions and injustices. As a symptom of relatively recent social and economic changes, the New Traveller emergence has shown an alternative way forward. The solutions that many have adopted and live by are totally at odds with the demands of a settled capitalist society. This is one reason why they fall outside the already existing 'net of fear and loathing': the DIY culture threatens the very socio-economic and political fabric that makes up sedentarist Britain. This 'alternative' community (like a virtual or cyber one) is not perfection but it does illustrate new ideas and beginnings which might just lead its followers and devotees into a 'new age' of harmonious living.

The modern British state has found, and will increasingly find, that by appearing to create problems for the New Travellers they have created a Traveller problem for themselves. One example illustrates this well. Until the annual People's Free Festival gathering at Stonehenge was effectively closed down in the mid 1980s, the internal Traveller economy had provided a living for most of those living on the road. Mo Lodge, a Traveller interviewed on a television documentary about 'the Battle of the Beanfield' commented that this economy was: "Anarchy in action and it worked, the Government just didn't like it".

Unfortunately, the festival economy has never really recovered from the loss of Stonehenge. The alternative Glastonbury Festival was no substitute for many seasoned Travellers who found that they were now not making enough money during the festival season to sustain the winter months. With this source of earned income denied to New Travellers, many have been forced into giving up their independence and were forced into disclosing personal circumstances in order to claim social security benefits. The irony in this seems overwhelming. The Criminal Justice and Public Order Act has made matters even worse for Travellers who rely on the festivals to make a living as they have become harder to organise with increased police attention and more legislative muscle. As far back as 1986 the DHSS Nomadic Claimants Working Party summed it up:

"Matters came to a head during the summer of 1985 when several large groups converged on Stonehenge for a festival that had been banned by the authorities. The resulting confrontation with the police *(the Battle of the Beanfield)* was said to have *disrupted the normal festival economy* and large numbers of claims to Supplementary Benefit *(as Income Support was then known)* were made." (DHSS 1986:3; my italics)

By creating the problem, the state had found itself with one.

Conclusion
Although in theory Travellers' claims for benefit should be treated in much the same way as those of any other 'customer' of the BA, there are certain socially constructed and legislative problems that do affect their access, take-up and receipt of social security benefits. These difficulties are a result of a combination of different factors, some of which have been alluded to in this chapter. The 'rabid antipathy' towards New Travellers is in part explained by their identity and non-conformity to the ascribed role of settled wage labourer and rejection of consumerism and materialism. The New Traveller lifestyle challenges the dominant familial ideology and offers an alternative form of domestic living. One of the main factors which needs further discussion is the very nature and framing of public policy and legislation. The example I have referred to in this chapter, social security, has been shown to be not only inflexible but in direct conflict with the nomadic way of life.

I have argued in this chapter that there are intrinsic sedentarist assumptions within the structures of the social security system. The main one being that to travel is to be not 'actively seeking work'. This is at odds with the reality of the situation for itinerants whose travelling is directly linked to their search for the types of employment they engage in: self-employed multi/flexi occupations. Both Traditional Gypsies and New Travellers prefer such forms of work, in keeping with their way of life. In the DHSS Nomadic Claimants Working Party Final Report of March 1986, it is stated clearly that:

"There is a widespread view that *because of their itinerant lifestyle, many of these claimants cannot be regarded as available for work even though they declare availability when claiming unemployment and supplementary benefit.*" (my italics).

It goes on to say that the availability test is: "ineffective for these (NAT) groups because of the large numbers of claimants involved and the lack of prospective employers."

Similarly, and more recently, an Employment Service circular (83/6,1992) stated that:

"Clients must be available for employment and must actively seek employment. However, clients who frequently travel from one place to another *put limitations on their opportunities to find work and reduce the chances for their availability to be tested.*" (my italics)

In sum, to say that to travel is *not* to seek work discriminates against nomadism: the system is culturally specific in catering for the needs of settled people whilst excluding and further marginalising nomads. The operation of social security in theory and practice is anti-nomadic leaving so-called unsettled customers at best with problems in claiming benefits and at worst excluding them altogether from the welfare safety net and wider society itself.

Acknowledgements

The bulk of the empirical data used in this paper was gathered during fieldwork I conducted for my PhD thesis. All other references, where not otherwise sourced, refer to this data which was collected between November 1993 and December 1994 in England and Scotland.

I am grateful to all the participants of the ESRC-funded seminars on Romani Studies held during 1993-4 at the University of Greenwich for the lively sessions which helped generate this paper. All were a continual source of help and support. I am particularly grateful to Thomas Acton, Judith Okely and Roy Hannigan who provided useful comments on earlier drafts of this chapter. Above all, there are Margaret and Fergus who made it all possible. Respect.

A note on the title

As Pat Gooding, National co-ordinator of the DSS/BA-led Task Force which deals with New Traveller 'customers' succinctly put it to me in a letter: "the phrase New Age Traveller (NAT) is one coined by the media and used for convenience." (Personal Communication 5/10/93). Throughout this article I occasionally make use of the acronym out of convenience but I am consciously aware of its hidden meanings. It is a term which has largely came into being via popular press headlines and is used as a tabloid codeword for 'scrounger' (in much the same way as 'underclass' is used as a racial codeword for 'black' in America). Most of the people who are living on the road and get called New Age Travellers do not see themselves in this way. Some of the self descriptions I heard during my fieldwork included hippy, punk, vagabond, itinerant, medieval brigand (as Douglas Hurd called them in 1986) or just plain Traveller, but New Age Traveller is not accurate and has a number of pejorative connotations attached to it. Self-ascription must be taken into account and although I go into this in more depth later in the article I felt it was necessary to point this out with regard to the title of the chapter.

References

ACTION GROUP FOR IRISH YOUTH 1993 *Identity Crisis: Access to Benefits and ID Checks* AGIY, London

ACTON T 1974 *Gypsy Politics and Social Change* Routledge Kegan Paul, London

ACTON T 1994 "Modernisation, Moral Panics and the Gypsies" *Sociology Review* September pp.24-28

BBC TV 20/5/93 *Roaming Free?* 'Heart of the Matter' BBC 1 Film Transcript Benefits Agency 5/10/93 Personal Communication from Pat Gooding, Benefits Support Branch Quarry House, Leeds

BENEFITS AGENCY 1993 "New Age Travellers" *Income Support Bulletin* Issue 24/93

BURTON R 1972 *The Anatomy of Melancholy* Dent, London

CHANNEL FOUR TELEVISION 14/2/91 *Operation Solstice* 'Critical Eye' Film Broadcast

CHATWIN B 1987 *The Songlines*. Cape, London

CLARK C 1997 "Assessing the Quality of Benefits Agency Services to those with 'An Unsettled Way of Life': Claimants, Vagrants or Customers?" PhD Thesis Edinburgh University of Edinburgh

COOPER S 1985 *Observations in Supplementary Benefit Offices: The Reform of Supplementary Benefit* (Working Paper C) Policy Studies Institute, London

DAILY EXPRESS 1993 'Pitchfork Rebellion' 2nd December

DAILY STAR 1992 'Sponging Scum' 27 July

DELEUZE G and GUATTARI F 1987 *A Thousand Plateaus* University of Minnesota Press, Minneapolis

DEPARTMENT OF HEALTH AND SOCIAL SECURITY 1986 *Nomadic Claimants Working Party: Final Report* DHSS HQ (RD9) March

EARLE F, DEARLING A, WHITTLE H, GLASSE R and GUBBY 1994 *A Time to Travel? An Introduction to Britain's Newer Travellers* Enabler Publications, Lyme Regis

EMPLOYMENT SERVICES 1992 *Advising clients: Dealing with bulk claims from Transitory Clients* Circular 83/6 September

FRASER A 1992 *The Gypsies* Blackwell, Oxford

THE GUARDIAN 1994 "Police Act to Halt Raves" 25 February

GRIFFIN C 1987 "Space, the final frontier: New Age Travellers in Gypsy and commune contexts" Unpublished conference paper

HANSARD 1993 The House of Commons adjournment debate, 26 July cols. 970-76

HARRIS J 1972 *Unemployment and Politics: A Sudy in English Social Policy* Clarendon Press, Oxford

HAWES D and PEREZ B 1995 *The Gypsy and the State: The Ethnic Cleansing of British Society* SAUS, Bristol

INDEPENDENT 1993 "Police Keep Tabs On the Travellers" 16 May

IRISH COMMISSION ON ITINERANCY 1963 *The Report of the Commission on Itinerancy* Dublin Government Publications

LIPSKY M 1980 *Street-Level Bureaucracy: Dilemmas of the Individual in Public Services* Russell Sage Foundation, New York

LOWE R and SHAW W 1993 *Travellers: Voices of the New Age Nomads.* Fourth Estate, London

OKELY J 1983 *The Traveller-Gypsies* Cambridge University Press, Cambridge

POLICE REVIEW 1993 "Tracking The Travellers" 4th June

THE SUN 1992 "Hippy Scroungers Must Get Jobs Or Starve" 1 August

STONEHENGE CAMPAIGN GROUP 1993 Personal Communication 27 March

WHITESIDE N 1991 *Bad Times: Unemployment in British Social and Political History* Faber, London.

Chapter 10 The theory of Gypsy law

Thomas Acton, Reader in Romani Studies,
Susan Caffrey, Lecturer in Sociology and
Gary Mundy, Researcher, University of Greenwich

In 1993 a study of Gypsy law was published in the *Yale Law Journal* by
Weyrauch and Bell which not only brought the example of Romani social
control mechanisms into the mainstream of legal philosophy, but was
passed in photocopy from hand-to-hand by Romani intellectuals all around
Europe. Their examination, however, was limited to the system built
around the kris of the Vlach Rom and they failed to see the relevance of
other forms of social control such as the blood-feud, which they ruled out of
their discussion. This chapter presents a broader overview and argues that
there is a structural inversion between kris systems and blood-feud
systems which shows how similar value systems can be enforced via very
different forms of social control. It is suggested that the different forms of
social control are appropriate to different nomadic and sedentary modes of
life in different Romani groups and using the theories of Pashukanis (1929,
1978) one might theorise the kris as an embryonic state developing a
criminal law from the historically prior civil law embodied in the norms of
Gypsy groups regulating conflicts through the feud system.

At first sight no two systems of social control could be more different
than the systems of private vengeance and avoidance found among the old
nomadic Romani communities of north-western Europe and those public
tribunals (the *kris*). These regulate all civil and criminal disputes among
many of the Rom of Eastern Europe, especially the great Vlach Rom
natsiya, the *Kalderari, Lovari, Churari* and *Machavaya*, both in the
Romanian-speaking territories of their original settlement and in their
world-wide migrations of the last two centuries. These differences in the
way Gypsies in different groups seek justice have led both to radical
misunderstandings by Gypsies of the value systems of other Gypsy groups
with whom they come into contact, and a fragmentation of ethnographic

work as sociologists and social anthropologists have described the practices of 'their' group without locating them in any broader historical and structural context.

This chapter will draw on the literature to present and contrast two ideal-typical models which we will call the 'feud' model and the 'tribunal' model in order to show that they are polarised variations on a common structure. In other words, there are alternative ways of expressing and embodying *Romaniya* in social action and organisation which must be seen as sociological variables. The feud model belongs to a more anarchistic and nomadic lifestyle; the tribunal model to a more settled and structured one.

Often these alternatives present themselves to the individual Romani person as moral choices which other Gypsies have just made wrongly. Thus, commenting on the difference on marriage by elopement and marriage by arrangement, in our fieldwork, what we hear from the Romanichals "Those Rom – they sell their daughters, you know" is matched from the Rom by "Those English Gypsies – they steal their wives, you know". The variant a person chooses, or to which they have been brought up, becomes a vital part of their personal identity and integrity and is seen by them as a boundary-marker of Romani identity as such. This means that ethnographers often follow their informants to take particular forms of Romani social organisation as standard; that is to say they treat particular values of social control variables as being invariants. Such an approach was virtually elevated to the status of methodological principle by De Marne (1985) and provoked a detailed critique by Acton (1989) which underlies the present chapter.

We wish to suggest that when the social control systems of particular Gypsy groups are considered in isolation, something of the genius of Romani culture and its ability to preserve itself and protect its members, to adapt and contribute to social change in the world as a whole (dare we, under the shadow of post-modernism, say 'progress'?) is always going to be missed. Of course, individual Gypsy groups do not fit exactly to the ideal types we will present and may rang somewhere between them and vary over time, changing and dividing their identities. Indeed, in some exceptional situations, such as that of the *Baro Shero* among the Polska Rom (Ficowski 1990) the social authority may be embodied more in the judge than the tribunal, a status which presents a standing temptation to ambitious Kalderash and Lovari *Bare* who are aware of it and seek to emulate it, often with the most unfortunate consequences.

The current systems, however, which help to define each group as it is here and now, are inherently likely to present themselves as conservative, perpetuating an existing social order. We hope to show that a multitude of overlapping small-scale conservatisms may in aggregate constitute a suprising global radicalism, offering to those who are politically tough more choices and more access to the process of lawmaking and enforcing than is immediately apparent. Who would have thought even ten years ago that we would have seen a Romani womens' movement (Aziz 1994, Asociación de Mujeres Gitanas, 1994) constitute itself in country after country almost in the way that the "new Gypsy politics" constituted itself in the 1960s?

This has very broad implications for the theory of law and social control in general. Until the pioneering work of Weyrauch and Bell (1993) legal theorists largely neglected the implications of the existence of Gypsy organisations as an example of what Weyrauch and Bell call "autonomous lawmaking" taking place within the geographical boundaries of modern states. Their work has already provoked debate in legal circles: Reisman (1993) criticised them as "historicist" in presenting Gypsy law as the "organic and inexorable" outcome of tribal tradition, thus treating law "as a sort of felt experience, rather than conscious choice." He argued that this leads Weyrauch and Bell into an attitude of moral indifference towards various reactionary and individually oppressive particularisms of Gypsy society.

This debate reached a much wider audience than that usually attracted by the arcane pages of the *Yale Law Journal* as offprints and photocopies were passed from hand-to-hand in the Romani studies community and discussion still continues. Our view is that Weyrauch and Bell's work is flawed because its whole analysis is based on only one of the polar ideal-types of Romani social control. Citing Acton (1979) they say (p.335) "Because the Romanichals, Bashalde and Sinti have quite different customs, in spite of cultural similarities, academic literature neglects them. Therefore, unavoidably, so does this article."

The trouble is that they have misread Acton's 1979 assertion that *American* literature neglects them as suggesting that the literature *in general* neglects non-Rom Gypsies; and perhaps fail to realise that "much of the factual information" (p.59, note 51) they cite is from works on Romanichals, especially those from Acton, Okely and Trigg. That they are able to do so points to a greater commonalty in the *content* of Gypsy law than they recognise, a fact acknowledged by Sutherland (1986 p.xiii) when she cites similarities between her cleanliness prohibition data from Rom and Okely's data from Romanichals.

The authors of this chapter cannot pretend to be any exception to the rule that they can only understand – that is make sense of – the institutions of cultures strange to them by mapping them in some way onto institutions familiar to them. We hope to show, however, that deconstructing the unnecessary limitation placed on their analysis by Weyrauch and Bell will allow us a much freer and more flexible mapping which will allow us a much deeper understanding of Romani identity and of the nature of law and overlapping private and public jurisdictions. We hope to show that there may be values, which are embedded in culture and enforced in law, which yet can be shown to be more than cultural and more than legal, informing rather than created, by culture and law.

We shall try to show when one takes the varieties of Romani lawmaking together, one can use them to illustrate a much richer conception of the relationship between law and the state and the way in which the state is constituted through legal developments, through the construction of society as a fictitious legal personage with obligations, interests and rights. In this we will draw on some of the formulations of Pashukanis (1929, 1978), on the development of criminal law from civil law, without, we hope, succumbing to the definitional polemics of Marxist scholasticism as to when social norms 'truly' become law.

This broader view of Romani legal development, drawing explanations from real and contingent historical changes rather than 'tradition' in the abstract, can, we feel, strengthen Weyrauch and Bell's underlying thesis about the importance and inevitability of autonomous lawmaking by meeting Reisman's critique of their historicism. At the same time, by showing that a greater range of moral debate which informs Gypsy lawmaking, we hope to defend Gypsy law itself against the charges of oppressiveness that Reisman also brings.

Let us first posit our two ideal types:

Avoidance and private vengeance – the feud system

This system is most completely described by the one great ethnographer that Weyrauch and Bell fail to cite, Martti Grönfors (1977), who discusses the Finnish Kaale Gypsies. The rather sensational title "Blood-feuding among Finnish Gypsies" rather belies the content which shows that just as a prison sentence is still very much an exceptional sanction in modern industrial society so actual bloodshed is the exception in a blood-feuding system. It is only necessary when, in a sense, the system fails and social norms have not held. The system he describes is very similar to that which holds good among English Romanichals and as our own fieldwork proceeds we come across abundant case material although reconciliations seem to be more easily achieved among Romanichals than among Kaale.

In such a system individuals are responsible for asserting their own rights and the rights of family dependents who are weaker than they are, or friends or kin who are unjustly outnumbered. To appeal to the non-Gypsy state is generally unacceptable except in certain clearly defined exceptional cases (drug-dealing is frequently one such) and there are among Romanichals and Kaale no Gypsy authorities to appeal to either. Rather, if one is robbed, one must muster sufficient friends to recover the property oneself; physical or sexual assaults must be matched by counter-assaults leading to submission or in extreme cases, death; unhygienic behaviour by excluding the unhygienic person from one's personal space. Not to stand up personally for one's rights or those of a weaker dependant if one has been wronged is to be shamed, 'ladged' in English Romani.

It might be thought that such a system could lead to continuing endemic violence but most observers agree that English Romanichal life is rather easy-going and peaceable on the whole. The reason for this, as Grönfors shows, is that although there is no policing authority in such societies there are, nonetheless, socially prevalent norms which mean that individuals are quite aware whether any particular action is right or wrong and avoid actions that will provoke someone else to a defence of infringed rights, especially if they are anywhere in the near vicinity at the time.

What happens if one does commit an an action by which another perceives themselves as wronged? Then the other must demand satisfaction. For example, one young Romanichal man in our fieldwork, X, bought a car from another, Y. As he was buying he said, "To save me taking the carpets up, tell me the floor is sound." Y told him it was. When X took the car back to his own encampment he found that the floor was actually almost rusted through. He took the car back to Y and demanded his money back.

At this point Y was faced with a choice of actions. He could well have tried to appeal to the very strong Romani ideal that a buyer must take responsibility for his own actions – the principle of *caveat emptor*. Had the fieldworker (Acton) been bringing the car back, he probably would have been met with the taunt, "Go and deal with the children!" In other words, an assertion that he ought to have been ashamed to admit having been worsted in a deal, something very shaming (a *bori ladge-up)* to any adult. X asserted, however, that it was not a question of his having failed to check, in which case he never would have dreamt of complaining, but that Y had directly told him a specific lie which he regarded as theft, "You *chored* my bit of vongar". If Y did not refund the money, he would "beat it out of him."

As it happened X was on bail for attempted murder on charges relating to the discharge of a firearm on a London caravan site. Almost immediately Y accepted that he had gone beyond hard dealing into actual lying (*penning hokkapens*) and refunded the money. Y then had to accept and live with the shame of having backed down which he dealt with by keeping out of X's way for some time to come. And that was the end of the matter.

Why did Y not gather his own friends to resist X's demand? For a balance of two reasons. First, X's reputation as someone who would not back down meant "it wasn't worth the aggravation, mate." But second comes a fact which Y left unstated, that in fact most of Y's friends would have felt very ambivalent about his calling upon their loyalty to back him up in what was, after all, a *hokkapen*. And X would then have had little trouble in mustering his friends and the trouble could have spread endlessly.

Where someone comes to realise they have offended in a way that cannot be sustained by public opinion, it is down to them to keep out of the way of those who have a justifiable grievance against them. One of our Romanichal friends had to stay away from Epsom for years on end after an argument about a bet on a game of pitch and toss. In somewhat the same way as God used to defend the right in medieval trial by combat, because the wrong would be unmanned by their realisation God was not on their side, so among the Kaale and the Romanichals justice generally prevails, because those who are in the wrong come to know they are so and act appropriately by physically avoiding those they have wronged until some reconcilation is arranged. The characteristic social control mechanism in this system is therefore enforced avoidance; violence and murder are rare occasional ultimate sanctions needed to keep the whole system in being.

Such an account matches the classic Marxist position of Pashukanis (1967:168) that "the origin of criminal law is associated with the custom of blood vengeance" even though he extracts from Kovalevsky (1886) a lurid picture where: "Every offence, even that perpetrated in revenge, forms grounds for a new blood vengeance .... often to the point of total annihilation of the warring clans." In fact, far more characteristic of the stable system of private vengeance among Romanichals and Kaale is the picture Pashukanis presents (loc. cit.) of the decay of the practice of feuding: "Vengeance first begins to be regulated by custom and becomes transformed into retribution according to the rule of the jus talionis: an eye for an eye and a tooth for a tooth, at the time when, apart from revenge, the system of composition or of expiatory payment, is adopted." Perhaps, however, this decay of is more marked among Romanichals than among Kaale.

Where Pashukanis, however, presents theoretical speculations about systems far removed from his actual experience, Grönfors gives us abundant rich detail from painstaking and empathetic field work. The private quarrels of the Kaale are far harder to document than the public disputes of the Rom in the kris; Grönfors takes us to the heart of such personal emotions and actions to give us one really good ethnography of a vengeance system to stand alongside the many studies of the kris. He shows us that what at first might seem random and bloodthirsty is in fact a courtly and institutionalised system for minimising violence and maximising individual freedom, by making each individual responsible to the extent of their ability, for the freedom of all.

Such a conflict-resolution system is consonant with the marital, economic and political systems of the Romanichals and Kaale. Both groups practice marriage by elopement. Marriage marks the point when individuals take responsibility for their own lives. It is a public shame for parents even to consider the possibility of their children forming sexual relationships although, of course, there are private discourses where that is not so. The man and woman who wish to take each other have to do just that – and then a well-documented game-like practice of formal reconciliation with the parents, similar to reconciliation after other offences – has to take place (Okely 1983: 154; Acton 1981:23; Salo 1987:91). The new nuclear family then becomes a political unit with its own sovereignty – even the nuclear family of origin of one's parents, is in the end no more than an ally. The nuclear family is also the independent economic unit – perhaps co-operating with others, but never forming the *kumpania* which marks economic organisation among the Rom.

It will be obvious that pursuing a commercial nomadic lifestyle facilitates such a system. Both avoidance and elopement are easier if one was planning on making a move anyway.

The tribunal system – the Kris
By contrast with the relatively inaccessible practices of private vengeance, the public proceedings of the kris have been well-documented in a literature which Weyrauch and Bell describe in some detail.

The kris is a public assembly held by many groups of Rom and in particular those Rom whom the Gypsylorists call *Vlach* and the Xhorakhane call *Gajikane* (see note on terminology at end) and who refer to themselves as the four *natsiya* of the *Kalderash, Lovari, Churari* and *Machavaya*. It can be held either to hear and resolve an accusation by one person or group of persons against another, or it can be held without there being a specific plaintiff or defendant to resolve some general issue of public policy which might become a cause of conflict, such as the allocation of business territories, or degree of reward permitted to those who assisted Romani holocaust survivors to make successful claims for individual war reparations. These assemblies are presided over by a small number of judges (*krisnitoria*) who possess no formal qualifications but are agreed and invited by the parties to the kris, some leaning to the plaintiff, some to the defendant, with an impartial president. These judges, however, do not deliver judgment as such but rather preside until the assembly reaches a consensus, with all the adult men present able to speak and be heard until the issue is exhausted. Sometimes women are excluded but varying degrees of female participation are sometimes found. Often the ethnographic reports present such female participation as wholly exceptional but in a system which is not based on written rules, to define female participation as *a priori* exceptional is to beg the question about how far the kris system *has* to reinforce patriarchal authority. The system promotes oratorical ability and ability to speak in this mode in Vlach Romanes is the major criterion for admission to and participation in the kris. (Perhaps this may explain why, in the West, where there is intermarriage between Vlach Rom and Khorakhane Rom, it is the Khorakhane rather than the Vlach who become bi-dialectal.)

The kris system regulates both marital and economic affairs. Both Vlach and Korakhane Rom have arranged marriages in which the father of the groom pays a bride-price to the father of the bride. Subsequent marital discord may thus easily lead to a kris about repayment of this bride-price. The extended family has an authority which it lacks among the Romanichals and the Rom work together in *kumpanias* which bring together several families which will make use of the kris system to assure their area of operation.

To draw out the contrast between the tribunal system and the feud system, let us imagine what would have happened to our friends, X and Y, had they been young Rom instead of young Romanichals.

In the first place, they probably would have been part of the same *kumpania* and so the question of buying or selling the car would not have arisen; it probably would have belonged to a father or an uncle and the question of who would use it would have been decided in the way that the use of goods within a household is usually negotiated, e.g. how do we decide who gets to sit in the seat with the best view of the TV screen: at home this is decided by age/gender power in negotiation, in contrast to a seat at the cinema where the quality of one's seat is dependent on how much one pays.

Suppose, however, X and Y were acquaintances from different *kumpanias* and X did persist in an accusation of theft against Y. In such a case his correct course of conduct would be the very opposite of what we recorded above. To make a threat of personal violence would be, so far from a vindication of personal honour, as serious and dangerous offence as the original alleged theft. If the matter was not resolved by mediation by relatives, then X's senior relatives should say, "*Ame mangas kris*" (which means both "We demand justice" and "We ask for the holding of a kris".) At such a kris Y's action would be treated first of all as an offence against the community, to be admonished or punished by some measure ranging from bearing the expenses of the assembly to some degree of exclusion and only secondarily as an occasion for the making of restitution to X.

Pashukanis' conception of the relation between civil law and criminal law may illuminate this contrast. Pashukanis' general thesis is that law is formed and progresses as a reflection of the advance of commodity exchange relations. It might be thought that the kris presents a counter-example to this general account of legal development because in the kris system, (which, at least in contrast with the feud system, is an example of public law) there is a larger area of daily life in which goods are not commodified, compared with the private vengeance system. We shall argue, however, that the form of the kris emerges (as in fact Weyrauch and Bell suggest) as a form of law-making which is private compared with that of the overall non-Gypsy state. We shall further suggest that it does so because of the commodity values that have been established in its general social environment.

Arthur (1978) sums up Pashukanis' distinctive position against other Marxist legal theorists in the 1920s as pointing out that not only civil law but also "public law relations, e.g criminal law, are an extension of forms generated by relationships between commodity owners". This must be seen within the general concept of historical progress (which Pashukanis shared with most of his contemporaries) of legal relations developing as Maine (1861) phrased it, "from status to contract". Human groups were seen as having originally socially constructed conceptions of right and wrong as personal obligations which individuals feel and expect to and from each other within the group. This is civil law, constructing individual subjects (through the development of commodity relations, say Marxists) as bearers of legal claims. Only when the community itself is actualised as the state, as a "fictitious bearer of right" against whom the individual can offend as well as against another individual, do we have criminals and criminal law. Finally, we may expect the collective institutions which enforce criminal law also to seek the monopoly of enforcing civil law, to outlaw private vengeance.

Among the Romanichals and the Kaale we find only civil law, not criminal law and the ultimate sanction against its breach is private vengeance, the feud, although the power of morality (or shared concepts of shame) and public opinion is such that, in general in feuds, fortune favours the righteous. These groups, therefore, although individualistic and even anarchistic in contrast to the Kalderash and Lovari (whose collectively regulated society possesses in the kris an embryonic form of the state, a 'fictitious bearer of right') nonetheless have an articulated social morality. We thus see a structural inversion: remarkably similar conceptions of morality, property, cleanliness and honour enforced in quite different ways.

Postulating a historical relationship between the feud and the kris

For most of the Vlach Rom who come to any understanding of Romanichal or similar social control systems, their perception of its historical relation to their own kris system is very simple: they see these 'other' Gypsies as having 'lost' the kris. Such a view has, on the whole, been followed also by those anthropologists who have taken Vlach Rom Gypsies as their major or only informants. The kris has been seen as a primitive, authentic and essential form of Romani culture if not, indeed, a survival of something like the Indian panchayat system.

Acton (1993), however, argues that it is far more plausible to see the theoretical relationship which we have drawn from Pashukanis as also a historical relationship. The Vlach Rom are so called because of the influence of Romanian on their Romani dialects. They were among those Gypsies who were (for periods probably varying between the different natsiya) enslaved or continuing in slave status under the Romanian neo-feudalism which developed from the sixteenth century onwards (Gheorghe 1983; Panaitescu 1941). The distinctive character of Romanian neo-feudalism has been brilliantly dissected by the father of Romanian social science, Henri Stahl, who used an exemplary mixture of anthropological fieldwork on surviving non-feudalised village assemblies and local archival research on feudalised villages to analyse the transition to neo-feudalism. In the 1980 English selection of Stahl's material the account given of the manners of village assemblies is startlingly reminiscent of the way in which the kris operates among the Vlach Rom today.

We can hypothesise that among enslaved communities practising avoidance mechanisms, as do the free commercial-nomadic Romanichals and Kaale, is not so easy. It is necessary for the slave communities to present a common front to their masters to try to avoid the extremes of extraction of surplus value. What could be more natural than that they should use the political forms available to them, which made sense, in terms of the rural Romanian polity of the day, even if the purpose and content of those political forms was derived from Romani and not Romanian culture ? Perhaps, as noted above, relations of exchange between individual Rom of some goods move from commodity exchange to domestic negotiation, but that is within the context of chattel slavery where they themselves, their actual physical bodies, have become commodities which can be sold in the market place. If some man wishes to find a wife for himself or his son and the women desired belongs to another master, then their own master must actually purchase the woman for them. The payment of the bride-price between co-parents-in-law (*xhanamiki*) today might thus perhaps be seen as a definitive statement that slavery no longer exists – the Rom own themselves (but in a way in which Romanichals are not owned at all.)

We must be careful, however, not to overstate the historical case for the priority of one or other system. Sixteenth century European sources may be seen as suggesting the existence of an internal justice mechanism amongst the earliest Romani visitors to Western Europe; but the repeated attempts of Scottish Gypsy leaders at that time to get the Scottish State involved in their quarrels suggests that if they had a tribunal system, it cannot have been exactly the same as the modern kris (Fraser 1992:119). Functional needs within different sections of the Romani diaspora and historical catastrophes breaking up established symbioses may have shifted social practices in both directions between tribunal and feud systems more than once.

Nonetheless, we may see the kris originating in response to the way in which commodity relationships developed within and around chattel slavery as an adjunct to Romanian neo-feudalism. It has to consider the interests of the Romani community as though they were those of a fictitious bearer of the kind of rights and obligations already defined in looser and less structured forms of Romani social life. In contrast, however, the feud system is appropriate and functional for many groups of free commercial-nomadic Gypsies.

This does not necessarily mean, however, that either of these systems are set in tablets of stone, or that they are inherently conservative or reactionary, as Reisman suggests of the kris. The kind of criticisms which Reisman makes of conservative American Rom uses of the kris may also be found among European Rom. One English Kalderash Rom specifically told Acton (Acton 1971:117) that he had settled in England because he felt American Rom were trivialising the kris, following recondite matters of gender pollution while ignoring important issues such as a young person getting involved in drug dealing. Pentecostal Rom in New York and some other cities have specifically rejected the kris as an institution in conflict with the Christian gospel, an attitude which contrasts markedly with the attitude of many European Pentecostal Rom. In Western Europe sometimes the krisnitoria have been specifically balanced between Pentecostals, Catholics and Orthodox; we are even aware of one case where a kris was threatened in a dispute over bible translation between Pentecostal Rom. To a sociologist, rebels, dissidents and subordinates, whether male or female, must be seen as much authentically members of their own cultural groups as conservatives and patriarchs. All cultures are arenas of conflict and all present possibilities of reconciliation; all law and polity is the object of struggle. Romani law and polities give us living examples of a theoretical variety we can rarely find elsewhere. In the end we may have to acknowledge that we can trace a master value-system in Romani cultures, building on notions of propriety and honour which, as Pan-Romani politics and a Romani intelligentsia have developed, can be recognised as intersubjective realities between Gypsies from different groups, despite their own prejudices, insults or even legal prescriptions as to the content. Although relations with the state are beyond the scope of this chapter (cf Grönfors 1979), there is a standpoint from which Gypsies in general may expect Gaje to acknowledge that they have been treated wrongly. Perhaps, as so often when looking at Gypsy history, we have to acknowledge that fundamental questions of right and wrong may be something more than local etiquette.

A note on terminology

A problem of terminology arises from the Vlach Rom's tendency to use the word 'Rom' to describe both themselves and the broader category of Gypsies who call themselves 'Rom' but are not seen as 'our Rom' by most of the Kalderash, Lovari, Machavaya and Churari. 'Vlach' is a convenient label attached by non-Gypsy experts referring to the Romanian influence common to the dialect of these four groups; Romanes *vlaxikane* is a modern back calque from this. *Gajikane* is used by many of the Muslim (*Khorakhane*) Rom of the Balkans to describe the Orthodox Vlach Rom with the implication that any form of Christianity carries with it a certain de-Gypsification; but in the Balkans time has often robbed this terminology of its offensiveness so that, in context, *"Me sim gajikano Rom"* can mean simply "I am not a Muslim". In the US, however, those who are *gajikane Rom* in the Balkans use the term to mean non-Gypsy, or to stigmatise non-Rom groups such as the Romanichals, as de-Gypsified.

References

ACTON T 1971 "The functions of the avoidance of *mochadi kovels* among Gypsies in South Essex" *Journal of the Gypsy Lore Society* Series III, Vol.50 (3)

ACTON T 1979 "Academic Success and Political Failure" *Ethnic and Racial Studies* Vol.2 (2) pp 231-6

ACTON T 1981 *Gypsies* Macdonald Education, London

ACTON T 1989 "Oppositions théoriques entre 'tsiganologues' et distinctions entre groupes tsiganes" in P Williams ed. *Tsiganes: Identité, Evolution* Etudes Tsiganes/Syros Alternatives, Paris pp.87-97

ACTON T 1993 "Rom Migrations and the end of Slavery" in *Journal of the Gypsy Lore Society* Series V, Vol.3 (2) 1993 pp.77-89

ARTHUR C 1978, "Editor's Introduction" to Pashukanis 1978, pp.9-31

ASOCIACIÓN DE MUJERES GITANAS 1994 "Las actividades del año 1994¡"

AZIZ C 1994 "We will not go into houses – It will drive us Mad – Sylvia Dunn, founder of the new Association of Gypsy Women talks to Christine Aziz" *The Independent on Sunday* 5 June, p.24

FICOWSKI J 1990 *The Gypsies in Poland* tr. E Healey, Warsaw, Interpress

FRASER A 1992 *The Gypsies* Blackwell, London

GHEORGHE N 1983 "Origin of Roma's slavery in the Romanian Principalities" *Roma* Vol.7 (1), pp.12-27

GRÖNFORS M 1977 *Blood feuding among Finnish Gypsies* University of Helsinki, Helsinki

GRÖNFORS M 1979 *Ethnic Minorities and Deviance: The Relationship between Finnish Gypsies and the Police* University of Helsinki, Helsinki

KOVALEVSKY M 1886 *Sovremenny obychay i drevny zakon* St.Petersburg, tr.D Nutt 1891 as *Modern Custom and Ancient Law of Russia,* London

MAINE Sir H S 1861 *Ancient Law* Routledge, London

MARNE P de 1985 "L'organisation d'un groupe tsigane" *Etudes Tsiganes* Vol.31 (4)

OKELY J 1983 *The Traveller Gypsies* Cambridge University Press, Cambridge

PASHUKANIS E 1929 *Allgemeine Rechtslehre und Marxismus: Versuch einer Kritik der juristischen Grundbegriffe* Verlag fur Literatur und Politik, Wien und Berlin, translated B Einhorn, 1978 as *Law and Marxism* Ed. and Intro. C Arthur, Ink Links, London

PANAITESCU P N 1941 "The Gypsies in Moldavia and Wallachia" *Journal of the Gypsy Lore Society* Series III, 20, pp.58-72

REISMAN W M "Autonomy, Interdependence and Responsibility" *Yale Law Journal* Vol.103 (2) pp.401-17

SALO M T 1987 "The Gypsy Niche in North America" in A Rao ed. *The Other Nomads* Böhlau, Geneva

STAHL H H 1980 *Traditional Romanian Village Communities* Cambridge, Cambridge University Press

SUTHERLAND A 1986 2nd ed. *Gypsies, The Hidden Americans* Waveland Press Prospect Heights, Illinois

TRIGG E B 1973 *Gypsies, Demons and Divinities* Sheldon Press, London

WEYRAUCH W O and BELL M A 1993 "Autonomous Lawmaking: The Case of the "Gypsies" *Yale Law Journal* Vol.103 (2) pp.323-399

Chapter 11 The social construction of Romani identity

Nicolae Gheorghe, Researcher, Institute of Sociology, Bucharest, and Vice-President, International Romani Union

There is an increasing demand for the kind of knowledge that we have accumulated about Roma over the years. Successive resolutions from the Council of Europe and the European Community (Danbakli 1994) mean that we academics may now more easily find a market for our products; but we also have a better chance to fulfil our humanitarian aspirations. It is this that we have been trying to do during our association with the International Romani Union during the last two years, using knowledge to militate for recognition of our people in national and international politics in such a way that, while restoring the dignity of the people, we can also explore the academic work that has been done on this people and in the name of this people.

In the past five years Jean-Pierre Liégeois and I have also lobbied intensively, almost aggressively, at the Organisation (formerly Conference) on Security and Co-operation in Europe (OSCE) and have achieved a sort of political recognition for our people in documents which express commitments and engagements from almost forty Governments covering territory from London to Vladivostok.

This lobbying began in Copenhagen, in June 1990 at the CSCE Conference on the Human Dimension, where the participating states recognised the particular problems of the Roma Gypsies in the context of a section in the final report on preventing intolerance, xenophobia, anti-semitism and every kind of ethnic violence. The process continued in a series of meetings in Geneva, (the Expert Meeting on Ethnic Minorities) Moscow, (another conference on 'the human dimension') and Oslo (a seminar on democratic institutions).

At the CSCE in Helsinki in 1992, the work done at these meetings was followed up by incorporation into the final text with a good section regarding the need to have programmes in the economic, social, administrative and legal fields in order to ensure equality of opportunities for Roma with the rest of the population. The governments gave commitments to co-operate in investigating the issues.

Knowledge and the political process

All these commitments have one common shortcoming. They are paper commitments but not legal obligations. Nevertheless, they are a recognition of Roma as a people. The fact that we appear in the section of the final document which is about combatting racism, intolerance and xenophobia means that the condition of our people should be recognised as a particular human rights issue. Activists can take advantage of this recognition to make a place for the Roma in the struggle for human rights and so encourage a different path, a new political tack for our people.

Of course, we have to follow up these texts ourselves. As a direct result of our work for Eastern and Central Europe at least we managed to mobilise governmental interest and financial support to organise a series of conferences on the situation of Romanies in Central and Eastern Europe starting with one in 1992 in Slovakia. These have tried to explore controversial issues and examine the social policies of everyday life, with representatives from Roma communities together with the representatives of governments and governmental agencies from twelve different countries. Such meetings must be as pragmatic as possible, to explore and re-evaluate existing programmes and projects in the community and in schools and educational establishments and in cultural activities and so on, to formulate what might be a desirable social policy for the authorities and for the Roma themselves.

These meetings challenge us, the Roma communities and Roma representatives, with the fact that we have a chance to express what we want. Usually the discourse of Roma leaders and representatives is to criticise the programmes of the different governmental agencies because they do not take into account the cultural aspects and desires of the people. Of course, we do not reach our objectives immediately just by holding conferences but at least we try to provide a chance for representatives to express their wishes, to articulate ways of approaching their troubles and problems according to their culture.

But at this point we must ask: what is this culture? What difference does it make if we approach the questions of housing and education and everyday life, taking into account the wishes of those who are directly involved?

I think that from the CSCE/OSCE documents we see that there is a link between cultural discussions and political practice. We do try to follow up all these political steps and put them into practice. CSCE meetings create for us the chance to put political pressure on national governments. At least that was my intention and my strategy coming from Romania and trying to deal with the many authorities in solving problems of conflicts between our Roma communities and local people in different villages.

Since 1990 there have been a number of attacks on Roma communities which stem from difficulties with the complex legal and social structure within which people are competing for land. Roma sometimes occupy land which belonged to the private owners and which was passed to co-operative farms. These are now no more and the people want to reappropriate their former properties. The only way to claim the land seems to them to be to expel the people who are there. The Roma had settled in these places in the decades after the Second World War.

We did not want these incidents to pass unnoticed. We wanted to bring to trial those guilty of the destruction of houses. We came into conflict with local people, local authorities and the national government who do not wish such controversial issues to become associated with the country's image abroad. Nonetheless, we put pressure to have these cases brought to trial in Romania and in some instances we succeeded. It is, however, a high price that our society has to pay for the actions of these people in a country which is not used to having such kinds of enquiry about what constitutes racism and ethnic violence. Where is the responsibility? It is not only Romania that is in this predicament. People who exist in a suddenly liberated society feel themselves to be entitled to behave in an aggressive way and overtly express prejudice aimed against Gypsies. They make no attempt to make a critical examination as such when they are thinking about the Roma people. Some feel that it is normal, natural, to say that they are lazy, parasites, thieves, everything bad.

So we wanted to start a debate, an enquiry in order to stimulate a sense of responsibility within a society aspiring to the rule of law. It was a community activity, working at local level and then taking our experience to the CSCE meetings to give information on how to put into practice what had been expressed in documents to save them from being only paper aspirations.

Another arena for realising the dynamic of the aspiration of our communities and people is the United Nations. Here we can report that in the last few years we also achieved something. First, in 1991 the Sub-Commission on the Protection of Minorities recommended Resolution No.65 for the protection of Roma and Gypsies to be agreed by the Commission on Human Rights (UNCHR) which took place in March 1992 (text available in both Romani and English in issue no.1 of the magazine *Patrin*). In the 'positive' paragraph of this resolution the Commission on Human Rights approaches the issue under the heading of "protection of minorities". In persuading them to do this we have tried to break the idea that Roma are not a minority or not a people.

This was not easy, as we found a number of delegates to the Human Rights Commission who expressed the opinion that Roma are not a minority. Nonetheless, we fought our corner and the resolution as passed did open the way for stronger recognition of Roma as a minority and possibly as a subject of international law and international politics – something that is lacking in the world at present when the issue of national minorities is played out in intergovernmental politics. At present the basic framework of such intergovernmental politics is that nation states make representations to other states when something affects members of their 'nation' who live as a minority in those other states. This adversely affects minorities such as the Roma who have no such resource, no 'fatherland' to back them up. We still have to work out an adequate concept under which Roma can be recognised as a subject of international law protection.

(One example that comes to mind here as a possible precedent is that of 'indigenous peoples'. Under this concept people have created or constructed identities which then have found political recognition and resources from within existing political institutions.)

Through hard work we have managed to crystalise an acceptance and awareness of the Gypsy problem both nationally and internationally. The UNCHR resolution demanded the appointment of a special rapporteur to the Sub-Commission for the Prevention of Discrimination and the Protection of Minorities. This special rapporteur (who was the Director of the Norwegian Institute for Human Rights) was charged to produce a report about possible ways and means of facilitating a peaceful and constructive solution of minority problems, paying special attention to those countries in which the Roma Gypsies live. His report (Eide 1992) should influence the thought of the Commission of Human Rights in the next three years, indeed the next decade, from the point of view of ways and means to facilitate peaceful solutions to the problems.

This progress requires that we move to a more positive approach than that of merely seeking to prevent discrimination which inevitably looks at a minority from a primarily negative point of view, tagging them as a problem in themselves. We did, in fact, seek to do that in the original wording of the resolution recommended by the Sub-Commission which called on states "to take, in consultation with Roma communities, all necessary legislative, administrative, economic and social measures to ensure de jure and de facto equality for members of those communities". Despite the Sub-Commission's recommendation, however, the national delegations refused to accept this positive wording and so we had to take a step backwards to the more negative language content of "prevention of discrimination", instead of positive affirmation in economic and administrative measures.

I raise this, not as a pedantic exercise in discussing United Nations terminology, but to show that the national governments are not yet prepared to think concretely about what might be done in economic, social and administrative ways. This is not a resistance based on bad will but because they are not well informed; they are conservative, they do not accept easily new ideas without being informed about what they might mean. I think that here there is something to be done and we can use our knowledge and expertise, especially when it has been evaluated by grass roots communities, to provide governments with ideas and to prepare them to accept something which might go in a positive direction for our communities.

The terms of the 1992 UNHCR resolution did advise states who may wish to do so to avail themselves of the advisory services of the Centre for Human Rights in Geneva for that purpose. This is a bit complicated because although this Centre exists to provide advisory services on request to governments – at present there are very few national governments willing to ask for their services to solve the problems of Roma in their countries – because they are not ready to recognise that such problems exist. Nonetheless, there is a potential opportunity to press people in government to ask for such services. But if we did find some government ready to ask for the services of the Centre for Human Rights, I wonder what this United Nations agency could offer by way of consultation at the moment on how to deal with this problem. Here again we have something to do. I think we must work with all agencies who might have something to contribute to help the Centre for Human Rights to prepare advice.

If we act together in this way, this means that in some sense we are playing with our identities. It is clear to me that I do play with my own identities. Sometimes I am a sociologist travestying a Gypsy, sometimes a Gypsy travestying a sociologist – so I play with it, as people are playing with their identities all the time; that capability is part of the resources with which we meet necessities.

So we put pressure on the one hand on governments to create a need for more knowledge but on the other hand we ourselves have to produce that knowledge in order to meet the requirement. That's one lesson that has to be learned especially by those from eastern Europe, where the problem for the Roma is more salient, and more significant because of the greater number of people involved and the fact that we are confronted with ethnic states which are in the process of becoming more nationalist than they were some years ago.

Playing with our identities

The first part of this paper presented the political work through which has evolved the requirement for the establishment of certain forms of knowledge about Roma. Now we turn to the substance of the question about how the image of Roma communities is socially constructed. When we play with these identities, institutions, resources and so on, what is happening ? What might be the consequence of this? Here is a key question. It is clear that we are in a process of ethnicity building similar to that termed in political science 'nation building'.

This constructed identity is a crutch, a political crutch. We are trying to build now a political identity of being Roma, being Gypsies, working with political institutions. Is this an artificial exercise? This is one of the first questions because those involved in these projects are people like me, educated Roma. I am not an exception. There are many like me in eastern European countries and some in western European countries too. There exists a stratum of Romani people integrated into society who are able to maintain a dialogue with the different establishments – political, administrative and academic – who nonetheless suspect that we are not 'true Gypsies' because we no longer live in the traditional conditions which are documented by ethnographers and anthropologststs.

There is therefore a crisis of legitimacy for our (i.e. Romani intellectuals') own 'ethnic identity', towards our own constituency which sometimes refuses credit and in the questions of the 'Gaje' establishment regarding who exactly we are. Who is the actor promoting this kind of new Gypsy perception? Is it a legitimated actor who does this? Here again, bearing in mind the experience of eastern European countries I think that the reality which is now appearing is that of a small Gypsy bourgeoisie, an important group of people, educated and articulate,and sometimes integrated within the surrounding society and exposed to the ideological discourse in the political structures of these European countries. Many of us are part of this establishment, created by socialist or communist parties which did have a discourse with the poor, the disadvantaged and those who suffered from the fascist regimes. This happened in the 1950s and 1960s and it opened the doors of schools and social mobility for different ethnic groups including some Roma individuals who were promoted to different levels of political bureacracy and administration.

I have been curious now to meet and recognise this type of person, educated, part of the establishment, who could create pressure within the establishment for us to be recognised as Gypsies. Many of them hardly spoke about their Gypsiness before 1989. Then, their main strategy was that of masking themselves, being assimilated as Romanians or Czechs or whatever. They hardly spoke the Gypsy language. All of this again raises the question of what kind of Gypsies are they who present this social background which was a stigma some years ago and yet now exhibits itself as a resource, something positive to be built upon. It can be a resource even at the level of careers because there are people who are now building careers in Gypsy politics. They are parliamentarians who have joined or even created political parties for contesting elections; there are people in bureacracy, in offices of minorities, offices of ministries of culture or labour. Like other intellectuals of eastern Europe they found promise in the ethnic discourse and in a national minority politics.

I do not wish to elaborate further at this point but clearly this new stratum of Gypsy intellectuals is a phenomenon of wider interest in the study of ethnicity and the role of intellectuals and should be a subject of scholarly investigation and research. How many are there of this new kind of actor, these Gypsy entrepreneurs in the field of politics and administration? What will be the outcome of their actions? This needs to be studied and evaluated.

I am associated with them in their political activism although I have my own criticisms of this kind of actor, criticisms rooted in the tradition of university academic life but also fuelled by the tensions found in the politics itself. Such reflexive critical thought needs to be contextualised within the study of political anthropology or political science or sociology.

Now, what has this to do with building ethnic identity? I think that, to pick on one of several possible terms from the jargon of political science, we Roma, Gypsies are in a process of 'ethnogenesis'. Ethnogenesis, at least in one interpretation, means a social group, previously occupying a despised and inferior position, moving from this position to some kind of respectability with a sort of equality with other social groups in the hierarchy of social stratification on the basis of a revised perception of their identity. The achievement of this movement is a project for us because of Gypsy experience of marginalisation, of inferior social position, of carrying a stigmatised identity in society in general, especially in Eastern Europe, where words like Tzigan, Zingaro, Zigeuner always carried a stigma of inferiority.

When, however, we speak about ethnogenesis in such terms we have to identify why they were despised and in a position of social inferiority, where they are coming from. The clearest example is in Romania where Gypsies were slaves until the mid nineteenth century. They were slaves in the full technical sense of the word, treated like chattel property in the jural codes of the Romanian principalities. The codification of Gypsy slavery became clearer towards the eighteenth century. Tsigane in the Romanian language was equivalent with *rób* which might be translated as 'slave'. So it was a social identity, much more than an ethnic cultural identity, marking, I repeat, an inferior social position, a legal segregation between Gypsies and non-Gypsies and between Gypsies belonging to different owners. So the fragmentation of the Gypsy population was reinforced by the legal treatment of them as property, starting from the Middle Ages.

These phenomena should also be of interest to economists. It appears to me from my reading of the literature that we have never studied exactly the economic impact of the Gypsy labour force in the Romanian principalities and in Eastern Europe. They were an important resource which had to be put under a harsh dependency in order to be used/ exploited. But they were useful and made a contribution which has never yet been properly studied. Studying it will also be part of the process of re-thinking our past.

This re-evaluation has also happened regarding Black slavery within the political economy of the southern United States, as part of the affirmative movement of Black identity. We have to locate the process of emancipation of Gypsy slaves within the examination of their contribution to the economy.

Although my main purpose here is to examine ethnogenesis and the processes of legal and social emancipation, I would also note that we can speculate endlessly on the problem of why Gypsies became slaves in the Romanian principalities in the first place. I myself have tried to do so using the theories of Wallerstein (1974) about the capitalist world system to look at why the enslavement of Gypsies was necessary and the re-establishment of a type of feudal domination (known as the second peasant serfdom) over the majority of free Romanian villages by the Boyars from the sixteenth century onwards in Moldavia and Wallachia which were then under Ottoman Turkish suzerainty (Gheorghe 1983).

We could illuminate this discussion by contrasting the east European situation, where societies needed an intensive exploitation of labour, with what has happened in western European countries which produced the nomads, who were marginals, in contrast to the slaves who were incorporated in the economic division of labour and in society as such. But I have not time here to go too far into the varieties of stigmatisation; I wish to examine how the conceptualisation of ethnogenesis means that we must re-evaluate the process by which a social identity is transformed into a cultural ethnic identity.

First of all we must note that this is not something unique to Gypsies; it also happened to Romanians. In fact, not only in the Romanian principalities but also in other European countries, what became in the nineteenth and twentieth centuries national identities, were initially social identities. For example, nowadays we just think that we are living in Romania, therefore our nationality is Romanian, but the *rumain* during earlier historical eras just meant a peasant in an enserfed position. So, the process of 'nation building' in eastern Europe had as one effect among others the promotion of old social identities as new national identities. As Gypsies were never part of this political process of nation-building, their identity remained largely a social identity and not a cultural one.

Only now are we perhaps approaching such a project to change a social identity into a cultural one, to transform a stigmatised identity into something different – to move from Gypsies to be Roma or Romanies. But this project must be carefully examined and analysed in a comparative context. Who are those who are concerned for, who care about this project?

Every time it is this new petty bourgeoisie, this intellectual and political élite who are trying to refashion the image of their roots and origins.

If the Roma intellectuals and political élite in eastern European countries are trying to do this, what is the image they are trying to promote? What are the alternatives open to them?

For the moment one leading alternative is to promote ourselves as a national minority. The important alteration in the political situation of Romanies in eastern European countries today is that they are often recognised, at least formally and legally, as a national minority – and there are many associations which have been and are promoting this trend. As a consequence of this they want to be treated equally with other groups which have already enjoyed the status of national minority for a long time.

What does it mean, to be a national minority in an eastern European country? There are now resources that are distributed to Gypsies, publications, broadcasting rights, associations, cultural centres, etc., as part of the policies with which states address their minority problems. Gypsies are part of the remit and membership of Commissions for Minorities in Hungary and Slovakia. In Romania, the constitution provides one special seat for a representative of each minority. This has led to an increase in the number of minorities. For instance, the Italians in Romania discovered that they might have a place in Parliament and so promoted their Italian identity. So at least we now have a Roma representative in Parliament – this is one of the meanings of being a national minority. This means that within this context of ethnogenesis today the Gypsy identity is presented as an ethnopolitical identity, the shape of which is highly determined by its articulation within the larger process of building, or at least demonstrating, political pluralism in eastern Europe.

I personally am critical towards this trend in the Romani movement which seeks to fashion Romanies as a national minority because I consider that in reality, the true concept of national minority is only a by-product of nation-state-building. The discourse of national minorities is another way to reproduce and to reinforce the nation-state. The fact that the nation-states are so generous now with these 'minorities' is just one device to reinforce the legitimacy of these states as ethnic states, states which actually belong to an ethnic 'majority'. So, ethnic minority policies are exhibited as if in a display cabinet, like a showcase in international politics to make sure that the Council of Europe and the western democracies think that things are good in eastern Europe.

I think that there are some intellectuals and political associations of Romanies in eastern European countries that are trying to exploit this niche provided by the political ecology of our society to insert themselves at this level of national minority policies. Acton (1994) commented on this point about the systemic nature of national minority politics. In my opinion participation in this system may tend to skew or deform the process of ethnogenesis, investing it with a false perspective which does not stem from our needs.

My intellectual motivation here is that we need to criticise nationalist ideology as such. Within our criticism of the nation-state is implicit a criticism of what might be a Roma nationalism fashioned in the tradition of east European cultural nationalism. We need to look empirically to see how in politics some Roma groups/leaders try to participate within the dynamic of nation-states and their nationalist discourse and politics – to which maybe they will pay a new tribute of suffering in years to come.

Are there any alternatives to this? Let me present my own political Utopia in which I must acknowledge the influence of Liégeois' (1976) book *Mutation Tsigane*. It is that of transnationalism.

Here I am beginning to reach the limits of my ability to conceptualise verbally in English. How can we try to conceptualise the situation of Roma being a dispersed people, non-territorially-based and distributed across many countries and so on. Why have I used the word 'transnational' from the array of concepts which are on offer to describe non-territorial or cross-stata or dispersed minorities? The idea, the meaning, is to indicate that we can evolve in a different way from nation states and national minorities. I wish to assert that we can build up an ethnic dynamic and a new image by reference to and in interaction with non-national institutions or supra-national institutions.

From here comes the energy of working through the Council of Europe, the European Community and the United Nations, trying to explore this niche which is provided by supra-national institutions which can contribute towards a new form and identity which is forged in this dynamic and not that of the nation-states. How is this possible? What resources can be collected? From wherever we can find them. I do not quite know how to render the French term *bricolage* but that is what it is, a collection together of different elements. It is a stimulating exercise with assured political benefits from our point of view – but for those who are not politically engaged it might also be a challenging exercise to see how a minority is created today in an actual political context. There is little literature to consult on the subject, however, which perhaps marks a lack of intellectual imagination.

How can we ground a political strategy in such a conceptual vacuum? Essentially we have to prophesy it! We prophesy, going here and there, exploring the byways of international politics, as amateur politicians, not even full-time politicians. At the seminar at the University of Greenwich where this paper was first delivered, I had just arrived from New York where the International Romany Union had just successfully applied to upgrade its status from the humble category of a 'roster' NGO (non-governmental organisation) to Category II; it was not much but nevertheless it was an upgrading. We are going in this direction to promote our image to the United Nations as a symbol of our universalistic identity.

These lobbying exercises are good because they oblige us to promote an organisational identity. We have been accustomed to carry out our political exercises in a language and ideology of affirmation that dates from the 1960s, 1970s and 1980s in the Romany International Union. The basic discourses date back at least to 1971 in London, when the Romany Union was founded and are based on the concept of discrimination. Much of this discourse about the discrimination against and the victimisation of Romanies is highly ideological. They are realities but there is also a political exploitation of these realities in creating a language to promote it. I have found this language less and less satisfactory. It has become a ritualistic presentation and interpretation of history only from the point of view of discrimination and victimisation of the group. This is part of the reality but I don't think that it is the full reality.

To create more positive alternatives, however, we have to build up an official organisation – to set criteria for organisational performance, to have a staff, to have a budget, to be able to implement our programme and to make the Commissions of the International Romany Union active, the language commission, the encyclopaedia and information commissions and so on. But despite long debates, we still find a crisis here in our union because we are not yet prepared to meet these requirements. Nonetheless, if we want to go further in this direction we have to grow as an organisation, qualified enough to represent the interests of the people and to express and conceptualise in a language which is acceptable with national and supra-national institutions. Whether we can do this or not I do not know but this is the challenge:are we able to organise an efficient international association? That is my goal in working for a transnational identity.

Let me stop here again for a moment to think again about the utility of encounters such as the ESRC seminar series which gave rise to this book, where we have the space to talk about and find new ideas. I came to the first seminar with my imagination a little exhausted. Life had been the promotion of one resolution after another. At the United Nations once we had Category II, we were already thinking about how to achieve Category I. It is becoming a routine and I do not find myself sufficiently satisfied. Personally, I feel we need to have this experience of learning from each other; political goals are not enough. Of course, we go in that direction but this does not mean that academic work has to be partisanly motivated. Just because you want to resist pressure from the government, it does not mean that you have to serve a political party of Roma or an association like ours. We should respect the freedom exercised by intellectuals. I think that we need more independent conjectures and interpretations of the situation of our people, valorising the culture. Even studies of kinship structure should ask how the family life of Roma communities is affected in situations where they are being prised apart as in the split between Czechia and Slovakia and in the migrations of Roma leaving eastern Europe. The spiralling effects of the migration of refugees throughout various states has resulted in much change and transformation which needs to analysed by a political science of Roma, not only a 'traditional' analysis of ethnography and folkore as has been the usual intellectual approach. In fact I see a diversity of trends in the field with some continuing their traditional Gypsyiology and others moving towards what might be termed a post-modernist discourse in analysing Roma communities.

Hence there is much to do in the academic community, as part of the effort of collecting ourselves. As a way to accomplish this, we began in Bucharest a small group for research studies on social policies. This was created within the Roma Association, as part of it but in association also with the Institute of Sociology where I am working and in correspondence with the Centre de Recherches Tsiganes in Paris. We want to create a kind of knowledge which combines academic expertise with documentation and social action. I am not a social worker but I find myself carrying out social work or community development work without having a clear image about what I am doing or in what direction we are going. Are we engaged in the integration of the Roma in the community? Is this the image that we want to promote about our people and, if so, what kind of integration and integration into what kind of societies? Societies dominated by nationalist discourses? Or into societies which are heavily controlled by the state, as was the condition and still is in many of our east European societies? Is 'integration' a legitimate concept from the perspective of the dynamic of Roma communities? Here social work, although rewarding because it has a direct effect to heal wounds which are visible, has to be reinterpreted and questioned from the point of view of more general premises. Nevertheless, in Bucharest we have tried to use expertise in our own interest but drawing on people in academia who are willing to volunteer the kind of knowledge that will enable us to present alternatives to local, regional, national and international authorities which are willing to give us a hearing.

References

ACTON T A 1994 "Modernisation, Moral Panics and the Gypsies" *Sociology Review* Vol.4 (1)

ACTON T A and GHEORGHE N 1992 "Minority, Ethnic, National and Human Rights" Paper to British Sociological Association Annual Conference (published in M.Reidy and S Udodesku 1993 *eds A call for a new community: racism and ethnic conflicts in the countries around the Baltic states,* World Council of Churches, Geneva pp. 29-36)

DANBAKLI M 1994 *On Gypsies: Texts issued by international institutions* CRDP Interface Collection, Toulouse

EIDE A 1992 *Second Progress Report, Addendum to United Nations Commission on Human Rights Report on the Protection of Minorities* United Nations Document E/CN.4/Sub.2/1992/37, New York

GHEORGHE N 1983 "Origins of Roma slavery in the Romanian Pricipalities" *Roma* Vol.7 (1)

LIÉGEOIS, J-P 1976, *Mutation Tsigane* Presses Universitaires de France, Paris

SKLAIR L 1991 *Sociology of the Global System,* Harvester, London and John Hopkins UP, Baltimore

WALLERSTEIN 1974 *The Modern World System* Academic Press, New York

WOITYLA K. (Pope John Paul II) 1991 "Di fronte alle minoranze etniche so consolodi una cultura dell'accoglienza e della solidarieta" *L'Osservatore Romano* CXXI(223) 27 September

Appendix
Edited transcript of the debate following the first presentation of this paper

Editors Introduction
The debate which followed the first delivery of Nicolae Gheorghe's paper was such that the ideas presented in it are best presented in the original flow of argument, rather than by being worked into a single set of comments or amendments which would suppress their dialectic. It started with a question from Sir Angus Fraser about the implications of the concept of 'transnational identity'.

"First, I can understand your impatience with the nation state; but are you laying claim to a status different from other populations which willy-nilly in real life are governed by and have to identify with nation states? Are you asking for rights and privileges which would transcend those of citizens of nation states? Conversely, isn't there a risk in your position in which if you identify a kind of loyalty which is greater than the nation state you are saying you have a lesser loyalty to that state than other citizens, so you are almost inviting discrimination from the governments of those states because you are not fully part of the nation?

"Secondly, where does it lead you to in terms of definition? It is difficult enough to define Gypsies even in terms of individual countries. If you are going to have this global concept, will it not create even bigger problems of definition? How do you create a concept of 'Gypsy' which embraces Travellers in England, Ireland and so on, as well as Gypsies in Romania, Germany and elsewhere?"

Nicolae Gheorghe replied,

"That's a difficult problem. My first reaction, as you say, was one against the nationalist discourse, for a non-territorial, non-traditionalist discourse, which is a bit of a definition by negation – not that we should necessarily repudiate negative definitions, as witness the modern Indian tradition of non-violence. I cannot fully answer your question but I can explore the difficulties a little. First of all, there is the problem of the relationship between nationality and citizenship. Here in Western Europe the two concepts are much more related than in Eastern Europe, where it is very easy for the two to differ; for example, you can be a Romanian citizen of Hungarian nationality. The creation of nation states in Eastern Europe was never finished, one reason for the unrest in the region. So I can seek to exploit this circumstance by saying that I can be a loyal Romanian citizen, without being myself a Romanian. I can be loyal to the state while still claiming an identity which transcends its boundaries.

"Traditionally in eastern Europe nationality has more to do with culture and less to do with the state. For example, you are Polish because you are a good Catholic and you speak Polish, not because you are a citizen of the Polish state which is actually quite a recent invention. Nationality in eastern Europe is culture, not citizenship. So at one level we can exploit this disjuncture to say that transnationality does not mean disloyalty to the state. But strong criticism of this position has come from the German Sinti, who opposed my approach as dangerous because of the memory of the Third Reich when citizenship was withdrawn from Jews and Gypsies leading to policies of extermination. At the same time however, there are Roma now in Germany who do not have the option of achieving legitimacy through citizenship because they are refugees. One of their leaders, Rudko Kacwynski, has suggested the idea of transnationality should mean a status of statelessness for all Roma, thus giving them some legitimacy within German society through a licence or freedom to refugees to travel in various countries.

"How can we accommodate these different political strategies? The answer comes from the dynamic of political development in western Europe. When you are a citizen of France or Germany, you are also a citizen of the European community – a little bit symbolic today, perhaps but a hope for the future. The academic study of the concept of citizenship shows it has always been a developing thing. Why should we not all be citizens of the United Nations – and have a Romani representative there as a representative of a dispersed people in various territories? This is my dream. But this would depend on a recognition in international law which for the moment doesn't exist. For the moment we are in the position of a non-governmental organisation alongside trade unions, environmental lobbies, professional associations and so on. At the moment you have to have a territory to qualify you as being a people – which is why we have people fighting for territory so violently, to qualify themselves for a voice in the world. I am prepared to look for something different."

Thomas Acton intervened to refer to two other possible sources of theory about transnationalism.

"The term is used (1) in international economic sociology, where Sklair's (1991) globalisation theory defines transnational firms in a way differentiated from international firms. International firms work in many countries but have a base in one, whereas transnational firms are those who have got beyond the control of any one government. So there is a need to theorise institutions beyond the sovereign control of the nation state. (2) In the Pope's statement of September 1991 (Woytila 1991) the Gypsies are defined as a transnational minority, with moral rights which are not dependent on their being granted national minority rights by particular nation states. In some sense those rights must exist even if national governments don't recognise them – and that's actually not all that surprising from an organisation which is itself paradigmatically transnational. In the sixteenth century the Catholic church was defeated politically and only able to survive by accommodating the nation state, allowing kings to appoint bishops and so forth and abandoning the claims to universal authority it pursued in the Middle Ages. That also involves a political conflict over the sovreignty of the nation state."

Nicolae Gheorghe pointed out that the Council of Europe Resolution on Non-Territorial Languages also marked a breach in the nation-state ideology, in article 586 which grants non-territorial languages equal rights *mutatis mutandis* with territorial languages – a way of recognising realities but without promising to do too much about it, using the Latin phrase to hedge their bets. In fact, every time it is a case of *mutatis mutandis*. Every time Roma and Gypsies are said to be *like* national minorities, or *like* indigenous people but never definitely *in* some category, singing their own tune. But we cannot invent a position and a status for one people only. We have to investigate the position of similar people in other parts of the world. The category of Travellers, for example, is used as a proxy for Gypsies in Western Europe but it doesn't apply so well to the Rom in Eastern Europe. This is why CSCE documents began to speak of Roma and (people commonly called) Gypsies, as a way of accommodating all the partial identities and to reassure Sinti and Jenisch that they are not excluded by Rom hegemony. But we cannot clearly list a complete and mutually exclusive list of Gypsy groups. Is Travelling a style of life, or a definition referring to the notion of dispersal? We still have many challenges to see how human rights can be implemented on a personal base rather than a territorial base.

Sinead ni Shuinear agreed that there were problems of using the word 'Rom' which was often seen by non-Rom Travellers as delegitimating them. It also leaves it open to officials to delegitimate people by saying they are not real Rom. She had been at a UNICEF conference recently where many of the delegates declared they did not have any real Gypsies on their territory; but where a Romanian delegate had declared with a straight face that Roma could not be declared a national minority in Romania as there were too many of them. We should, therefore, have some more simple and enforceable category.

Nicolae Gheorghe expressed sympathy but said as long as the definition of ethnicity was part of a competition for resources it was bound to be a complex issue.

Charlie Smith (chair of the Gypsy Council for Education Culture, Welfare and Civil Rights) declared that down the centuries Gaujos had always drawn lines around Gypsies to define them but these boundaries had never really been recognised by Romany people. It seemed obvious to him that the problems of a people who live all over the world could not be sorted out unless there was a world government. Gypsies, in fact, were ahead of Gaujos, pointing out the way to them, emphasising to Gaujos who were obsessed with bits of land they can never finally own, that human rights were more important. Gypsy identity should not be dependent on what territory they happen to live in. This does not mean, however, that Gypsies cannot be loyal citizens of particular states.

Peter Mercer (president of the Gypsy Council for Education Culture, Welfare and Civil Rights) agreed, adding that many Gypsies, such as himself, looked on themselves as 'Gypsies living in England' but were still prepared to join the British army and acknowledge national loyalties. Most Gypsies did not have any aspiration to create, let alone live in a mythical 'Romanestan'. "Nationalism about who we are doesn't take away from our loyalty to the state". People are entitled to have split loyalties as had the Irish in England. At the same time, the freedom of travel within Europe should be implemented equally for all but it was not being equally implemented for Gypsy people. "I'm much more likely than a Gaujo to get stopped at any border once people realise who I am."

Donald Kenrick echoed tributes paid by others to Nicolae's courage. When he had visited Romania twenty years before, Nicolae had let him sleep on the floor of his room, at a time when he could have faced severe penalties for harbouring a foreigner overnight. But if we are studying the position of Romanies "we have to study it as it is now, not as it might be in twenty years time. This morning I was at London Airport to try to help a Polish Gypsy woman coming here as a refugee. There would have been no point my saying to the customs officer that this woman is a supra-national and therefore she has got a right to come in." He had had to show that she had a possible case for political asylum as part of persecuted ethnic minority. Similarly with English Gypsies we have to fight for sites within planning law as it is not as we would like it to be.

Sylvia Dunn (now president of the National Association of Gypsy Women) intervened at this point saying that having just been told to leave her own land and, having nowhere legal to stay, she did not see where working within the laws as they stand was getting her at all. (She has, however, since gained planning permission.)

Donald Kenrick acknowledged that we needed to change laws where we could but where we cannot (which is most usual) we have to take advantage of them. National minorities had not been a traditional status in the West but various race relations laws were in the process of creating such categories by various legal judgments as to whether Sikhs or Rastafarians count as a 'race' in English law. So long as ethnic or racial or national minority status exists and gives a claim on resources, Gypsies will be proving their right to it. In the West, also, whether or not one has a homeland is not so important. The fact that there is a Turkey doesn't give Turks in Britain, France or Germany many advantages, because Turkey isn't supporting them. And there are many minorities from Kurds to American Indians who have to carry on their struggle without a territorial state to back them.

Nicolae Gheorghe responded that all national minorities in Eastern Europe and Rom in particular, had problems with being suspected of disloyalty. Nonetheless "to confuse you more", he said that his civil rights work in Romania had very much emphasised the Romanian citizenship of the Rom. Civil rights work was essentially a building of citizenship, stimulating the mutual responsibility of the state and the citizen. And clearly one had to live certain contradictions between approaches to national and to international organisations in order to demonstrate the qualifications of the Roma community for various kinds of help. "Romania is not yet a member of the Council of Europe but by being a member and representative of the International Romani Union I can have a voice there, I have been allowed to speak there in spite of our people being not well-defined yet, as a representative of a European minority." So, of course, he worked within the system but that did not mean one had to stop thinking about the system and possible alternatives.

Penny Vinson pointed out that another aspect of the use of the idea of transnationalism which required caution was that if nation states didn't like what local Gypsy leaders were saying, they might call in foreign Gypsy leaders from an international movement to say something more favourable or to reinforce a local pro-government Gypsy faction. Thomas Acton said he had just seen that happen effectively in Hungary but the fact that the (former) conservative government in Hungary was seeking to build Gypsy electoral support was still a more hopeful phenomenon than that of right wing movements which just seek to expel Gypsies; and in fact the status given to the international movement would be unlike to disappear even if the centre left (which probably has much greater Gypsy support) won the next elections. General discussion of international politics followed, points being made about countries being able to take pride in Gypsies who were their citizens helping develop international work and the fact that Gypsy festivals and art are often promoted as tourist attractions.

Judith Okely intervened to support the thrust of Nicolae Gheorghe's speech but to ask why a previous paper by Acton and Gheorghe (1992) had lumped her together with "the old racist Gypsylorists".

Thomas Acton replied that this paragraph referred to writers discussing racism, not examples of it; they were contrasted with the racist Gypsylorists. He and Nicolae had not intended to accuse Judith Okely herself of racism at all. The point was rather that within the nation-state there were a variety of political discourses. During the morning there had been discussion, for example, of the adequacy of the anti-racist perspective, as though anti-racism was a primitive and self-evident concept. But it is not. It has been constructed within the context of a particular style of politics, usually one where there are race relations laws. To work anti-racist politics in Britain, you have to work with constructed racial categories with which, as a social scientist, one can't actually be happy. There is, therefore, a certain amount of cognitive dissonance involved in this for Romani intellectuals, for example, at the points where Nicolae wriggled by saying, "This goes beyond my imagination." The Acton and Gheorghe (1992) paper was not intended to back one side or the other but to point out a genuinely paradoxical disjuncture. At this point Charlie Smith asked for a translation. Thomas Acton replied that he meant that Gypsies work in very different ways from different political imperatives and from different political problems in different countries and, therefore, when Gypsy politicians met from different countries they really often do not understand why they are doing what they do in particular countries which makes the work of Romani intellectuals in bringing them together very important. Nicolae Gheorghe had spoken about this in a very daring way as intellectuals "playing with their identity" but we do need to balance different versions of reality at the same time.

Judith Okely re-emphasised the need during such discussions for academic courtesies to be observed, avoiding vehement or slighting language in disputes. She gave the example of decolonisation in Africa where a lot of those who had supported anti-colonial struggles had also supported African nationalism. Now, however, there was extreme scepticism about the notion of nationalism because boundaries had been carved out by the colonial authorities, paving the way for exploitation of national minorities by the new nation states created. The danger of non-Gypsies studying Gypsy representatives is that the non-Gypsies find themselves, however politically scrupulous, over-caricaturing, for example, anthropologists and setting them up as straw men. She drew attention to other examples in Acton and Gheorghe's (1992) where she felt sneering references which pilloried traditional social anthropologists were unnecessary.

There was then some general discussion as to whether particular writers had or had not been caricatured or pilloried and as to whether a dispute between academics could be represented as a dispute between Gypsies and Gaujos and to pick up concerns expressed in the morning about the accuracy of information circulated either by governments or by academics. Thomas Acton asserted that our only hope for fairness was to develop our own collegiality. Our collegiality could not bring about consensus; but it could develop our mutual understanding. More dialogue, not greater restraint, was the cure to the evil identified. We did live in a world of governments and oppositions and different Gypsy intellectuals will find niches within different partisan approaches. To that extent, the existence of people who caricature each other is a guarantee that the people in power will find some spokesmen they like, rather than rejecting all Gypsy spokespersons.

Nicolae Cheorghe endorsed the need for co-operation.

"There was a traditional, sort of ritual opposition between Gypsies and Gypsiologists. It's part of the Gypsy discourse in our Gypsiology. It is a tradition in our field. We do need to clarify the problems between the two groups; we need to come to terms with this. The solution to it is the fact that you now have Gypsy partners. I don't know how much you recognise educated or intellectual Gypsies as proper Gypsies even when they are not ethnographically typical but that this doesn't matter. Whether considered legitimate or not, we are actors in the situation, we are politically active. We are creating a discourse which, of course, also deserves to be studied and criticised. We can't be exempt. I have sometimes caricatured the positions of others and have been caricatured myself. For instance, when I denounce the Roma petty bourgeoisie I am trying to deconstruct their rhetoric and politics. That's how politics works. Sometimes criticism is aggressive; but the intention is not to hurt but to further understanding.

"There is another development which I have not mentioned yet. It has been suggested that there is a sort of Gypsy sovereignty which is trying to reaffirm (or perhaps even, to caricature) itself. We have now in Romania a 'Gypsy king' and a 'Gypsy emperor'. I see you smiling: we know this is a media event, an artefact but for all that it is still interesting to see how the media have treated it, for the insights that it can offer about the development of utopian political imagery. Of course, this king and emperor are self-appointed, and now we see in Slovakia another example, Farkas, has appeared of a self-appointed Gypsy king who has even sought the blessing of the Vatican. These are stories for the TV and the media but there may be more to it than this. In Romania, both the king and emperor come from one of the most traditional Gypsy groups, the Kalderash. Perhaps we are observing the development of a new Kalderashology. These two men are first cousins, they are *xhanamikhi* [co-parents-in-law] but long-term rivalry between the two families has now been crystalised in public by one being crowned king and another being crowned emperor. The ceremonies were very well broadcast, much better than the humble Human Rights activism of some of us, with some official recognition – which is kind of symbolic.

"They have tried to make use of tradition. We need to elaborate on how this can be possible. For instance, what is the institution of chieftainship in the Kalderash Gypsy world? How are cultural items now being mobilised in order to legitimise power in the world of Roma Gypsy politics?

"Let me refer here to the concept of Max Weber about three types of leadership which have developed in the modern world: charismatic, traditional and rational-bureaucratic. We can see all three of them at work, or at least being used as models. As charismatic leaders we may take some of the religious leaders who might also develop a political message and political organisation. We have as traditional leaders the king and the emperor. We have also the beginnings of the rational-bureacratic approach within the organisation of Roma communities.

"One interesting development with the emperor, which might conceivably be emulated by the king, was that he went to India. He went at the end of February/beginning of March 1992 with a team of journalists. He was received by some Indian officials who appeared with him on Indian TV. This is a sort of valorisation of the past; it's also congruent with the dynamic of east European nationalists who always look for a homeland; a territory of reference for a kind of mythical prestigious past.

"Anyway, I wanted to inform you about this kind of development because both the emperor and the king are claiming to be the king/emperor of all the Gypsies of the world. So watch out, English Gypsies: you might have to pay tribute!"

A number of participants then recalled 'Gypsy kings' they had met and posed the questions as to why such 'kings' thought they could get away with it and what actions should be taken. Nicolae Gheorghe replied that he had with others initiated legal action against these claims to royalty in Romania and the various government officials who had colluded with them, because they are unconstitutional and a derogation of Romanian sovereignty. It might be thought to be merely amusing but within such caricatures there is a dynamic that challenges (undermines?) the reality which contributes to make people aware about their identity as citizens.

Political identities are also being crystalised by other experiences. Roma who are going from Romania to Germany discovered a political identity there because they are claiming the status of political refugee. They became political Roma. In Romania they are discriminated against and persecuted; they are refused entry into Germany and then repatriated to Romania. They arrived from Romania with a vernacular consciousness not so much thought about but they returned to Romania, after all the pressures on them, much more concerned about what they are and they try to define themselves and they try to promote identities: composite identities – many of them being contrary to one another. It is a very awkward field of research.

Thomas Acton commented:

"Of course, this difference of consciousness transcends the difference between the Rom who have the *kris* (the Vlach Rom tribunal system) and chieftainship and the Romanichal groups and others like them who in fact always had private systems rather than public systems of justice (cf. Acton and Caffrey, in this volume). But each of these groups, when they come to have politicians seeking bureacratic forms of politics, can borrow the traditions of the others to impress the gaje. So there's a double layer of complication and manipulation. It seems to me that the independence of individual political judgement, and judgement about right or wrong, among

English Gypsies is different from the way a Kalderash Rom conducts himself with respect to his own community because the possibility for Kalderash of drawing on traditional communal structures of power are different from that of the English Romanichal who has, instead, to appeal to a public sense of fairness in a conflict which will be seen as personal. In the end you have got to stick up for yourself if you are an English Romanichal."

Peter Mercer repeated the question as to how it was possible that 'King' Ion Cioba could think he could get away with appointing ambassadors to the UK. Thomas Acton replied that he could only think that possible or in any way helpful because he was coming from a rather different sociopolitical tradition.

The debate ended with further discussion of the responsibilities of academic researchers. Robbie McVeigh said that he was a little worried at the drift to post-modernism, and the idea that "anything goes". He thought that we had to make it clear that there were some academics to whom we would not extend the courtesy of colleagues, scientists and scholars had collaborated in mass murder under the Nazis, and we should not automatically treat all academics as within the pale of our collegiality. Good scholarship could not excuse complicity in genocide, or lesser crimes; we did have to decide where to draw the line.

Afterword *Sir Angus Fraser, Researcher and Consultant, London*

The aim of the ESRC seminar series that gave rise to the bulk of the papers in this collection and its companion volume was stated to be: "to provide a meeting-place where academics, policy-makers and Gypsy activists can share experiences and locate their own work within a research tradition, and to relate academic research to current UK and European policy initiatives". This formulation suggested a desire to pass beyond the constraints of sometimes tightly knit academic disciplines towards the wider frame of reference necessary in the area loosely labelled "Gypsy studies"; to establish some balance between academic detachment and pragmatic needs; and perhaps, indeed, to attenuate understandable impatience on the part of Gypsies over any tendency to regard them simply as an interesting subject for research and the testing of theoretical models, regardless of the consequences. In a field where scepticism about the reliability of sources is vital, given the undiscriminating nature of much that has been produced, and where judgements need to be founded on an accumulation of solid evidence, the series invited a variety of practitioners from different backgrounds to submit their work in hand to the judgement of peers.

When the programme was first planned at the University of Greenwich, it could hardly have been foreseen that a major UK "policy initiative" was going to be acted out during the entire period occupied by the successive seminars. Two days after the exchanges started in March 1993, the Department of the Environment announced proposals for legislation that would criminalize unauthorized camping and at the same time repeal the duty, placed upon local authorities twenty-five years before but never fully honoured, to provide caravan sites for Gypsies. The Criminal Justice and Public Order Bill, chosen as the incongruous setting for these measures, had a stormy reception. By the time of the final seminar in September 1994, the Bill had still not completed its much delayed passage through Parliament, but a powerful (and perhaps rather unlikely) cross-party alliance in the Lords, led by two hereditary peers with support from the National Farmers Union, the Country Landowners Association, Tory backbenchers and Opposition peers, and which appeared to hold a monopoly of all the good arguments, had managed to secure a majority vote against the Bill's attempt to abolish local authorities' responsibility for sites and the central financial aid that underpinned it. A month later, the Bill returned to the House of Commons, and the Lords' amendments were reversed. It received Royal Assent on 3 November 1994, and overnight all Travellers not on authorized sites could in effect be regarded as criminals. The analysis which Luke Clements and Sue Campbell have subsequently provided shows how decades of gradual progress have been set at nought by this volte-face towards travelling Gypsies, carried through in the teeth of informed opinion.

Many minorities have known the ill effects of the human tendency to judge and value everyone else's way of life by one's own, and the various chapters in the present volume have been in large measure an anatomy of stigmatization, not just of Gypsies, but also of Travelling people in Ireland, New Travellers, and the Burakumin in Japan. Gypsies have suffered from such ethnocentrism ever since they arrived in eastern Europe centuries ago, and the results are still all too visible. In 1991-94, the American Jewish Committee sponsored a series of surveys of attitudes towards Jews and other minorities in nine European countries. In reply to a question about which minorities the respondents would prefer not to have in their neighbourhoods, the answers invariably put Gypsies in the least favoured category – below Arabs, Asians, Blacks, Jews, Turks and a variety of others. The recorded degree of antagonism ranged from 48 per cent of respondents in Russia to 94 per cent in Slovakia. In Britain the figure was 65 per cent. Gypsies were given similarly negative ratings on the question of whether the minority was thought to behave in a manner provoking hostility. A number of European countries with large Gypsy populations — such as Romania, Bulgaria, Spain and Serbia — were not included in these surveys, but there is every reason to suppose that trends there would have shown no difference. So extraordinary a depth of hostility towards Gypsies wherever they live cannot but be deeply disturbing, whether it takes the form of anonymous opinions gathered by pollsters, or is translated into the direct menace of physical violence, or is reflected in the legislative apparatus of the state administration.

The "how" of discrimination is copiously documented. The "why" is more difficult to pin down, though sedentary/nomadic tensions have formed a salient part of the answer, as Robbie McVeigh argues. In a few countries, national and local authorities appear increasingly to recognize a prudent need for informed advice as a prerequisite for decision-making in this area. For Gypsies, the important point is to draw on laboriously acquired knowledge and experience so as to preserve their individuality. Politically, they have been the weakest of peoples, but flexibility and adaptability have long been their instruments of survival. In contrast to earlier strategies of shunning publicity and remaining inconspicuous, some have recently taken to active pursuit of basic Gypsy rights and making their case publicly against policies of rejection and assimilation, while at the same time laying stress on what Gypsies have to offer when given the chance. Nicolae Gheorghe's ruminations on Gypsy ethnicity and identity set out one approach to the political conundrum and show how, though still working as mediators within the system as it is, he and fellow Gypsy activists are seeking to forge a link between cultural debate and political practice by focusing attention on what needs to be done economically, socially and administratively. His own concept of "transnationalism" may not command universal allegiance, since some are wary of potential risks of intensifying nationalist hostilities, but his remarkable extemporization in the seminars provides a fitting coda to the discourse on interaction between Gypsies and their surroundings.